Compromising Scholarship

Compromising Scholarship

Religious and Political Bias in American Higher Education

George Yancey

BAYLOR UNIVERSITY PRESS

Cover Design by Cindy Dunne, Blue Farm Graphic Design

Library of Congress Cataloging-in-Publication Data

Yancey, George A., 1962-
  Compromising scholarship : religious and political bias in American higher education / George Yancey.
      p. cm.
  Includes bibliographical references and index.
  ISBN 978-1-60258-268-2 (hardback : alk. paper)
  1. Postmodernism and higher education--United States. 2. Christians--Political activity--United States. 3. Church and college--United States. I. Title.
  LC111.Y36 2010
  378.01--dc22
                        2010020196

Dedicated to all scholars who are willing to think outside the academic box and who refuse to limit themselves by the social pressures of our current academic generation.

Contents

List of Figures and Tables

COLLEGIALITY SURVEY

Acknowledgments

In many ways this book is a return to important issues that originally attracted me to academia. My dissertation was based upon an exploration of the social backgrounds that sociologists tend to share, and I made the argument that those circumstances help to shape the social biases in the field. Soon after finishing my dissertation, a series of events led me into research on interracial families and then to multiracial churches and racial identity. I am immensely grateful for the start that was given to me by my dissertation committee and especially Norval Glenn (chair), Lester Kurtz, and Christopher Ellison for the extra work they did with me as I earned my doctorate.

I am fortunate that I work at a university that supplied me with the opportunity to complete this research project. The graduate students that the University of North Texas provided for me aided greatly in the preparation of the survey instrument. These students include Karen Kaiser, Kenan Bayhan, Oguzhan Basibuyuk, and Mimoza Ahmeti. I also wish to thank Dale Yeatts, the chair of the department, for his support of my research while I was writing this book and for allowing me to find internal funding for the project.

Finally, it also was important to get perspectives from other scholars as I conducted this research. I received wise advice from Louis Bolce, Michael Emerson, and Elaine Ecklund. I also thank Nicole Dash for answering some of my methodological questions in the early construction of the project. To the degree that anyone finds value in this book, they should thank these individuals. Any errors or omissions in this work are solely my responsibility.

CHAPTER ONE

Introduction

On May 1, 2009, U.S. District Judge James Selna issued a ruling that James Corbett violated the establishment clause of the First Amendment when he called creationism "superstitious nonsense" during a high school history lecture. The lawsuit cited more than twenty statements made in the classroom that, according to the plaintiff Chad Farnan, favored "irreligion over religion." However, only the statement on creationism was found to have violated Farnan's rights. The ruling ended this particular conflict, but this type of complaint has become quite common at educational institutions. A group finds evidence that it is being insulted or faces bias and complains about intolerance. Usually the complaint does not rise to the level of a court case, but the objectivity of the educational institution is quickly called into question by that group, and social conflict ensues.

At the other end of the political spectrum, on May 12, 2006, the California Senate passed a bill requiring school instruction material to contain discussions on the contributions of homosexuals, bisexuals, and transgendered people while banning teaching or books that denigrate people based on their sexual preference. The argument by Sheila Kuehl, a state senator from Santa Monica, is that ignoring such individuals is similar to the way the contributions of people of color and women have been ignored. Thus a perceived bias against sexual nonconformists was the stated reason behind such a law. Here a different group, based on sexual preferences and not religion, makes claims of bias within educational settings and attempts to find a solution to that bias. Thus members from both the Left and Right make claims that they face intolerance in educational institutions.

The above cases concern issues surrounding high school students, where the potential for influencing underage individuals brings additional levels of scrutiny. However, charges of bias and intolerance are also quite common in institutions of higher education. While professors enjoy protections of free speech that high school history teachers do not have, concerns about bias against certain social groups remain a hot topic. This is so not only because of how the possibility of prejudice may affect students in college classrooms, but also because institutions of higher education are the places where science is conducted. If bias and intolerance influence professors in the classroom, then they also likely affect the way they conduct scientific research and knowledge discovery.

Intolerance has become the new curse word in contemporary society. No one wants to be seen as biased toward members of other social groups. The cost for obtaining such an image is ridicule and social ostracism. Given such penalties, accusations of unfair bias have proven to be powerful mechanisms for motivating individuals toward social expressions of acceptance. Accusations of intolerance help to curb the use of racial, sexual, and gender epithets by encouraging individuals to accept members of different social groups into their friendship networks and to curb the most egregious workplace discrimination. The flip side of intolerance is the providing of undue favor for those in-groups that are admired. This favor allows some individuals to profit at the expense of others. Thus bias toward those similar to ourselves in appearance or ideology also has been seen as an undesirable trait. In this way, charges of bias have taken on much of the same moral weight as accusations of intolerance.

The notion of intolerance, or bigotry, has generally been used for those who opposed equal rights for people of color and women. But as we saw in the above examples, accusations of bias are not merely tied to those who seek to victimize racial minorities and females. Political conservatives and liberals are often quick to accuse the media of biased treatment in favor of those they disagree with (Alterman, 2004; Brock, 2004; Coulter, 2004; B. Goldberg, 2001; McChesney, 2004; Medved, 1993; Olasky, 1988). Both religious (Howse & Reagan, 2005; Medved, 1993; Olasky, 1988) and nonreligious (Bishop, 2007; Dawkins, 2006; Gey, 2006) individuals argue that they are the victims of bad treatment due to unfair bias. Individuals with lifestyles that differ from the norm in sexual preference (Leland, 2000; Long & Sulton, 1987; Padilla, 2004), eating habits (Iacobbo & Iacobbo, 2004; McColgan, 2005), and even clothing choices (Ince, 2005) argue that society is unfairly biased against them as well. Charges of bias are often used in an attempt to humiliate those who oppose certain social groups and so to obtain social power for those groups. But the question still remains: who does truly face disadvantages in our social institutions because of bias?

Because of the undesirability of being labeled as intolerant, it is often difficult to document the existence of intolerance in contemporary society. For example, although racial bigotry may be the most undesirable type of bias in modern society, there is evidence that racial bias still exists in the United States (Bobo, Kluegel, & Smith, 1997; Bonilla-Silva, 2003; Feagin, 2006; Gallagher, 2004; Kinder & Winter, 2001; Sidanius, Singh, Hetts, & Federico, 2000). But efforts to measure individual prejudice tend to run into problems since prejudiced individuals have a powerful social incentive to hide their racism. Likewise, attempts to discover other types of biases and prejudices are often limited by our inability to determine whether individuals who dislike those in other social groups are willing to disclose their displeasure. We know that intolerance and bias exist in our society, but social pressure to reject those qualities has made it difficult to document them.

Obviously those with relatively little power will do less damage with their tendency toward bias than those with more power. We may agree that any undue prejudice or bias is always detrimental to having a healthy society, but certain individuals can do a lot more damage with their prejudice than others. Among those who can do a lot of damage with their bias, or a lot of good by being unbiased, are those with positions in higher education. In contemporary society, acquiring education is linked to the ability a person has to obtain social prestige and economic resources. If individuals controlling institutions of higher education have intolerance against certain social groups and bias supporting other groups, then some social groups will gain undue influence in our society.

The purpose of this book is to explore the contours of bias and tolerance within institutions of higher education. To be specific, I am particularly interested in bias among scientists and their scholarly supporters in the humanities since it is within scientific exploration that the academy may have its most powerful societal impact. I will specifically look at the discipline of sociology to gain an in-depth understanding of these contours. I use quantitative research to document if any social bias exists in this discipline as well as qualitative work to discover the social and philosophical forces behind this bias. However, I will also explore other disciplines so that a breadth of possible prejudice and bias can be more fully documented. The results of this work will help us to comprehend the potential social bias that may exist within academic circles. Once we have that understanding, we can begin to assess if, and how, we need to tackle this problem.

Complicating the task of investigating tolerance in higher education is the fact that previous research has suggested that education is positively related to tolerance (Coenders & Scheepers, 2003; Kane, 1995; Loftus, 2001; Phelan, Link, Stuene, & Moore, 1995; Vogt, 1997). Because of this fact, there may not be enough evidence of intolerance among the highly educated so that biases in academia can be empirically documented. But it remains to be seen whether those with high levels of education are relatively free of bias or merely are able to hide their bias from noisy researchers. Finding innovative ways to measure the potential biases within the highly educated is vital if the purposes of this book are to be fulfilled.

What Is Tolerance?

Before we begin our examination of the possible sites of intolerance and bias in academia, it is important to explore a couple of philosophical issues about tolerance. For example, does tolerance mean that I must accept any idea that someone provides to me? If I am a Democrat, must I accept political conservatism to be tolerant of Republicans? If I am a Christian, must I accept the teachings of Mohammed to be tolerant of Muslims? Must I suspend my right and ability to critique ideas I disagree with in my effort to be tolerant? I suggest that this sort of approach does not and cannot reflect an accurate understanding of tolerance. Tolerance cannot mean that I give up my own ideas and beliefs, or else those ideas and beliefs do not have much meaning for me. In that case, I would have to be intolerant of my own ideas and would have to change them so as to be "tolerant" of others.

Furthermore, we can ponder whether tolerance means not forming any judgment about the actions in which others are engaged. In other words, must it be the case that I perceive the lifestyle of a drug addict to be just as valuable as the lifestyle of a professor? I hope not. I feel comfortable in asserting that, for the most part, professors add more positive value to our societies than drug addicts.[1] If tolerance means that I have to equate the value that society gives to a drug addict with the value it gives to a professor, then I will lose any ability to promote actions I believe are good for society. Tolerance cannot mean that I have to turn a blind eye to the consequences of a person's beliefs or actions. If becoming tolerant forces me to make such assertions, then surely efforts to eliminate bias lead me to ignore common sense and reason. I must retain freedom of my own thoughts and convictions even as I work to accept those with different ideas.

A better way to think about tolerance is as the ability to treat those one disagrees with respectfully and to not act in a prejudicial way toward them. Tolerance means that we do not react in irrational ways to those who differ from us because of that difference. In other words, a person may not want his or her offspring to marry someone of a different religion if maintenance of their religious culture is important to them. They are making an assessment about the real cultural consequences of these religious differences. However, if they were to resent their offspring marrying someone of a different race, such cultural conflict is not inevitable, and there is little reason to oppose such a union except for a desire for racial purity. As such, it is much easier to see the latter situation as intolerant rather than the former situation. Of course, one can argue about the correctness of discerning the consequences of a particular situation. Some can argue that the maintenance of religious culture should not be important enough to oppose an offspring's interfaith relationship.[2] Such ambiguous decisions are mingled with an individual's values and cannot be determined by scientific analysis. However, there clearly are situations in which no reasonable person could find a rationale to oppose those of a different category. It should not matter whether the person moving into the house next door is of a different race, religion, or has a different sexual preference. It should not matter if that person is a hunter, vegetarian, comic book collector, or has some other different lifestyle as long as the person is reasonably quiet, does not lower the property value of the neighborhood, and makes his or her house payments. Resistance toward individuals one lives with in the neighborhood or that one works with is a measure of intolerance, as there is no rational reason for such resistance. This resistance must come from a bias against such individuals.

This brings up another important dynamic of tolerance. For tolerance to be fully realized, it has to be directed at someone with whom one disagrees. The Baptist may be tolerant of the Church of Christ member, but if he or she agrees with that person 90 percent of the time, then how much tolerance has been exhibited? Not much. If the Baptist accepts the atheist or the Buddhist, then we can begin to discuss tolerance. Likewise, there has been a tendency to look at attitudes toward certain groups (gays and lesbians, Muslims, people of color) as measures of tolerance.[3] The problem with this tendency is that individuals who are philosophically supportive of these groups will score much higher on such tolerance measures, even though they may be intolerant toward other social groups. Before we can assess the level of bias, we have to assert with which groups one disagrees. This observation is particularly relevant concerning individuals in higher education since these individuals have likely been socialized to become tolerant toward certain, but not all, social groups in our society.

The ideal of tolerance I am describing does not require us blindly to accept whatever idea or action is sent our way but allows us to value our own beliefs. However, we do not devalue others' beliefs to such an extent that we punish those who differ from us, as long as that difference does not overtly impact how they may treat us. In other words, I reasonably can discriminate against seeking a romantic relationship with a hunter if I am a vegetarian and my beliefs about animal cruelty would inhibit my ability to find a deep interpersonal connection with such an individual. On the other hand, it would be intolerant for me to refuse to purchase the services of a plumber, lawyer, or mechanic because of their hunting habits since those habits would not affect their ability to serve me. Tolerance means that we take our beliefs seriously but live in a world with others we disagree with in a hospitable way. Practicing this type of tolerance should lead to a society in which individuals are free to seek out their own personal pathways, even if those pathways diverge from the rest of the society, as long as they are not harming others.

As I look for evidence of bias in academia, it is important that these principles of tolerance are taken into account. I must not place the burden upon professors of agreeing with all philosophies that they may encounter to escape being labeled biased. However, it is vital to explore situations where bias is irrational and linked to resistance one may have based on hostility toward certain social groups. It is also critical to discover what groups those in higher education may find distasteful. It is only by exploring the attitudes individuals in higher education have toward social groups they disagree with that we can truly learn about the extent and boundaries of bias in academia. To meet these criteria, it is my intention to explore the willingness of academics to hire individuals from distinct social groups. Asking academics about whether they are willing to work with members of a given social group does not force those academics to agree with a given lifestyle or personal philosophy. However, membership in these social groups has little or no impact on the ability of potential job candidates to perform their occupational duties. Thus hesitation to hire members of a given social group should indicate a propensity toward intolerance of those groups. Such a measurement allows me to assess the level of bias among academics according to the dynamics laid out in this section.

Bias and Academia

As we consider the possibility of bias in academia, we need to recognize that we are not in totally uncharted waters. If social biases in academia are not qualitatively different than social biases in other areas of our society, then we can draw on previous literature to think more deeply about how we can address the possible social biases of scholars. Bias can develop from our perception of individuals we perceive as part of our in-group. Superficially, one may argue that the in-group for academics is other scholars. Indeed, academics do share a certain number of common experiences (e.g., attending graduate school, writing a dissertation, seeking publications with original research or ideas) that can bind them together. However, what may be more important than these experiences are the social groups to which academics belong. The fact that scholars are more likely to be politically progressive and irreligious (Ecklund & Scheitle, 2007; Klein & Stern, 2004–2005; Ladd & Lipset, 1975; Larson & Witham, 1998) also produces a certain subculture that influences the values of academics. Membership in these social groups may be more likely to influence academics to develop social biases than the unique organizational aspects within academia.

It has been argued that ethnocentrism may be a part of the human condition (Sumner, 1906; Taifel, 1981). Societies may rely upon ethnocentrism to produce social cohesion by convincing the members of that society that the norms and values embedded in that society are the best ones available (Catton, 1961; Durkheim, 1965). Out-groups are inevitable since part of how we define ourselves is through negative reference groups. This ethnocentrism does not merely apply to entire societies, but it is also likely to manifest itself within our subcultures. Subcultures, like entire societies, have similar needs of definition and justification, allowing them to be inflected with an ethnocentric bias. Because scientists pursue knowledge through logic, they may naturally believe that their values are the result of critical thinking and logic when in fact their work is inevitably influenced by certain social and political values.

The implications of such ethnocentrism in the academic subculture are significant. For example, ethnocentrism produces an in-group bias by which a group emphasizes information that dehumanizes out-group members or refutes the philosophies within out-groups while it screens out information that humanizes out-groups and supports those philosophies. This tendency generally occurs without the individuals engaging in this bias even realizing it. For them it is normal and natural to perceive certain groups as less human, moral, and decent than individuals in their own group. Because they are trained in the scientific method, some academics may be tempted to believe that scientists are able to rise above this bias and to make more objective assessments of those in social out-groups. But we have to ask whether the training of academics truly has enabled them to escape the influences of group membership.[4] If academics are unable to escape from the ethnocentrism that plagues other social groups, then there is no reason to believe that their failure to accept out-groups is purely based on scientific criteria. Ideas and individuals from certain social places in our society are rejected not because they do not have merit, but rather because they challenge the internal norms and values of members within the academic community.

Previous Attempts to Assess Bias

Since charges of bias carry such a heavy moral weight, it is not surprising that several groups have perceived themselves as victims of bias. As noted earlier, these charges bring with them the possibility of gaining social power in our society. Documenting potential bias has been a challenge for the proponents of groups perceiving themselves as the victims of bias. Often political conservatives base their arguments that they face unfair bias upon anecdotal observations of certain authors (Goldberg, 2001; Goldberg, 2008; Horowitz,

2006). But such claims have failed to convince supporters of academia that certain social groups suffer from unfair bias (Kimura-Walsh, 2008; Lazere, 2004; Lee, 2006). The problem is obvious. As research into perceptions of media bias has demonstrated (Dalton, Beck, & Huckfeldt, 1998; Gunther, 1992; Lee, 2005), we are especially attuned to the potential bias against a social group to which we belong. There is a natural tendency for individuals to interpret the actions of others in a light most favorable to them and their own social group. Thus legitimate criticisms of or arguments against elements within one's own social group can be reinterpreted to indicate an unfair bias against one's group. Furthermore, creating perceptions that one's social group has been unfairly punished or has not been fairly compensated can produce a situation where one can make social and economic claims on others, so there is material motivation for seeking out examples of unfair bias against one's own group whether that bias exists or not. This type of motivation makes such claims suspicious to out-group members.

Anecdotal evidence is also suspect for a more subtle reason. While we are highly sensitive to how others may mistreat us, we are not always as sensitive to how out-group members are treated. This insensitivity may grow as we encounter social out-groups with which we have less in common. I am likely to be quite aware of how African Americans face prejudice and bias, for example, but less aware of how those issues are manifested for Hispanic Americans. I am probably especially unlikely to have sensitivity toward how European Americans face prejudice since research suggests that the social distance between African Americans and European Americans in the United States is greater than between most other groups (Bogardus, 1968; Gallagher, 2004; Yancey, 2003). So assessment of bias based an anecdotal assertions is likely to be incomplete, as it will only take into consideration those who belong to an observer's social groups. It is fair to question the accuracy of claims of bias from members of the possibly victimized group if they only offer anecdotal evidence. It is not that individuals making such accusations are lying, but rather that the group's interpretation of events has distorted the events themselves. Efforts to discover the presence and limitations of intolerance in our society have to include more than assertions based on subjective interpretations.

Schmalzbauer (2003) goes beyond simple anecdotal evidence with an interview of twenty Catholic or evangelical journalists and twenty Catholic or evangelical social scientists who are prominent in their respected fields. He documents how they have been able to maintain their religious identities in their work. While his work does provide some evidence that religious individuals may experience success in academia, it is a selected sample in that it includes individuals who are already accomplished. His work is clearly not a systematic examination of the power of social bias in academia. It is unable to document the individuals who may have been discouraged from engaging in scientific endeavors because of bias against them. Even among these successful individuals, Schmalzbauer documents some tensions that have arisen because of their religious faith. If such tensions are present for successful academics and journalists, then they may be much more powerful for religious individuals who have not experienced such success.

The need to utilize systematic observations to document evidence of bias has led some to use studies of political or religious affiliation instead of personal observations (Horowitz & Lehrer, 2003; Klein & Stern, 2004–2005; Klein & Western, 2004–2005; Weaver & Wilhoit, 1993). For example, Klein and Stern (2004–2005) observe that only 7.9 percent of academics in six major disciplines are Republicans, while Weaver and Wilhoit (1993) document that only 16 percent of journalists are Republicans. As it concerns religious ideology, Ecklund and Scheitle (2007) show that only 2.9 percent of academics at elite universities are conservative Protestants, although Ecklund and Scheitle make no claims of religious bias as the culprit. These studies can imply that academics are predisposed to have prejudice against Republicans and Christians. I will document in the next chapter that there are historical and cultural reasons why such a political and religious discrepancy may exist among academics. However, merely documenting the level of underrepresentation of some social groups does not illustrate that prejudice against those social groups is rampant, and merely because a group is underrepresented does not provide us with assurances that this group experiences prejudice. In fact, if there is a strong cultural value of tolerance among scholars, members in academia may go out of their way to not practice prejudice against social groups to which they do not belong. Research on the correlation between education and tolerance suggest that such a value exists (Bobo & Licari, 1989; Kassing, Beesley, & Frey, 2005; Lynch, 1987).

A recent survey does suggest that academics may possess some level of animosity toward evangelicals (Cooperman, 2007). But even such surveys do not confirm that academics act on such bias. Scholars may operate out of a norm of academic freedom, and while they may personally favor some social groups over other social groups, they may not show that favoritism in their interactions. Such individuals may have such a thirst for accuracy in scientific endeavor that their biases for or against certain social groups do not also shape the findings that emerge from their work.

Some have debated whether the political disparity in academia is as great as some would argue. Cohen-Cole and Durlauf (2005) point out that measures of political affiliation do not measure the degree of political extremism and thus are not a good assessment of the degree of progressiveness among scholars. They also point out that since so many individuals are not registered as either Democrats or Republicans, looking at political party affiliations leaves out measuring the attitudes of too many scholars for us truly to know the political makeup of academia. Furthermore, Hamilton and Hargens (1993) provide empirical evidence that the percentage of politically conservative academics actually increased by about 7 percent between 1969 and 1984. While these criticisms do not neglect the basic argument that political progressives outnumber political conservatives in academia, they do challenge the notion that such overrepresentation is linked to a serious problem of bias among scholars. Merely having a higher number of progressive academics is not evidence of bias against non-progressives (Giroux, 2006; Lee, 2006).

Furthermore, there may be another reason why political and religious progressives are relatively likely to be in scientific disciplines. There may be a self-selection factor in which those with a more conservative religious and political orientation are less likely to be attracted into scientific inquiry (Ames, Barker, Bonneau, & Carman, 2005; Lee, 2006). Religious and political conservatives may be less comfortable with the open nature of scientific inquiry (Ames et al., 2005), and so academia may not be an attractive profession for them. If conservatives are less comfortable with the rules of the sciences, then their relative underrepresentation may be due to their own choices rather than to prejudice and bias on the part of religious and political progressives.

Finally, some have attempted to analyze the products produced by supposed biased actors to indicate the level of intolerance located in an institution. This is an attempt to go beyond the mere statement that certain political and religious groups are overrepresented in certain occupations and to indicate that this overrepresentation has created unfair assertions that support certain groups and disparage other groups. For example, research has investigated whether there is a liberal media bias by exploring whether the actual news coverage does favor progressives over conservatives (Dalton et al., 1998; Domke, Watts, Shah, & Fan, 1999; Fico & Soffin, 1995; Kohn, 2003; Niven, 2002). Generally such research has failed to find evidence of this potential bias. There have been some attempts to assess academic bias through the analysis of course descriptions (American Council of Trustees and Alumni, 2006) and Web sites (Balch, 2006). This is a difficult technique to use to discover bias within academia for two reasons. First, it is unclear how to assess whether an individual's research is the result of bias or of an accurate examination of reality. The documentation of sexism is well founded (Bonvillian, 2006; Edwards, Reich, & Weisskopf, 1978; England, 2001; Folbre, 1985; Rose & Harmann, 2004; Tichner, 2002; Wharton, 2004) in academic research. Political conservatives may argue that there is extraordinary attention to the existence of sexism which shows liberal bias when in reality it is merely an accurate reporting of our current society. Individuals who prefer to perceive scientific findings as biased may not be able to accept that scholars are merely providing a frank assessment of the social, biological, or physical reality before them. Second, we would be wise to question the potential bias of the researchers who construct measurements of bias. If a field is truly dominated by those of a certain political or religious perception, then how they measure bias may favor their in-group. For example, an anthropologist with a culturally relativistic perspective may fail to measure how this presupposition leads to work that is biased against a traditional religious value system simply because his or her experiences do not produce an understanding of how such a bias can develop. But if efforts to measure bias in anthropology fail to account for a tendency against religious traditionalists, we are unlikely to get a complete picture of social bias within this discipline.[5]

To document the contours of intolerance in academia, research must be conducted that is systematic in nature and not limited to a few personal observations. This work must assess the potential for prejudice among a variety of different social groups. Research that explores the bias against only certain types of social groups (i.e., liberal groups, religious groups) ignores the potential of bias against other types of social groups. This work cannot be based on the development of subjective measures that require interpretation by a third-party researcher. The measurements must clearly indicate that an unwarranted degree of favoritism or hostility has been accorded to certain social groups. Finally, such work must deal with what academics actually believe or do. It cannot merely be based on the level of representation of certain social groups among academics since there is no guarantee that a lack of representation lends itself to negative bias against those groups. In chapter 3, I will introduce my research design, which meets the conditions set in all of the above criteria.

Why Study Higher Education?

Studies of bias have been conducted in a variety of social settings. Clearly political and media institutions have a powerful influence in our society and are worthy of systematic study. My exploration of institutions of higher education does not mean that there is not also value in exploring the possibility of bias in other social settings such as entertainment and mass media, primary and secondary education, and political institutions. However, I have chosen to study institutions of higher education because these institutions are among the most important venues in which long-term social change can take place. The presence of bias within them has important ramifications as to the future direction of the United States.

Three basic general functions are accomplished within institutions of higher education. The most obvious function is the teaching of academic knowledge provided in our colleges and universities. Such teaching can influence young minds and in doing so impact the philosophy and ideology of future generations. Because the value of academic freedom is generally trumpeted on campuses of higher education, academics can organize their instruction in a variety of ways. They can emphasize certain scholarly realities while ignoring others. Thus the social biases academics bring into their teaching roles are likely to be transmitted, in some form, to the students they have in their classes. This impact is not always immediate, but, because our educational institutions disproportionately influence younger individuals, the potential for long-term effects is difficult to overestimate. The messages sent by our education system may help determine the social attitudes in our society for some time to come. If our system of higher education is promoting bias against certain social groups, then those groups are likely to suffer for quite a long time. The second function that is linked to institutions of higher education is research. The type of research conducted at academic institutions not only produces material innovations to our society, but also often produces social and cultural initiatives. Such research provides legitimacy for social and intellectual movements and can thus encourage them. For example, academic assertions about the innate nature of homosexuality have provided support for civil rights movements for homosexuals in the larger society. Clearly the manner in which research is conducted and subjects are chosen for study can have real ramifications on the social and cultural direction our society takes. The third basic function concerns service to the community. How academics decide to serve the community also has important implications to the social direction of the larger community. Academics obviously have many social resources that they can provide to social organizations. If certain community organizations receive more support from academics than other community organizations, then the former organizations possess a significant advantage in accomplishing their stated goals. For example, if proponents of building a new factory have a more difficult time finding academic experts who will support their goal than the opponents of that factory, then they will be at a disadvantage in influencing the public of the wisdom of building the factory. Academics do possess a certain amount of social prestige which can be useful in persuading the general public.

My research will concentrate on understanding the potential biases within academia. To this end, I will seek to capture the attitudes of scholars in college and university settings, whether they are adjunct instructors, part-time teachers, or tenured or tenure-track professors. They are the ones who deal with students in academic classes and so have a great deal of influence with their teaching. While there are research organizations not directly connected to a particular college or university, the vast majority of the research conducted is done on academic campuses. Thus, those who set the research agenda for most scientific fields generally work at colleges or universities. By surveying those who work on these campuses, I will capture the attitudes of those who are influential in shaping scientific research. Finally, colleges and universities have some emphasis on service to their community. It is not an accident that communities often desire to attract educational institutions since the services and economic opportunities provided by them almost always outweigh any additional costs they may bring to those communities.

Different types of colleges and universities have contrasting effects within these three basic academic functions. It is plausible that liberal arts and community colleges have a more powerful impact on the teaching of undergraduate students than research institutions. They may be more likely to influence the larger society through teaching than research. However, research institutions clearly are more likely to produce the influential research that shapes our social direction than are other types of educational institutions. As such, they have their own sphere of influence. Assessing professors and instructors in general, whether they teach at a city community college or an elite Ivy League school, is vital to gain a view of the power of academic bias to influence our larger society.

To be sure, there are many different areas of instruction and research provided at institutions of higher education. Some of these areas are more vocationally focused, such as preparation to engage in a trade or to work in the business realm. While these elements of instruction and research are important, the core of higher education is scientific inquiry and critical thinking development. There is value in exploring all of the different types of instruction and research that are possible in institutions of higher education, but I will limit my inquiry to more scientific disciplines and the humanities, as I argue that doing so will allow me better to gauge the type of impact that academic institutions produce. Furthermore, concentrating on disciplines that focus on science and critical thinking will enable me to make general assertions about the nature of science itself.

Studying Academics—A Two-Pronged Approach

To explore the attitudes of academics, I will utilize a two-pronged approach. First, I will undertake an in-depth exploration of the discipline of sociology. This exploration will enable me to understand the tendency of academics to possess biases for and against certain social groups. I will collect both quantitative and qualitative information about sociologists. The quantitative work will be based on a systematic sample of members of the American Sociological Association. These members were encouraged to fill out a Web survey that assessed their potential biases. The systematic collection of these responses will allow me to generalize about the potential ways in which biases exist among sociologists and to identify what factors are related to the propensity to possess social biases.

After I have established these factors, I will then conduct a qualitative exploration of Internet blogs that have been written by sociologists. These blogs are put out by sociologists for public consumption, but they allow the scientists to explore issues affecting the social groups toward which they may have biases. Examining these blogs is an unobtrusive method that examines the sociologists' attitudes in a natural social setting. Such an examination allows me to understand the nature of the biases, how they manifest themselves in the thinking of sociologists, and the possible sources of those biases.

I will then engage in the second prong of this research design, which is a quantitative exploration of other scientific disciplines.[6] I have collected smaller samples of scholars from other academic disciplines that allow me to learn whether the factors for possessing social bias discovered in my examination of sociologists also are viable as ways of understanding other disciplines. By collecting data from scholars in the humanities and physical sciences and other social science disciplines, I will be in a better position to determine whether different qualities across contrasting scholarly fields influence the types of bias and levels of intolerance found among sociologists. I will also be able to test whether previous assertions about the different social attitudes across different types of sciences (Ladd & Lipset, 1975; Wuthnow, 1985) are still an accurate way to understand academia.

The quantitative portion of the research endeavor corrects a number of problems evident in previous attempts to document the level of bias in social institutions. First, this work systematically collects samples that are relatively random. While the directories used in this research have their limitations, I use probability techniques to maximize the participation of academics as potential respondents. As such, the findings will be able to be generalized to the larger academic population. Second, this research design allows me to assess the social attitudes toward a variety of different groups. With this research design, I can focus on documenting which groups actually experience bias rather than merely hypothesizing which groups suffer from bias. Even if I create potential hypotheses, I am unable to ignore disconfirming findings from this design that may refute my hypotheses. Suppose that I am a political Libertarian. I may only be interested in prejudice against Libertarians, and so I am tempted to look at only the results as they concern Libertarians. But I must also take into account the scores of other social groups in my society. If Green Party members face more hostility than Libertarians, then that is evidence of this political bias and I must report it. Finally, I will document the actual prejudicial attitudes of academics and not merely make inferences about their social attitudes and the potential prejudices they have. I will not merely assume that because certain groups are overrepresented in a given field members of these groups must have bias against certain out-group members. The questions used will indicate whether academics likely engage in an unreasonable prejudice against certain social groups. If they do, then we will be forced to consider what the real-world implications of such prejudices may be.

It can fairly be asked why I will spend so much time analyzing the attitudes of sociologists as opposed to other academics. There is a danger that, as a sociologist, I may be too close to the discipline to determine objectively the degree of bias in it. On the contrary, I submit that my familiarity with the discipline will allow me to have a better comprehension of the findings discovered by this work. I possess an understanding of the history and nature of this discipline that I do not possess in other disciplines. Furthermore, my time in the discipline will help me to anticipate potential biases, though I will use a research design that allows for the assessment of multiple social groups. Finally, it is worth noting that I do not possess the social background of most sociologists. Thus, while I am an insider in this discipline, I also have enough outsider credentials that allow me to make a legitimate assessment of the discipline.

Outline of Book

The outline for the remaining chapters in this book is as follows. In the next chapter, I look at some of the epistemological work that has questioned the ability of scientists to develop an objective approach to their research. This lack of objectivity is not limited to the social sciences and humanities, but also affects the physical sciences. Thus biases embedded in scientific research are likely to shape scholarly inquiry across disciplines. Thus, I will explore the historical and social context of academic study in general and of sociology in particular. This exploration will help us to understand the types of social pressure that may create contemporary biases among scientists. Finally, I speculate about the possible differences that may exist across the different types of scholarly inquiry (humanities, social sciences, physical sciences). These arguments set up the hypothesis under which this research can be conducted.

Chapter 3 begins my research into the discipline of sociology. I use a question asking the respondents whom they are willing to let into their workplace. The sample of sociologists will be sufficiently large to allow me to probe deeply the different ways bias and tolerance play out among them. I found that sociologists prefer not to work with individuals who are fundamentalists, evangelicals, National Rifle Association members, and Republicans.[7] The results of this work indicate that sociologists are significantly more hostile toward religious conservatives than to political conservatives but there is hostility directed at both types of social groups. I also found that sociologists who are older, female, and who study marginalized populations are more likely to possess these biases than other sociologists. Furthermore, sociologists tend to favor individuals who are Democrats and/or members of the ACLU. Thus it is not only the case that these scientists may treat certain individuals unfairly, but they may also provide an unfair level of preference for other individuals. However, the strength of the negative bias against religious and political conservatives is stronger than the positive bias toward progressives.

It is not only important to determine the degree to which sociologists are biased against members from certain groups, but also what that bias may look like. Chapter 4 utilizes a qualitative assessment of blogs written by sociologists. These blogs allow sociologists to express their perceptions and affection (or lack of affection) for given groups. I found that sociologists generally express a significant amount of hostility toward individuals with conservative political beliefs. To the degree that they conflate religious conservatism with political conservatism, sociologists also express hostility toward religious conservatives. I speculate that an important reason chapter 3 indicates that fundamentalists are more likely to be rejected as potential coworkers than political conservatives is that religious fundamentalism may indicate a higher degree of certainty of extreme conservatism, as opposed to moderate conservatism, within a potential job candidate.

In chapter 5, I go beyond the exploration of sociologists to investigate the evidence of bias or tolerance in other academic disciplines. The disciplines I explore are anthropology, political science, history, language, philosophy, chemistry, experimental biology, and physics. Such an examination helps to determine whether the findings about sociologists can apply generally to other academics. I also explore different types of disciplines to see if the social biases scholars exhibit are unique to the type of academic work they do or if it is a general feature of academia. I found that in other disciplines, fundamentalists and Republicans are also the least desired colleagues among the social groups. This rejection is less powerful among academics in the physical sciences than among those in the social sciences and humanities, but this tendency is still present. The bias documented among sociologists is not exceptional but is rather a reflection of the academic subculture, although it is more prevalent in certain disciplines. While I only document this quantitatively, it is also plausible that the qualitative results of chapter 4 are applicable as well. Thus other academics may conflate religious and political conservatism to justify their rejection of fundamentalists and evangelicals.

In chapter 6, I discuss the implications of the findings in this work. Clearly the idea of objective scientists who are open to all possibilities is further problematized by these results. Nevertheless, scientists often promote this image of objectivity to legitimize their work. But the presence of these social biases has very real consequences that have to be addressed. Because of these biases, contrasting viewpoints cannot be explored and individuals from disfavored social groups are discouraged from entering academia. Another problem that comes from these biases is that nonscientists often see through the efforts scholars make to have objectivity, and thus the status of scientists to speak to the larger society is compromised. Until we face the full costs of ignoring the social biases present in academia, both science and the larger social community will lose out on the opportunity to enjoy the full benefits of an academy that confronts all scientific possibilities.

In chapter 7, I conclude with some suggestions on how to address the issues brought up by this work. While fundamentalists, evangelicals, and Republicans may not suffer from minority group status outside of the academy, they likely suffer from that status inside of academia. Measures should be taken to ensure that the talents and voices offered by members of these groups are respected. In this chapter, I suggest some of these potential corrective measures and speculate about future work in the study of academic bias.

Finally, in a book about bias, it is only fair that the reader should know up front the possible bias of the author. The reader should be free to use that knowledge to assess the accuracy of the author's findings. Although I have taken steps to maximize the chances that my findings will be based upon the real existence of bias, and not my subjective concerns about it, this does not mean that I am immune to the possibility that these findings are tainted by my own perspective. In fact, I do have religious and political perspectives that differ from most social scientists. I am a Christian in the spirit of the New Evangelicals as described by Quebedeaux (1978), which provides me with a traditional religious belief that most of my academic peers do not share, and yet I have several progressive social and political values as well. Thus my traditional theological beliefs do not always translate into traditional social beliefs. Perhaps some of my religious differences come from the fact that I also differ from most of my academic peers in that I went to high school in the South and come from a home of lower socioeconomic status,[8] which are both predictors of higher levels of certain types of religiosity. Nevertheless, I do hold to a religious belief system outside of the mainstream of most of my colleagues. Politically, I am an independent. At times this has meant that I have voted for Democrats, Green Party members, Libertarians, and Republicans. While I do not consider myself a political conservative by any stretch of the imagination, I know that, compared to other social scientists, I am quite conservative. I have no membership in the ACLU or the NRA, and I am neither a vegetarian nor a hunter. I added those activities to my survey, as I believed that they would be controversial enough to elicit information about the possible social bias among scientists. As we will see in the following chapters, I was correct to include these organizations and activities, as they do elicit responses that reflect some of the social bias in academia. I do not, however, belong to any national organizations that readers would recognize as conservatively oriented, and probably my most controversial activity is wearing my Texas Longhorn clothes at the different Texas public campuses where I work.

CHAPTER TWO

Historical and Social Bias within Academia

I remember a time when my image of scientists was that of old white men with grey hair that spent all their time in the laboratory. I guess today we would call them nerds. It was also my perception that these men were only interested in the truth, and that as such, they were open to any possible findings of their research. Since then, I have obviously come to realize how wrong I was with my assumptions about scientists' age, race, and sex. I am glad to have been wrong about those assumptions. But now that I am in academia, I also realize how wrong I was about the objectivity of scientists as well. I am not, of course, the first person to realize this. There is a large body of academic literature that has explored the impossibility of objectivity in scientific inquiry. The types of biases that may influence academics do not just occur. They develop within a given social and historical context. Before I explore the location of social biases within academia, it is important to assess the nature of the academic community and issues surrounding the social and historical development of academic inquiry.

Biases in Scientific Inquiry

Epistemology is the study of knowledge. Scholars in this field argue that we have certain social biases that shape how we understand what we think we know. These biases reinforce themselves over time and make it difficult for us to gain an objective understanding about reality. For example, a person may be convinced that individuals in a certain occupation, such as auditors, tend to be mean people. This idea may arise from the fact that every time a person encounters an auditor, the auditor is rather insensitive to the concerns of that person. Furthermore, this hypothetical person may hear from friends and family members about other unpleasant experiences they have had with auditors. Over time, all of this information convinces a person about the meanness of auditors. However, these experiences are the result of social forces that have shaped a person's ideas about auditors. In reality, this person does not know if auditors are any more unpleasant than other individuals, but that person's experiences seem to confirm this as social fact and so the person accepts it. In fact, it is often because an individual has already developed a stereotype about the meanness of auditors that he or she will discount contradictory data. Thus any pleasant experience the person has with an auditor is seen as the exception that proves the rule. Likewise, scientists also bring in their own presuppositions into their studies which may or may not comport with reality. This bias may convince scientists to emphasize certain findings that support those presuppositions while they minimize the importance of other findings that work against those presuppositions.

Marx has sometimes been credited with the initial development of epistemology. His arguments about false consciousness imply that our economic conditions often convince us to accept a certain set of social beliefs, regardless of whether those beliefs are true. Thus our knowledge is socially constructed rather than based on a logical assessment of the social reality around us. Mannheim (1954) built on Marx's work with his argument that ideas are bound to a certain social position in society. Marx dwells on the economic conditions that permit the development of philosophies that will allow society to evolve, but Mannheim is not restricted to claims about our economy. He contends that many different social forces such as occupations and status categories also help to shape the ideas emerging within a certain culture or subculture. The implication of his work is that acquisition of knowledge is also conditioned by the social structures surrounding scientists. Academics, like members of other occupations, are shaped by social forces that make some ideas accessible to them, while other ideas are beyond their perception. Thus, scientists are not objective seekers after reality; rather, they document a reality as shaped by the social dimensions that influence those participating in scientific inquiry.

At its core, epistemology implies that we are unable to make logical and objective assessments of our social surroundings, because social forces produce biases in the way we acquire our knowledge. Yet theoretically, this is where scientific inquiry should be able to help us get past such biases. In theory, scientific inquiry forces us to develop workable hypotheses that we can test. Our hypothetical person does not have to rely on his or her previous experiences with auditors, but can use an external test to see if they really are mean people. Perhaps that person has had a bad run of auditors or keeps such lousy books that he or she infuriates auditors with sloppiness. But scientific analysis of the personality traits of several auditors can help us not to be trapped by the unique social situations this person has encountered. We can hypothesize that auditors will score as meaner than others on a psychological test. However, if they do not put up such scores, we will have to come to a different conclusion about their hypothesized meanness. Scientific inquiry has developed as a way to counter the social biases that often distort our ability to gain an accurate view of social reality.

The only problem is that scientists themselves still have their own personal and social biases which can affect science even with use of the scientific method. Polanyi (1958) developed the idea that scientists have to develop personal skills that help them do their research. These skills include the ability to conduct research but also the ability to convince others of the rightness of their findings. Thus highly persuasive and charismatic scholars are able to convince others that their ideas are best, and we are no longer relying upon pure scientific inquiry in order to find logical answers. Kuhn (1962) built on this work by pointing out how paradigms, or worldviews, develop to dominate scientific fields. These paradigms are ways of thinking that take on a life of their own and determine where scientists are supposed to look for answers. Solutions that do not fit into the given paradigm of the day are generally discarded and not taken seriously until the current paradigm is found to be insufficient for dealing with the contemporary information found in a scientific field. These and other classical scholars of epistemology argue that scientific inquiry is not an objective search for truth. Rather, such inquiry is dominated by the personal and social biases that shape the researchers of the day.

Such lines of analysis have been adopted by some contemporary scholars as they attempt to find new paradigms and worldviews that can be used to understand our social and personal reality. For example, feminist (Grosz & de Lepervanche, 1988; Harding, 1986, 1987; Hubbard, 1983) and Afrocentrist (Asante, 1998; Karenga, 2001; Semmes, 1981) scholars have complained about a male, Eurocentrist approach to research. They argue that such an approach is blind to the social realities experienced by women and individuals of color. For example, discussions of the beneficial nature of economic growth in a society take on new meaning if one considers the marginalized position that women and people of color continue to hold in this expanding society. As a result of their critiques, we have seen the rise of scholarly inquiry that takes into account alternative perspectives to the dominant scientific paradigms of the day.[1] It is not my argument that these challengers are either correct or incorrect. But these critiques illustrate that how we view social reality is tied to the biases that arise out of our social position, seen in this case in terms of race and gender. Whether it is possible to overcome these biases and to gain an objective assessment is unclear, but it is critical that we accept the reality of such biases or we will place too much stock on the ability of scientists to understand objective reality.[2]

These biases are important not only for understanding which perspective scholars tend to adopt, but also because they tend to attract others who share those perspectives. Weber's ideas of elective affinity (1958) suggests that certain ideas or philosophies tend to reproduce themselves within a given subculture by attracting those who deeply support them. Research into religion suggests that this may be the case since followers of a certain religion tend to be drawn from a given subculture and their religion reinforces perspectives benefiting that subculture. We have evidence of this as it concerns the religious perspectives of blacks (Lincoln & Mamiya, 1990; Washington, 1964; Wilmore, 1972), feminists (Berger, 1999; Ruether, 1975), and the upper class (Niebuhr, 1957; Pope, 1942; Roof & McKinney, 1987). In each of these cases, certain religious institutions disproportionately attract members of certain social groups because they attend to the wants and needs of individuals in those groups. Likewise, certain philosophical perspectives in the sciences may attend to the wants and needs of individuals with certain social biases that disproportionally draw those individuals into certain scientific fields. Perhaps just as important, individuals who do not share those social biases are not drawn into a given scientific field or are even discouraged from engaging in scientific work. Thus scholarly analysis is done in a way that excludes possible alternatives to the dominant paradigm since individuals likely to consider those alternatives are turned away from scientific work.

If scientists work in fields where individuals with alternative perspectives cannot easily participate, then it becomes vital to understand which biases dominate scientific inquiry. Because of the difficulties of working through one's own biases, we should know the nature of those dominant in scientific disciplines. To undergo this assessment, it is important to look at the development of scientific inquiry. It is in the development of our scientific institutions that we can discover clues as to the sort of affinity that exists to draw certain individuals into scientific work. In the following section, I offer a quick look at the development of scientific inquiry with special attention to how this development may create incentives for certain biases among academics.

The Development of Scientific Inquiry

Marie Boas Hall (1958) discussed a time before the advent of science as a period in which societies attempted to understand forces beyond their control through magical beliefs. Perhaps the earliest application of what we may call science occurred in early civilizations located in the Mesopotamian and Nile valleys. We entered a period of modern science in the sixteenth century with the work of individuals such as Leonardo da Vinci, Andreas Vesalius, and Galileo Galilei (Gordon, 1995). These and other scientific thinkers began to use methods of experimentation and rationality to understand the biological and physical world around them. This led to a scientific attitude that began to emphasize reason over previous supernaturalist beliefs. In other words, science presupposes that humans are capable of learning about their physical and biological environment and have a responsibility to engage in such learning.

Before the development of scientific inquiry, humans relied on supernatural beliefs to understand their physical and social reality. The use of otherworldly religious beliefs allowed humans to answer questions about physical processes they did not understand, to glimpse the nature of humanity, and to form the type of moral values that would benefit them. As scientific inquiry developed, it quickly became a competitor with religious beliefs as the legitimator of knowledge. This conflict was illustrated by Galileo's excommunication from the church for his insistence that the earth circled the sun rather than vice versa. His punishment served as a warning to scientists that their ability to engage in open inquiry would be limited as long as religious leaders possessed control of the larger society.[3] These events also illustrated the potential conflict between scientific inquiry into the natural world and traditional religious authority. This conflict between physical scientists and religious advocates continues today over issues such as evolution and embryonic stem cell research.

In response to such dangers, scientists and freethinkers of their day helped to develop what would be known as the Enlightenment movement. This social movement pushed for the freedom of scientists to engage in inquiry without the interference of religious institutions. With the French Revolution, these individuals discovered social power they had not previously enjoyed. The Enlightenment movement not only fought for the rights of individuals to learn about physical and biological phenomena, but it also allowed social scientists to question the social and moral order of the religious organizations of their day. Comte (1896) founded the discipline of sociology as a way to develop societal morality scientifically. He saw scientifically developed morality as superior to the religious superstitions that dominated society. Thus, the social sciences developed as a way to use scientific methods to understand societal constructs and tendencies. From Comte's work, and the work of other scholars, social scientific disciplines also emerged as counters to the traditional and religious social structures of their day. Scientists within these disciplines offered the scientific method as a way to deal with questions of societal values and organization, which often came in conflict with supernaturally based traditional values and social organization.

Disciplines in the humanities also developed alternative, and nonreligious, ways to construct our philosophical and social understanding about reality. Humanities such as linguistics and philosophy challenged the idea that the way we conduct our lives in our culture is the only, or even the best, way to conduct our lives. The disciplines in the humanities also tended to question traditional supernaturalist understandings of our social reality. In the humanities there was less emphasis on using the scientific method and more emphasis on developing multicultural comprehension about social and cultural worlds that differed from the dominant group. To the degree that supernatural religion served as a major component of that dominant culture, studies in the humanities served as a challenger to traditional religion. Since the humanities do not rely upon scientific methodology, scholars in these fields are not necessarily scientists, but they often provide philosophical and theoretical frameworks under which a good deal of social scientists and even some physical scientists operate. Thus understanding the humanities is a valuable way of understanding the cultural context in which scientists operate.

As such, scientific inquiry in the physical and biological sciences, social sciences, and humanities has developed as a competitor to religious thought. In different ways, these disciplines sought to position themselves as authoritative mechanisms to deal with questions that were previously answered through supernatural sources. Religious explanations of how and why our physical world developed were challenged by the development of the physical sciences. Arguments about the best way to organize society and the moral values that should drive that society awoke between religion and the social sciences. Finally, the value of understanding alternative views of reality produced distinct answers between scholars in the humanities and adherents of otherworldly beliefs.

This bias can be seen in the transformation of the American university from one dominated by religious ideology to one that tends to dismiss the influence of religion (Marsden, 1996; Ringenberg, 1984). Even religious colleges have started limiting the influence of their founding churches in an effort to gain more credibility with their secular academic counterparts (Burtchaell, 1998). Smith (2003) goes as far as to argue that academics simply assumed a zero-sum reality whereby the decrease of religious superstition would be correlated with more reliance on scientific rationality. With such an understanding of the relationship between religion and science, there is little wonder that academics are less likely to have religious belief than nonacademics.

This illustrates one possible bias of academics—an antipathy toward religious thought. Since science is a competitor with supernaturalism, it is logical that scientists will resent and seek to reject claims made by religious institutions. This resentment may explain why scientists are less likely to have supernatural religious beliefs than nonscientists (Ecklund, Park, & Veliz, 2008; Larson & Witham, 1998; Leuba, 1934, 1921). This has especially been true for social scientists, who are less likely to adhere to a supernaturalist belief system than physical scientists. However, scholars of all different types may be less open toward working with individuals of faith if they perceive such individuals as threats to their status as arbitrators of knowledge.

There is another potential bias among scientists worth exploring. A very important characteristic of science is that it is an institution that values progress. The scientific method advocates the use of experiments to eliminate inaccuracies so that we can progress toward a more accurate knowledge of our world. As we gain this knowledge, the natural reaction is to make changes to our society in regard to what we have learned. As individuals in the social sciences and, to a more limited extent, the humanities begin to adopt scientific mechanisms, they do so with the idea of discovering knowledge that allows society to progress, or move forward. Social groups that support a static idea about society are antithetical to such efforts. This creates the possibility that social science and humanities scholars are more open to working with individuals with similar progressive attitudes toward social change. They may resist working with individuals who are generally satisfied with the societal status quo, as they may perceive such individuals as hampering their ability to promote the idea of societal progress in light of new scientific evidence.

This bias may not be limited to the social sciences and the humanities. Those in the physical sciences often conduct work that has important societal implications (e.g., cloning). Even scientists who do not conduct such controversial work may philosophically desire the right and freedom to perform their research as they so wish. This desire to conduct work without the constraints imposed by traditional societal notions may also influence those in the physical sciences to have a more negative view of individuals who seek to maintain the current societal structure. If this is true, then individuals in the physical sciences would have a relatively low desire to work with individuals who want to maintain our current societal values and ethics, although their resistance may be lower than that of scholars in the social sciences and the humanities. Political conservatism is generally seen as a political philosophy that maintains the status quo or seeks to return society to a treasured time in the past. Thus, scientific disciplines, to various degrees, may possess an antipathy toward political conservatism if science tends to influence individuals toward progressive changes in the larger society.

In short, there are sociological reasons why scholars are more likely to favor those who have no religion or who have more progressive societal ideas. It is possible that individuals of minor religions are less threatening to scholars since their competition for social legitimization is with the dominant religious ideology in a given society. Thus we would expect academics to be less likely to have traditional religious faith or to have a static notion about societal change. If individuals prefer to interact with others who are similar to themselves, then scientists also may be more likely to reject those who have traditional religious faith or are not supportive of societal change. This rejection would be the potential source of negative bias among academics.

Scientists, the New Class, and the Culture War

Some theorists (Berger, 1986; Ehrenreich & Ehrenreich, 1977; Gouldner, 1978; Kristol, 1979) have argued that we have seen the development of a "new class" shaping social attitudes. The theory of the new class suggests that professionals in industries that help to produce culture or are affiliated with government work can be called a "knowledge class." These are qualities that clearly describe scholars and thus make them prime candidates for membership into this new class. "New class" individuals not only deal with the construction of culture and knowledge but also move away from traditional social values and become attached to a more progressive ideology. This attachment is due in part to the economic interest that members of the new class have in progressive governmental philosophy, but also to their desire to resist the limitations placed upon society by notions of traditional morality (Gouldner, 1978; Kristol, 1979). Thus scholars may be disposed toward political progressiveness simply because of their social position in society.

Once antitraditional values become enshrined within scientific occupations, scholars become part of what has been labeled the culture war. Hunter (1991) popularized the notion of a critical struggle in the United States between individuals with contrasting ways of constructing meaning in their lives. On one side are traditionalists who perceive that the highest meaning of life can be found in a supernatural order. On the other side are modernists who perceive meaning as coming from the choices individuals make for themselves. Issues such as abortion, same-sex marriage, and embryonic stem cell research represent tension points over which advocates of both sides engage in conflict. The conflicts may not really be directly over those issues, but they represent the different cultural worlds that each side would desire to create.

In the context of the culture war, members of the new class inevitably become supporters of the modernist position. Their potential hostility toward traditionalists and conservative cultural values positions them in the modernist camp. Scholars may play a vital role in this struggle since they possess the role of legitimating knowledge in society. This allows them to support the "discovery" of knowledge that supports the perspectives of modernists in their cultural struggle with traditionalists. Many of these traditionalists base their cultural understandings on religious justification. Thus the cultural war easily can become the latest installment of the historical conflict between religion and science. For example, the attempts of traditionalists to incorporate notions of creationism into academic research have been conceptualized as part of a cultural, as well as scientific, war (Forrest & Branch, 2005).

If academia becomes a critical front in a culture war that rages in society, then the stakes are much higher for maintaining scientific purity. Scientific purity may not only indicate the need for academic rigor, but it may also create the desire to ensure that proper social and cultural values are promoted through scientific work. Scholars possess a powerful incentive to filter out those who do not support such values. Thus social biases can possibly lead to discrimination against individuals who do not share these values. Political and religious conservatives (Coulter, 2004; D'Souza, 1991; Kimball, 1990; Sykes, 1990) have argued that such discrimination has taken place. Horowitz (2006) claims that politically radical professors unfairly punish politically conservative students. There is also research that attempts to back up those assertions. Rothman, Lichter, and Nevitte (2005) provide evidence that political conservatives with similar academic credentials are not able to teach in as prestigious positions as political progressives. Ecklund (2010) also finds that a significant number of elite scientists believe that religion is either irrelevant or even dangerous to the mission of science. Other research (Hodge, 2002; Ressler & Hodge, 2003) indicates that evangelical social workers may have faced discrimination at the hands of social work academics. Gartner (1986) comes to a similar conclusion in his examination of religious bias in admission to doctoral programs in clinical psychology. If such discrimination is taking place, it is not only religious conservatives that suffer. The sciences also suffer from a dominance of viewpoint that prevents the sort of dialog that reduces extremism and that allows for a sharpening of different perspectives (Nieli, 2005).

Yet claims of liberal bias by nonacademics have generally been linked to work that looks either at isolated incidents of bias (Elder, 2003; Goldberg, 2001; Limbaugh, 2004) or a few cases in unique situations (Bozell, 2008). What such works fail to do is demonstrate that there is a systematic bias that pervades entire scientific disciplines. If academics are foot soldiers in a larger culture war, then one would expect to find powerful biases that clearly shape what are acceptable products from scientific work. There would be ways in which scientific work that does not serve the goal of furthering a progressive position in the culture war is discouraged. The discouragement of work that does not support progressive causes would allow members of a given scientific field to concentrate their energy on supporting their progressive viewpoints.

Some have argued that notions of a culture war have been vastly overblown. Fiorina (2005) argues that moderation, rather than extremism, is the typical response of most Americans. He contends that there is conflict among the elites but not among the vast majority of Americans. Furthermore, Demerath (2005) contends that any potential cultural war present in the United States pales in comparison to other societies where such cultural conflict is more pronounced. Thus he contends that arguments of cultural polarization have to be understood in a historical context in which the struggles in the United States are not nearly as pronounced as what would be expected in a full-blown culture war. However, Abramowitz and Saunders (2005) find that while some of the claims of the culture war are overblown, there are still deep divisions in the United States. Furthermore, it has been demonstrated (Knuckey, 2005) that cultural divisions that buttress voting patterns emerged in the mid to late 1990s but were not present before that time, indicating that recent cultural conflict fuels a significant portion of the political struggle in the United States. Finally, even if notions of the culture war are overblown, the fact that polarization is still prevalent within the elites suggests that scientists and scholars, who are part of that elite, are likely to be caught up in the culture war. Fighting the culture war may be an important task of scientists that can interfere with their ability to discover and disseminate knowledge.

The culture war and the position of scholars in the new class both provide possible motivation for academics to exercise their social biases within a context of potential discrimination. However, merely because scholars have motivation to discriminate does not mean that they engage in discrimination. Overrepresentation of political and religious progressives in academia can be due simply to the desire of such individuals to engage in scholarly work as opposed to other possible occupations (Ames et al., 2005; Cohen-Cole & Durlauf, 2005; Ecklund & Scheitle, 2007; Kimura-Walsh, 2008). A self-selection effect, rather than discrimination from other academics, may account for the unwillingness of political and religious conservatives to engage in academic research. Discovering the propensity of scholars to screen out those who are perceived as culturally undesirable is important for understanding if undue bias is a factor in the cultural makeup of academia.

Religious and Political Factors in Academia

It is well established that individuals in academia have political and social attitudes that differ from nonacademics. As early as 1902, an article in the *Atlantic Monthly* observed that academics tend to take on a more radical and critical political position relative to nonacademics. World War I briefly tempered some of the powerful progressiveness among scholars, but this did not last as many academics became disillusioned about the war and support for new ideas generated by the Russian Revolution began to grow (Ladd & Lipset, 1975). This movement toward political progressivism continues throughout the twentieth century. After World War II, Republican presidential candidates consistently received a smaller percentage of the vote from academics than from other professionals (Howard, 1958), and there is evidence that McCarthyism help to enfranchise radical activism rather than discourage it (Nisbet, 1971). Ladd and Lipset's (1975) work indicates consistent evidence of political liberalism in academia, with the social sciences and humanities having more liberalism than the physical sciences but the physical/biological sciences having more progressiveness than the fields of business, engineering, and agriculture. I later discovered (1994) these trends among sociologists, and there is little reason to believe that other academic professions are not also much more politically progressive than others in our society.

Religious belief, as well as political orientation, serves to distinguish academics from the rest of the population. Leuba (1921) documents the early trend of academics accepting a nonreligious belief at a higher rate than nonscholars. He found that this tendency toward religious apostasy was stronger among those in prestigious higher institutions. Surveys of academics between 1913 and 1933 indicated that irreligious belief had grown among them over those twenty years (Leuba, 1934). Stark's 1963 examination of graduate students also indicated that those in more elite positions were less likely to possess religious beliefs than other graduate students. Contemporary work by Larson and Witham (1998) also notes the pattern of elite scientists being more likely to reject religious belief. Other recent work indicates that social scientists are more likely to reject religion than other scholars (Stark & Finke, 2000; Wuthnow, 1985). Ecklund, Park, and Veliz (2008) reinforce the findings of overall irreligiosity among scholars, but discovered that the gap between the social scientists and physical scientists has declined with a fall in religious observance by the physical scientists. The rejection of religion is so powerful within academia that charges of anti-Catholic discrimination have been made (Alba, 2006; Greeley, 1973).

Beyond the ideological differences scholars have with nonacademics, it is also worth noting that there are demographic and social differences between these two groups. Ladd and Lipset (1975) document that scholars are more likely to come from families that are well educated and Jewish than are other individuals. My own early research (1994) indicates that sociologists are more likely than the general public to grow up in families with a high socioeconomic status (SES) that are educated and Jewish. Ecklund and Scheitle (2007) also have illustrated some of the social and demographic differences between scientists and the general public. It is important that scholars are less likely to grow up in families that are religious or from the South, as I noted at the end of chapter 1. At least part of the difference in political, social, and religious beliefs between academics and nonacademics is due to their distinctive social and demographic backgrounds.

The research cited in this section clearly indicates that individuals in academia disproportionally come from certain social groups and tend to have social and political attitudes that distinguish them from the rest of our society. These attitudes are not automatically tied to their role as scholars, but they do indicate that academics may be susceptible to certain religious, social, and political beliefs not directly linked to the research they conduct. Such an assertion is in keeping with the epistemological work indicating that our perspectives are deeply shaped by our social position in society (Bourdieu, 1988; Ladd & Lipset, 1975; Mannheim, 1954; Yancey, 1994). Thus, it is often difficult to determine whether the findings of scholars are determined by their personal propensities to engage in bias or whether they have indeed accurately recorded the data surrounding them.

These biases are not limited to affecting the ability of scholars to understand societal issues. They also potentially shape assumptions surrounding some of the theories in the physical and biological sciences since these theories can play a role supporting presuppositions that aid the subcultures these scientists come from. For example, the theory of evolution provides a useful philosophical tool for those who desire to distance themselves from the idea of an all-powerful deity (Dawkins, 1986; Desmond & Moore, 1992). This theory allows such individuals to conceive of a natural world that can develop without any supernatural aid. The theory has important socio-psychological implications for those who advance an agenda of human choice over otherworldly determinism. The philosophical and psychological support that this theory provides to the irreligious does not indicate that the theory is false. It merely indicates that physical scientists may have personal motivations to advance this theory regardless of its accuracy. One should not critique evolutionary theory based on its social and political implications. It should be critiqued solely on how well it explains the physical and biological processes that we can observe. However, it is naïve to think that these implications, or personal motivations, do not interfere with the ability of scientists to conceptualize the origin of life, and we would be wise to monitor the ability of scholars to entertain alternative scientific perspectives.

There is stronger argument that these biases may affect the judgment of social scientists and scholars in the humanities. Religious and political biases can be connected to a need to promote a progressive social view in which there is a need to overcome historical stratification. This may indicate importance of a powerful government that addresses issues of inequality. Such a priority naturally arises from the politically radical philosophies, such as socialism and communism, which contend that movement toward a centralized government is desirable. This propensity to seek out support for public sector control can undoubtedly affect the way scholars critique private markets and extol the virtues of the public sector. Once again, the existence of this bias does not necessarily discount the argument for a larger role for the public sector. Scholars' concerns about capitalism and private enterprise may be well founded. However, we also have to consider the possibility that political bias within these academics removes alternative ways of conceptualizing social solutions.

These previous studies indicate that there are political, social, and religious differences between academics and nonacademics in the United States. However, these studies do not assess whether these differences have any sort of long-term effect on the research conducted by scholars. Assessing this effect is difficult since to do so one has to conceptualize the alternative scientific findings that would emerge if these biases did not exist. It is a task that I do not attempt with this current research. In such an assessment, the researcher would bring his or her own social biases into the analysis. Thus the assessor's argument that alternative scientific findings are being neglected because of the biases among academics would be distorted by his or her biases and we could not be sure which set of scientific findings (the assessor's or the rest of the scientific field's) is most plausible. However, if it can be demonstrated that alternative ways of understanding scientific reality are stymied even before they are offered, then one is in a better position to question contemporary scientific results. Such a demonstration has to be constructed in a way so that the potential biases of the individuals assessing the sciences play, at best, a limited role in shaping the conclusions. In other words, academics have to be provided an opportunity to reject or accept the opportunity to present alternative perspectives before new ideas have undergone proper scientific rigor. If we can test the willingness of academics to refuse consideration of alternative perspectives, then we can argue that scholars are using bias as they conduct their work. Rather than attempt to make the difficult argument of conceptualizing alternatives to current scientific findings, I will attempt to investigate whether individuals who may conceptualize such alternatives unnecessarily face barriers to their ability to conduct scientific work. We now must ponder how to conduct such an investigation.

Who Will Scholars Allow into Their Field?

Merely because academics are more likely to be irreligious and to have more progressive political attitudes than other individuals does not mean that they limit their research to ideas that support these perspectives. It is possible that these are the very perspectives that allow academics to consider possible scientific alternatives. For example, political progressiveness has been linked to social tolerance (Chandler, 2001; de Wijze, 2000; Moon, 2004; Sidanius, Pratto, & Bobo, 1996). Furthermore, individuals with lower religiosity are less likely to adhere to an exclusive notion about religion and may be more willing to embrace different ideas about social reality than strong adherents to a religious faith. Theories such as the authoritarian personality (Adorno, Frenkel-Brunswik, Levinson, & Sanford, 1950) and right-wing authoritarianism (Altermeyer, 1968) are built upon the notion that the very personal qualities documented in academics (political progressiveness and religious openness) are correlated to open-mindedness. The very disparities noted between scientists and nonscientists may lead to scientific disciplines that are more, and not less, willing to explore alternative perspectives.

Of course, it should be observed that the very individuals who discovered the virtues of political progressiveness and irreligiosity are the scholars who likely possess those qualities themselves. At least a modicum of skepticism must be tied to these findings. For example, the authoritarian-personality theory has been criticized as targeting conservative, but not liberal, intolerance (Eckhardt, 1991; Martin, 2001). To truly test the willingness of scholars to avoid the traps of bias, it is vital to assess their willingness toward showing tolerance for those with whom they disagree. The real question must be how open scholars are toward those that are not akin to them in their social beliefs. Do they allow those that differ from them socially, politically, and religiously to be legitimate competitors in scientific inquiry, or does their desire for homophilic associations (Cetina, 1999; Gieryn, 1999) inhibit the exploration of possible alternatives to the scientific field?

I am asking how willing scholars are to allow individuals into their profession who may develop ideas that challenge the revealed wisdom of their fields. This revealed wisdom is likely connected to the social and political worlds of academics, so competition from alternative perspectives may not only threaten a scholar's previous scientific work, but also challenge the very worldview a scholar bases his or her life on. Of course, there is no certain way that an individual can know if someone who is allowed into the profession will one day challenge its basic epistemological underpinnings. But clearly those from social groups that differ from other scholars (political conservatives and the highly religious) are more likely to provide such a challenge than other individuals. Therefore, this question can really boil down to the relative willingness of scholars to allow those from other social groups to participate in the search for and creation of scientific knowledge.

This leads to the key way in which we can operationalize a possible way to locate scientific bias. If scholars are willing to allow those from different social and ideological groups into their field, then it becomes clear that they allow those who can bring contrasting ideas into the discipline. If scholars are hesitant to allow individuals who differ from them in social and ideological ways into science, then a key reason for this hesitation may be fear that such individuals may challenge the revealed wisdom in the discipline. I have stated that the testing of whether a person has tolerance means the testing of ideas that sufficiently differ from that person's own ideas and whether the person has unjustified discrimination. If the purpose of science is to be an honest search for reality, then there is little reason why those with ideas that differ from other academics should not have the same opportunity to enter into scholarly work. Therefore whom academics are willing to work with becomes a key question for understanding the dimensions of bias and tolerance in educational institutions.

Scientific Bias

As stated in the opening chapter, rejecting those from a certain social group is not necessarily indicative of an unfair bias against that group. Individuals who reject friendships with those of different political perspectives may have learned that they fight often with those they disagree with politically, and such rejection can lead them to find more suitable friends. Those who have decided not to seek romantic entanglements with those of different religious beliefs may want to make sure that they are able to raise their children in their own religious tradition and an interfaith marriage may inhibit such socialization. There are legitimate reasons why individuals reject certain social groups. Rejection is not by itself evidence of unwarranted bias.

Given this reality, the question that has to be explored is whether the desire against interacting with certain social groups is justified for scientists. Are there reasons why members of certain social groups should not be able to work in academia? The answer to that question is yes. Individuals who have not completed the required amount of education are individuals who are unlikely to be prepared to engage in academic inquiry. Thus, for example, the social group of high school dropouts clearly can be discriminated against as it concerns entry into the scientific profession. Membership in groups of lower educational attainment can automatically disqualify individuals from participation in scientific work. However, once we get away from groups that by definition are lower in educational attainment, we have a hard time finding rational reasons why certain social groups should be excluded from participating in scientific inquiry.[4] If the disproportionate social and demographic makeup in the sciences is due to the rejection of groups that have lower levels of educational attainment to the sciences, then such disproportions may be justified. However, if these disproportions are not due to uneducated members of those social groups being rejected from the disciplines, but instead are due to adequately educated and trained members of those social groups being rejected, then we have evidence of unreasonable bias in scientific inquiry, unless some other rationale can be legitimated for this rejection. For example, previous work has shown that irreligious individuals are more likely to be scientists than those with high levels of religiosity. It may be the case that as individuals come into scientific disciplines, they tend to lose interest in religion. Science may be a powerful secularizing force. But it is also possible that due to the sociological and philosophical reasons provided in the previous paragraphs, those of high religious faith are discouraged from entering the scientific realm. Since there is no inherently logical reason why people with high religiosity should be excluded from participating in scientific inquiry, this would be a good example of an unreasonable bias affecting individuals with high religiosity and the institution of science as a whole.

Possible Disfavored Groups

Social groups that would test the possible biases among academics have to be groups qualified for conducting academic study but that may be rejected by academics for reasons other than their educational qualifications. Clearly political social groups fall into this category. Many would describe conservative political parties such as the Republicans as political forces that resist social and political change, and so members of conservative parties may face disfavor among scholars. Beyond Republicans and Democrats, it is valuable also to investigate other political parties, such as Libertarians and the Green Party, to see if there is a particular mix of political issues that is correlated with positive or negative bias within academia. Finally, scholars may approve of membership in the progressive ACLU more strongly than membership in the conservative NRA. There is no theoretical reason why members of conservative political parties are not qualified for engaging in scientific inquiry, but they may face a bias within an academic subculture that discourages them from engaging in that inquiry.

Beyond political social groups, there are also religious social groups that may encounter potential biases in academia. Irreligiosity appears to be a prominent characteristic of scholars. As such, there is the possibility of bias against individuals of faith. There is not an inherent reason why religious individuals are unable to engage in scientific inquiry. Bias against religious belief may discourage individuals with relatively high levels of religiosity from participating in scientific exploration. There is research that indicates that individuals belonging to religions with conservative theological orientations may have more powerful adherence toward their faith (Buell & Sigelman, 1985; Kelley, 1972; Longenecker, McKinney, & Moore, 2004; Noffke & McFadden, 2002). Those who possess conservative religious orientations, such as evangelicals and Mormons, may be seen as less acceptable by scholars than individuals who come from more moderate and progressive religious theologies, such as Jews. But the religious group that may face the highest level of rejection may be fundamentalists who can be conceptualized as even more religiously conservative than evangelicals and Mormons.

Finally, it is also viable to consider lifestyle choices when considering the possibility of bias. If scholars are prone to support social change, then nontraditional lifestyles may be seen as more acceptable to them. Individuals engaging in sexual practices considered nontraditional, such as homosexuality and bisexuality, may be relatively unlikely to experience negative bias. Transgenderism may also be a nontraditional lifestyle that is less likely to experience negative bias among scientists. On the other hand, transgenderism is a lifestyle that is conceptualized as being more public, and scholars may be more comfortable with unconventional lifestyles that remain private. Furthermore, there are political implications tied to certain lifestyles. Vegetarians are generally perceived as promoting social change through their dietary habits and can be seen as living a progressive lifestyle. On the other hand, individuals who engage in hunting can be seen as promoting a more traditional, or conservative, lifestyle tied to notions of the societal status quo. As such, vegetarians may be more acceptable to scholars than hunters. The higher level of acceptability of vegetarians may be more pronounced with academics than members of general society. But once again there is no inherent reason why scholars should favor those of a given sexual practice or lifestyle as it concerns their ability to engage in scientific inquiry. Ideally individuals with lifestyles one disagrees with would not affect the social atmosphere of the department as long as they do not bring aspects of their lifestyle into their work. But testing for the possibility that lifestyle bias is present in academia will allow us to see if scholars care about how their colleagues live their lives.

Social groups connected to conservative political ideologies, traditional religious values, and conventional lifestyles are groups that are theoretically not likely to be favored by academic scholars. If academics are likely to resist the incorporation of such groups into their occupations, then we clearly have evidence of an unreasonable bias in academia. This type of bias has serious social implications that should not be glossed over, but I am more concerned about the ramifications about the type of scientific inquiry that is possible due to such bias. Those ramifications will be discussed more fully in chapter 6. It is also important to explore whether certain social groups, such as progressive political, religious, and lifestyle groups, experience a positive bias by scholars. The research earlier in this chapter indicates that these progressive groups are more likely to be overrepresented in the academy and to have more social power among scholars than those from traditional groups. It remains to be seen whether members of these progressive groups who possess social power utilize that power to ensure that out-groups gain limited access to scientific inquiry or whether they truly live out their commitment to social toleration.

Conclusion

There are given biases that can be predicted among those who engage in scientific inquiry. The work from this chapter indicates that political and religious progressives are overrepresented among scholars of different disciplines. This overrepresentation is to be expected more within the social sciences and humanities than within the physical sciences. Given these historical biases, we are now in an excellent position to test the ability of scholars to include those from distinct social groups. If scholars are not willing, or able, to allow individuals of different social groups into their scholarly field, then we have to question how willing they are to entertain ideas that do not comport with their previously held conclusions. In this way, the arguments of early epistemologists such as Popper and Kuhn may carry a great deal of weight in disabusing us of the notion that science is an endeavor that conducts an open search for the truth. Rather, science may be just another social institution that seeks to sustain itself by creating a social atmosphere that provides cultural, ideological, and relational comfort for its members.

It is quite possible that scholars may avoid the propensity toward social homophily that is an important part of human society (McPherson, Smith-Lovin, & Cook, 2001). The nature of their occupation suggests that they may make up one of the few subcultures that prioritizes seeking objective reality more than maintaining its own social interests. In fact, because of their ideological progressiveness, scholars may even go out of their way to welcome those from different social groups, even at the expense of members of their own social group. Academics may desire to have interaction with ideas different from their own if they have a value system that encourages searching for knowledge no matter where it may be found. Such a value system would support debate among differing ideas and would allow scientists to be more broad-minded than individuals from other occupations. But since little recent empirical work has investigated the potential openness of scholars toward accepting individuals from different social groups, we previously have had no way of verifying such an assertion. In the remainder of this book I will address this research gap.

Previous efforts to assess the presence of bias within social institutions have tended to focus on anecdotal evidence. Without systematic assessments it is impossible to determine whether the bias displayed by such evidence is due to unusual circumstances or if it reflects a bias that dominates a given social institution. In the following chapter, I will begin a systematic examination of the possible existence of bias within academia. I will do this by using a question that determines the likelihood of academics to accept individuals from certain social groups as colleagues within their discipline. Once I have exhausted my exploration of sociology, I will be in a position to conduct a wider exploration of different scientific disciplines.

CHAPTER THREE

With Whom Do Sociologists Want to Work?

Exploring bias within the discipline of sociology will allow me to assess whether there are certain dynamics that facilitate or limit the emergence of social biases and intolerance that may be generalized to other academic disciplines. Once I have investigated the general trends in sociology, I will then consider whether those trends hold up in other scientific fields. If they do, it is possible to extrapolate some of the nuanced findings from my in-depth study of a single discipline to the other scholarly fields. This investigation will allow me to gain an understanding of the types of biases scientists develop and how they may construct their social biases. In this chapter, I will conduct a quantitative exploration of sociologists in the United States. In the next chapter, I will examine some of the online blogs written by sociologists to gain a qualitative perspective of their social tendencies.

Sociological History

I have chosen sociology for an in-depth analysis since it is the scientific field I know best. My knowledge of this discipline will allow me to appreciate some of the nuances that may emerge from my findings. Although some may wonder whether I am too much of an insider to provide an honest evaluation of the field, I contend that my inside knowledge of sociology and sociologists offsets any disadvantages I may have from the biases I have developed being part of the discipline. However, in no way am I asserting with this analysis that sociologists suffer more or less from social biases than other social scientists. Whether sociologists are more prone to adopt the biases that scholars possess can be evaluated when I compare the results of this chapter to the results of my quantitative analysis of multiple disciplines in chapter 5.

It is important to understand the historical and social context in which sociologists operate. It is commonly acknowledged that sociology was founded by August Comte. He perceived the need for a scientific way to develop the moral rules that should organize society. Thus from its inception sociology was a discipline that challenged the hegemony of religious order, which is true for many other scientific disciplines. However, early American sociologists tended to be clergy or sons of clergy, and in fact many sociologists overtly showed support for religious faith even while they sought to subvert the influence of religion in the larger society (Smith, 2003). Furthermore, early prominent American sociologists worked with social workers from Hull House in their endeavor to learn about society and to find applied ways to improve society. However, a schism developed between sociologists and social workers as the mostly male sociologists desired to escape the lower status possessed by the mostly female social workers (Deegan, 1988; Smith, 2003). The sociologists worked toward establishing their work as a scientific endeavor distinct from the work done by the social workers. To help them create this separation from social workers, these clergy and sons of clergy moved away from religious appreciation in their work and took a rather critical assessment of traditional religious thought.

This conflict with social workers illustrated an important early dynamic that would shape how sociologists would interact with people of faith. Smith (2003) divided early twentieth-century sociologists into reformers and academics. Reformers were more likely to have religious belief and sought academics as allies in their attempt to make societal changes. Academics regarded the reformers with some degree of professional embarrassment and were more antireligious in their outlook. Their understanding of religion was that it was a competitor for social influence. As the academics looked to gain status in order to use scientific information to address the social problems in society, they reframed religious ideology in an effort to stigmatize and privatize it. It was these academics, and not the reformers, who built upon the foundations of the early sociologists and developed American sociology into the institutions it is today. It is not evident that American sociology had to maintain a confrontational stance toward organized religion, but there were clearly socio-psychological aspects in the development of this discipline that inclined sociologists to develop such a stance.

American sociologists also focused on studying the demographic transition.[1] This helped to situate their work in a way that allowed them to understand processes of urbanization and industrialization. As they documented these processes, it is natural that sociologists perceived these changes as an acceptable path toward a more advanced society. Thus American sociologists developed ideas that facilitated, rather than resisted, social change. In this way it is not surprising that these scientists tended to support political initiatives that challenged the social status quo.

It is clear that the early sociologists fit into the progressive social and religious norms discussed in the previous chapter. There is little reason to believe that this pattern has changed for contemporary sociologists. Contemporary sociologists were known for their support of the progressive social movements that emerged during the 1960s. For example, the writings of contemporary sociologists and other social scientists have supported the progressive social movements of feminism (Benokraitis & Feagin, 1995; Chodorow, 1999; Gilligan, 1993; Hochschild & Machung, 2003; Plummer, 1995), environmentalism (Bell, 2008; Gould & Lewis, 2008; McCarthy & King, 2005), and racial justice (Bonilla-Silva, 2001; Carr, 1997; Feagin, 2000; Massey & Denton, 1996; Newman, 2003; Oliver & Shapiro, 1995). In addition to their support of political progressiveness, contemporary sociologists also have provided work suggesting that the nature of traditional religion is heavily shaped by social forces (Batson, Schoenrade, & Ventis, 1993; Durkheim, 1965; Geertz, 1966; Greeley, 1972; Roof & McKinney, 1987; Weber, 1958). Such work challenges the otherworldly beliefs of those with high religiosity. Furthermore, other research indicates that the highly religious may have less tolerance (Griffin, Gorsuch, & Davis, 1987; Hunsberger, 1995; Laythe, Finkel, & Kirkpatrick, 2001) and less openness to progressive social change (Altermeyer, 1968; Ellison, Echevarria, & Smith, 2005; Hayes, 1995; Olson, Cadge, & Harrison, 2006) than the irreligious. On the other hand, other social science work has suggested that personal religiosity is positively correlated with health benefits (Koenig, 1997; Levin & Chatters, 1998; Levin, 1996; Musick, 1996) and prosocial behaviors (Furrow, King, & White, 2004; Saroglou, Pichon, Trompette, Verschueren, & Dernelle, 2005; Shariff & Norenzayan, 2007; Sinha, Cnaan, & Gelles, 2007; Steinman & Zimmerman, 2004). Yet the documentation of such benefits does not have the ethical implications of the previous work on tolerance and the open-mindedness of the former studies. Contemporary sociologists appear to offer as little support for religious conservatives as they do for political conservatives.

Sociologists may not be the best representatives of scientists in general. But studying the sociological discipline in-depth will provide for a reasonable assessment of the social biases within the social sciences. Previous work has documented that sociologists possess the same general level of political progressiveness and irreligiosity (Ecklund & Scheitle, 2007; Hamilton & Hargens, 1993; Ladd & Lipset, 1975) as other social scientists.

Methodology

Understanding whether academics may screen out members of certain social groups as they attempt to gain a job in academia is a valuable way to test the existence of bias against these groups. But different types of academic institutions can have contrasting propensities to employ such screens. An educational institution not highly respected or expected to conduct cutting-edge research may not have the opportunity to use such screens as readily as elite academic institutions. Such organizations may have to accept members of disfavored groups since their positions are not highly competitive. It is plausible that scientists who work in more prestigious universities have the ability to act on their biases more easily than those in lower-status positions because they can be more selective about whom they allow into their departments. Furthermore, it is plausible that scientists in more prestigious positions may perceive themselves as possessing an important gatekeeping role for their discipline. Since the cutting-edge research that drives the discipline is more likely to occur in elite universities, screening out unwelcome social groups may help to ensure that these groups do not infuse the discipline with "unacceptable" ideas that may be embedded in those groups. Yet we also have to take into account the possibility that those at elite higher institutions may be more likely to adhere to scientific values of objectivity. As such, it is plausible that social bias is less likely to occur among scholars at prestigious higher education institutions.

To investigate which possibility accurately describes sociologists in higher-status positions, I need to gather the responses of sociologists from a relatively wide variety of academic positions. It is important to see if those who work in higher-status positions have a different propensity to accept social groups than those who work in lower-status positions. However, there are other institutional differences that may be important as well. For example, it is possible that there are different propensities to accept social groups according to whether the sociologists work in a religious educational setting or not. Those in religious educational settings may be more likely to accept highly religious individuals than those at nonsectarian educational institutions. However, those same religious institutions may discourage irreligious social groups, such as atheists, or groups with lifestyles that do not comport with traditional religious understandings, such as bisexuals. Furthermore, there may be valuable information to be gathered by exploring the type of specialization in which a sociologist works. Sociologists who work with issues of inequality (e.g., race, sexuality, gender) may be more sensitive to issues of rejection and more likely to accept members of social out-groups than other sociologists. Conversely, it is also possible that such scholars may be more likely to perceive individuals who are political conservatives and from traditional religions as barriers to the civil rights that they want to encourage. This may lead them to be more willing to reject religious and political conservatives. Finally, basic demographic differences such as sex, race, and age can also provide information about which scientists are most likely to engage in social bias.

It is quite tricky to investigate a highly educated population. A major problem is the possibility of a social desirability effect. A social desirability effect describes the tendency individuals have to make themselves look good when they are answering surveys or question-naires. Because of this effect, respondents do not always provide an honest answer, but rather answer in a way that they think is socially acceptable. This is especially true since the highly educated tend to per-ceive themselves as socially tolerant (Schaefer, 1996). Thus if directly asked about their willingness to accept those in other social groups, one would expect a higher number of them to exhibit social acceptance than would be the case in a candid setting.

Accordingly, I did not directly ask the academics in this research about their willingness to accept those in a variety of social groups. Instead, I couched this work under a rubric of collegiality. I sent out a survey that introduces itself as an attempt to assess collegiality in academia. Collegiality, or the ability to have a harmonious social environment, is an issue of great interest to many in academia, and it makes sense for an academic to conduct such a study. Labeling this study as such allows me to ask academics about whom they are will-ing to work with.[2] Research in race and ethnicity has indicated that being willing or not willing to work with a given social group is a key measure of social distance (Bogardus, 1968; Song, 1991). A question about whom one wants to work with can be a valuable way to assess levels of tolerance academics have toward social groups.

To conduct this research, I created an online survey. I used the Web site Survey Monkey to manage my survey. This Web site allowed me to send a link to the survey to each respondent's e-mail. Each respondent was able to fill out the survey and return it without my knowing who returned the survey. The survey I used, which was sent out on October 13, 2008, can be seen in the supplemental material. A breakdown of the demographics of the sample can be seen in figures 3.1, 3.2, and 3.3.[3] From these figures we can see that almost 50 per-cent of the respondents are over the age of 50, almost half are females, and over 80 percent are white. None of these demographics are sur-prising given that I am surveying a highly educated and established population.

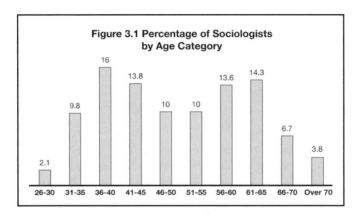

Figure 3.1 Percentage of Sociologists by Age Category

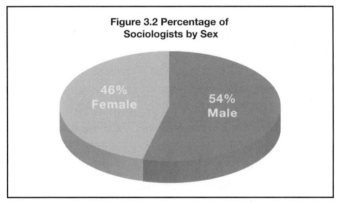

Figure 3.2 Percentage of Sociologists by Sex

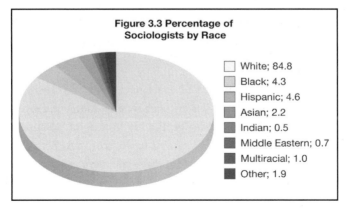

Figure 3.3 Percentage of Sociologists by Race

The response rate of the survey was 29 percent, as 435 respondents filled out the entire survey.[4] This was a lower response rate than desired, and yet the response rate was higher for sociologists than for any other scientific group I tested. Despite the low response rate, this research provides information about academic bias, which fills an important research gap since there have been no real previous systematic data that deal with this issue. As I discussed in chapter 1, previous attempts to address the possibility of bias in academia have not utilized systematic inquiry. This research has searched for systematic patterns rather than using anecdotal evidence subject to researcher bias. It is a step forward in our understanding of the potential of social, religious, and political bias among sociologists specifically and academics in general. For now, this study contains the best available data for addressing issues of bias. In the appendix, I show how the low response rate does not invalidate the data for determining the types of bias in academia but that it might challenge the accuracy of the data in determining the strength of the bias. Although I am very confident that the biases I have discovered with these data reflect the biases in the field, I am less confident that the strengths of the biases are as strong as the data suggest. Those readers with continued interest in the accuracy of these data and my confidence in the conclusions I have drawn from the study should consult the appendix, where I address this issue more forthrightly.

The key question on the survey is question 4, which asked whether the respondent is influenced by the social group a prospective new hire belongs to when considering hiring this person for a faculty position. The wording of the question is

> Assume that your facility is hiring a new professor. Below is a list of possible characteristics of this new hire. Many of them are characteristics that you can not directly inquire of prospective candidates. However, if you were able to learn of these characteristics about a candidate, would that make you more or less likely to support their hire? Please rate your attitude on a scale in which 1 indicates that the characteristic greatly damages your support to hire a candidate, 4 is that the characteristic does not make a difference, and 7 indicates that the characteristic greatly enhances

your support to hire the candidate. If you do not understand the
characteristic, then please indicate such with "n/a."

In a questionnaire about collegiality, this question is logical since
it investigates the type of individuals the respondent believes will
create a more collegial social atmosphere. The question allows me to
determine the type of individuals with whom a sociologist desires to
work. The attitudes of sociologists were assessed for twenty-six social
groups. Their answers were scored on a scale of 1 to 7, as described
above. Higher scores of the question indicate more acceptance of a
given social group. Respondents who indicated that they knew nothing about the social group were excluded from analysis.[5]

This question also gets at assessments of whether individuals
have an honest opportunity for an academic position given the social
group to which they belong. I assert in the question that academics
are not allowed to assess whether individuals belong to some of these
social groups before hiring them. Federal law forbids determining the
political attitudes, religious orientation, sexual orientation, and family status of individuals for the purpose of deciding whether or not to
hire them. Yet in real life, individuals undoubtedly do sometimes learn
about such characteristics, and if academics do have social biases, such
knowledge can come into play as hiring decisions are being made.[6]
Thus I am testing a potential bias that has very real consequences for
individuals in groups not accepted by others in academia.

Results

The mean scores measuring tolerance toward each of the social
groups can be seen in figures 3.4a, 3.4b, 3.4c, and 3.4d. To indicate
more clearly the contrasts between the social groups sociologists
favor and those they do not, I removed the middle category of "does
not matter" from these figures. Three groups are clearly not favored
by sociologists—fundamentalists, evangelicals, and members of the
NRA. Thus 49.4 percent of the sociologists surveyed indicated that
they negatively took into consideration the fact that a prospective
candidate was a fundamentalist[7] (figure 3.4c), and 41.2 percent of
the sociologists indicated that they negatively took into consideration the fact that a prospective candidate was a member of the NRA

(figure 3.4a). Furthermore, 39.1 percent of sociologists weighed negatively the fact that a prospective candidate was an evangelical (figure 3.4c). In addition to these groups, this information also indicates that Republicans are not desired by sociologists, as 28.7 percent of the sociologists weighed negatively the fact that a prospective candidate was Republican (figure 3.4a). The evidence of this work indicates that groups hypothesized for facing negative bias by sociologists do indeed experience the potential for rejection.

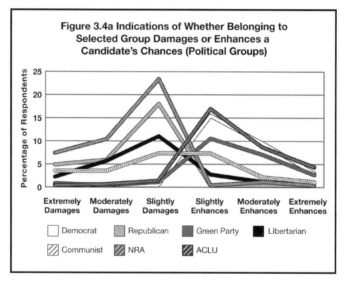

Figure 3.4a Indications of Whether Belonging to Selected Group Damages or Enhances a Candidate's Chances (Political Groups)

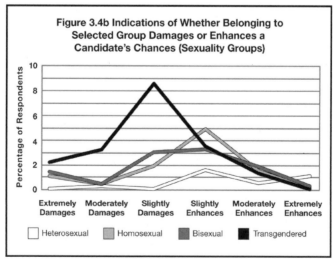

Figure 3.4b Indications of Whether Belonging to Selected Group Damages or Enhances a Candidate's Chances (Sexuality Groups)

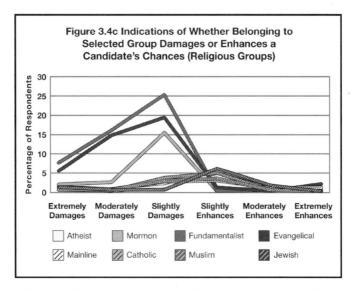

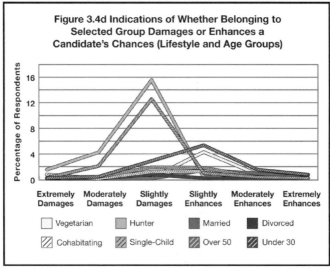

In contrast to these groups, others were seen favorably by the respondents. For example, 27.8 percent of the sociologists weighed favorably the fact that a prospective candidate was a member of the Democratic Party, 29.9 percent of the sociologists weighed favorably the fact that a prospective candidate was a member of the ACLU, and 20.2 percent of the sociologists weighed favorably the fact that a prospective candidate was a member of the

Green Party (all of these are in figure 3.4a).[8] If we accept the idea that the ACLU is an organization with progressive political as well as civil rights activism, then all three of these tendencies are tied to political progressiveness. Thus, there are definite political preferences that can enhance one's ability to obtain a position as an academic sociologist. Once again, previous predictions of who would be favored by sociologists were accurate.

In table 3.1, I indicate the percentages of sociologists who stated that a particular social group does not matter and the overall mean scores on the seven-point scale. We see here even more evidence of favorability of progressive political groups and disfavor of traditional religious and political organizations. The highest mean scores belong to the Democrats and members of the ACLU. Both scores are over 4.4 and are significantly higher, at .001 level, than those of any of the conservative political groups (e.g., Republicans and the NRA). The lowest scores belong to fundamentalists ($m = 3.207$), NRA members ($m = 3.379$), and evangelicals ($m = 3.423$). It is also of interest that these are the groups that have the lowest percentage of sociologists who state that membership in these groups does not matter. In fact, it matters to more than half of all sociologists whether the job candidate is a fundamentalist, whereas less than 3 percent of all sociologists care if the candidate is married, divorced, or cohabitating, or is single with a child. Clearly religion and political conservatism engender more hostility among sociologists than lifestyle or sexuality choices.

These findings are strong enough as they stand, yet they may underestimate the degree of social bias sociologists have. Many sociologists may indicate that membership in certain social groups is unimportant in a potential hire in an effort to be perceived as tolerant. They instinctively know that being in such groups does not influence how well a person can perform their duties as a professor. This can produce a social desirability effect despite my best efforts to minimize it.[9] About a third, or 31.5 percent, of the respondents indicated that none of the characteristics indicated in the survey matter to them.[10] These individuals either are truly unmoved by any of the social groups or their desire not to be seen as intolerant shows up in this question,

Table 3.1. Percentage of Sociologists Stating That a Particular Social Group Does Not Matter for Job Candidates and Mean Score on 7-Point Scale for Each Group

	Percent "Does Not Matter"	Mean
Democrat	71.0% (265)*	4.408
Republican	70.5% (263)	3.574
Green Party	77.5% (289)	4.279
Libertarian	79.4% (288)	3.761
Communist Party	75.3% (278)	3.905
NRA	56.9% (209)	3.379
ACLU	67.9% (252)	4.439
Heterosexual	96.5% (355)	4.054
Homosexual	90.0% (334)	4.019
Bisexual	89.7% (331)	3.997
Transgendered	81.1% (300)	3.846
Atheist	90.0% (332)	4.015
Mormon	79.3% (295)	3.745
Fundamentalist	49.7% (185)	3.207
Evangelical	58.0% (215)	3.423
Mainline	92.4% (341)	4.027
Catholic	93.5% (346)	4.005
Muslim	88.9% (330)	4.005
Jewish	90.6% (336)	4.049
Vegetarian	93.0% (345)	4.070
Hunter	77.4% (287)	3.733
Married	96.8% (358)	4.046
Divorced	98.9% (367)	3.995
Cohabitating	96.2% (357)	3.981
Single-Child	95.4% (355)	4.013
Over 50	83.5% (334)	3.852
Under 30	89.4% (356)	4.062

Number of respondents who state "does not matter" in parentheses.

which is typical when surveying the highly educated. I have no way of determining what percentage of those who indicated that none of the social groups matter have truly developed a perspective of complete tolerance and what percentage are being affected by social desirability bias. The latter group may indeed have hostility toward certain social out-groups, but this hostility does not come out in a survey. Thus for now, I can only assert that these current findings represent the lowest baseline of the percentage of sociologists who use social bias in their hiring decisions. I can assert that about half of all sociologists will utilize some degree of a negative social bias to hamper the ability of a religious fundamentalist to obtain an academic position, but it is possible that the actual percentage is much higher.

The implications of these findings are stark. When I advise graduate students in my department about going out on interviews, I tell them not to reveal any personal information that may be used negatively against their obtaining an offer. My reasoning has always been that individuals, no matter how well intentioned they may be, will inevitably bring their biases into their hiring decisions. This research indicates which characteristics students should hide in their interviews and which ones they should reveal. Students who are members of the ACLU and the Democratic Party should trumpet those facts during their interviews. Those who are conservative religiously and politically should hide that fact. The information in this research indicates that revealing one's political and religious conservatism will, on average, negatively influence about half of the search committee one is attempting to impress. Furthermore, if some of the survey respondents were less than candid with their responses, the percentage of those with a bias against political and religious conservatives may be even higher. This degree of influence is clearly powerful enough to significantly affect whether an individual is able to get a job offer.

Of political and religious conservatism, which one engenders more disfavor from sociologists? The percentage of sociologists who reject fundamentalists is significantly higher than the percentage who reject Republicans (49.4% versus 28.7%: $p < .001$). Such a difference may be due to the fact that fundamentalists are seen as extremists while Republicans are not. However, evangelicals can fairly be seen as more mainstream than fundamentalists. Yet the percentage of sociologists that reject evangelicals is significantly higher than the percentage of those who reject Republicans (39.1% versus 28.7%: $p < .01$). Thus religious conservatism is seen as less desirable to sociologists than political conservatism. While some sociologists are not favorable toward political conservatives, and are especially resistant to those who resist gun control legislation, sociologists most clearly resist the inclusion of religious conservatives.

Since the group most likely to be rejected is fundamentalists, there may be value in documenting the extent of the rejection they may experience. As noted above, about half of the respondents indicated some hesitation to hire a candidate who was a fundamentalist. To be fair, about half of these individuals indicated only a slight hesitation. It is difficult to interpret the quarter of the respondents who stated that knowing that a candidate is a fundamentalist only slightly damages their willingness to hire the candidate. This may mean that they have only slight apprehension that can be easily dismissed if the candidate is well qualified, or it could indicate the sort of lingering concern that could influence the respondent to actively look for reasons to reject the candidate. Either way, a fundamentalist candidate operates at a disadvantage in attaining the position. However, almost a fourth of all the respondents indicated that knowing that a candidate is a fundamentalist either moderately or extremely damages the ability of the respondent to accept the candidate. This indicates not just a minor concern but the real likelihood that the respondent will resist the candidate with some degree of vigor. Assuming that any given sociologist has the same propensity to reject fundamentalists, if a search committee is composed of five scholars, then it is likely that at least one of the individuals on the committee has a moderate to strong disdain toward hiring a fundamentalist candidate. Thus the fundamentalist candidate may start out the process with one "no" vote already lodged against him or her.

Yet it is not merely religious conservatism that is triggering animosity. If that were the case then Mormons and Muslims, two other religious groups known for their religious conservatism, would score at least as low as evangelicals. The fact that members of both of these groups are more likely to have their potential candidacies damaged by their religious beliefs than enhanced indicates that religious conservatism does contribute to their rejection by some sociologists.[11] But in both cases, the rejection is less than that experienced by fundamentalists and evangelicals, suggesting that there are other factors which contribute to the bias against conservative Christian groups. Those other factors may include the position of Christians as the dominant religious group in the United States, which may make some sociologists more likely to perceive evangelicals and fundamentalists as competitors for cultural power in a way they do not perceive Mormons and Muslims. It is not merely the supernaturalist perspectives of these Christian groups that generates the negative social bias exhibited in this study, but dynamics of competition of these groups as legitimators of social reality.

Given the higher level of animosity directed at religious conservatives, it is worth asking if this animosity is created by sociologists who work in institutions that have faith traditions. It is plausible that some of the sociologists of faith resent those of other faiths and that this is buttressing these results. This survey did not determine the religious preferences of the respondents, but given the well-established fact that the percentage of social scientists who are highly religious is relatively small (Ecklund & Scheitle, 2007; Ladd & Lipset, 1975; Stark & Finke, 2000), this seems to be an unlikely determinant of these findings. But some sociologists teach at religious schools, and such schools often have rules about hiring professors of different faiths. It may be the desire of such sociologists to adhere to their institutional rules, which create this religious/political bias. Since the respondents teaching at religious institutions only comprise about 14 percent of the sample, it is unlikely that they are a powerful factor in creating these results. Nevertheless, I decided to assess whether this was a possibility by comparing professors who teach at religious institutions with scholars who work in nonreligious settings. The results of these findings can be seen in figure 3.5.

The results in figure 3.5 indicate that sociologists who work in religious educational settings are less likely to accept members of the Communist Party, atheists, Muslims, Jews, and married and

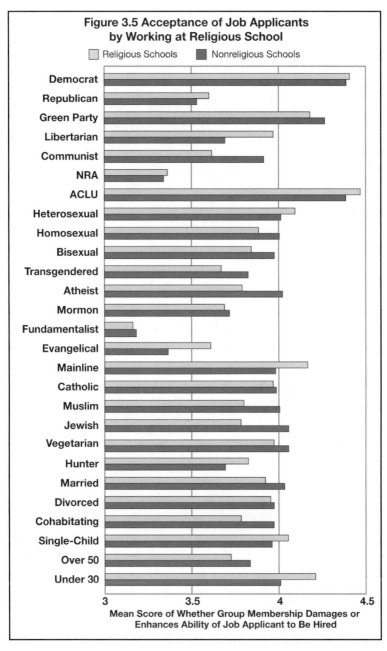

Figure 3.5 Acceptance of Job Applicants by Working at Religious School

cohabitating individuals than other sociologists. On the other hand, sociologists who teach at religious educational institutions are more accepting of members of the Libertarian Party, mainline Protestants, singles raising children, and those under thirty than other sociologists. Thus, it is unclear whether sociologists who teach at religious institutions have more of an overall propensity to reject social out-groups than other sociologists. There is a propensity for these scholars to indicate selectivity due to the religious orientation of the applicants. This may be due to the religious requirements at such educational institutions. However, as it concerns the social groups that prompted the most powerful biases among all sociologists—acceptance of Democrats and ACLU members and rejection of Republicans, NRA members, fundamentalists, and evangelicals—those at religious institutions did not significantly differ from other sociologists. Even sociologists at religious educational institutions follow the basic tendency to reject religious conservatives more than political conservatives. Among sociologists at nonreligious institutions, 48.9 percent exhibited some hesitation to accept fundamentalists and 38.9 percent exhibited some hesitation to accept evangelicals. For those at religious schools, the percentages that showed hesitation to accept fundamentalists and evangelicals were 56.2 and 42.6 percent, respectively. These percentages were lower as it concerned political conservatives, although 28.8 percent of those at nonreligious schools still would penalize Republican candidates to some degree and 41.0 percent would do likewise to NRA members. At religious schools, 31.2 percent of sociologists exhibited some degree of rejection of Republicans and 44.7 percent showed hesitation to accept NRA members. Thus the difference between acceptance of political and religious conservatives is not simply due to sociologists following the rules at their religious institutions. These social biases are embedded into the field deeply enough so that the institutional rules at religious schools have little effect on the potential of sociologists to hire those who are religious and/or political conservatives.

It has been suggested that scholars at prestigious higher institutions are more secular and progressive than other scholars (Leuba, 1934; Stark, 1963). But none of these previous studies has investigated whether these qualities lead to more social bias against political and religious conservatives. This research provides us with an opportunity to conduct such an investigation. The respondents were asked to indicate the type of setting in which they worked. The scores of those who worked in a setting with a doctoral program and the scores all other sociologists are seen in figure 3.6. The evidence in this table indicates that there

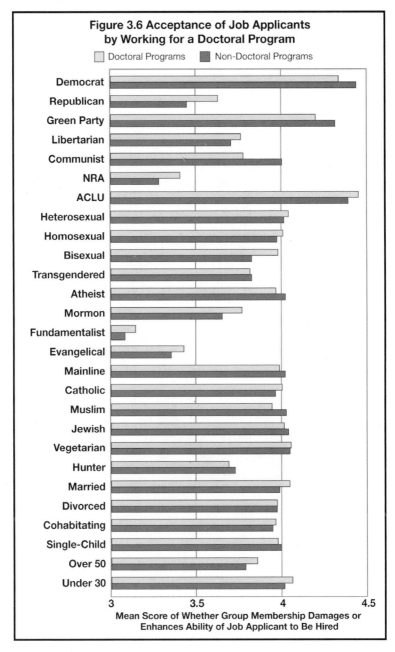

Figure 3.6 Acceptance of Job Applicants by Working for a Doctoral Program

Doctoral Programs   Non-Doctoral Programs

Mean Score of Whether Group Membership Damages or Enhances Ability of Job Applicant to Be Hired

is very little difference in the attitudes of sociologists who work in doctoral programs and other sociologists. The only members of a political group that sociologists at doctoral programs are significantly more likely to reject are members of the Communist Party. However, this finding is offset by the fact that such sociologists are significantly more likely to accept Republicans than other sociologists. Thus the prestige of departments in which sociologists work does not seem to be likely to increase their propensity to exhibit progressive political bias.

On the one hand, these results indicate that sociologists who are in more prestigious academic programs are no more socially biased than other sociologists. It seems plausible that, for such scholars, evaluation of a potential candidate's work is more important than the social group the candidate comes from. This may offset any possible effects that may arise from the higher probability that scientists at more elite institutions are more likely to be progressive or irreligious than other scientists or that they act as gatekeepers for the revealed wisdom in their discipline. This provides hope that the damage done by social bias is less than one might fear from the initial results of this study since those at more prestigious educational institutions do not reject those from stigmatized groups any more than do other sociologists.

But it has to be noted that 46.6 percent of all sociologists teaching at doctoral programs still use their negative perceptions of fundamentalists to influence if they are going to hire a prospective sociologist. The percentage is lower for evangelicals (35.3 percent) and Republicans (25.2 percent), but these figures are still high enough to create concern about the opportunities for individuals in these groups. Furthermore, it is quite possible that these particular data cannot fully capture a possible elite effect because of the crude measure of separating doctoral programs from all others. I am not looking at the top twenty or even top fifty programs in the field to investigate whether scholars in those programs are more intolerant than other sociologists. To safeguard their identities, I did not ask the respondents to name their schools, and so it is not possible for me to make such a distinction. It can be argued that only the elite doctoral schools truly act as the gatekeeping forces in academia and so research that explores the level of social bias in elite universities as compared to other doctorate-granting universities will be very important in assessing whether an elite effect truly does exist.

Possible Factors Shaping Social Bias among Sociologists

Beyond documenting the presence of social bias among sociologists in doctoral programs or religious schools, it is also valuable to discover what other factors may lessen or increase that bias. Investigating these institutional factors can inform us about the possible sources of social bias. Understanding the possibility that sociologists with different characteristics have contrasting propensities to engage in social bias will also provide us information about whether the demographic or social makeup of the sample has a powerful effect on the findings. This knowledge will be quite valuable when assessing the viability of these findings across different subcultures within the field of sociology.

For example, sociologists often are linked together by the specializations in which they work. It is plausible that sociologists within certain specializations may be less likely to operate from social biases than other sociologists. Those who directly study the effects of social bias on marginalized groups may be more sensitive to its effects on other groups. To assess this possibility, I have used three questions that assess the three top specializations of a respondent. Those that selected Asia and Asian America; Latino/a Sociology; Race, Gender, and Class; Racial and Ethnic Minorities; Sex and Gender; or Sexuality as one of their top three specializations were designated as those that studied marginalized groups. Since I am taking the top three specializations of the sociologists, I likely have created a measure in which individuals who study stratification to any significant degree will be captured by this dummy variable. This is admittedly a rough way to capture this effect, as it is possible that some sociologists in other specializations may still study these subjects, but it nonetheless provides for a conceptual separation

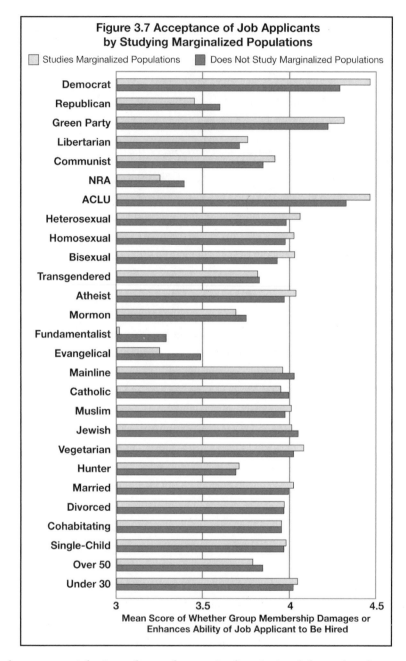

Figure 3.7 Acceptance of Job Applicants by Studying Marginalized Populations

between sociologists who study marginalization and those that do not. In figure 3.7, I compare these sociologists with those who do not include any of the "marginalized" specializations.

These results indicate that scholars who study marginalized groups are indeed sensitive to the inclusion of certain social groups. They are more likely to accept Democrats and members of the ACLU than other sociologists. However, this acceptance is not spread out to all social groups. In particular, there seems to be a propensity of such sociologists to exhibit a religious bias. Individuals who study these marginalized groups are more likely than other sociologists to reject evangelicals and fundamentalists as potential coworkers. Thus, even as sociologists in general tend to reject these groups, individuals who study marginalized groups are even more biased against such individuals. It is plausible that the rejection of fundamentalists can be linked to the subjects that such scholars explore. Since there is evidence that fundamentalists have less progressive attitudes toward women (Hayes, 1995; Martin, Osmond, Hesselbart, & Wood, 1980; Peek, Lowe, & Williams, 1991), sexual minorities (Altermeyer & Hunsberger, 1992; Fulton, Gorsuch, & Maynard, 1999; Marsiglio, 1993), and possibly even people of color (Griffin et al., 1987), these scholars may reject a fundamentalist colleague simply because they fear he or she may not support the marginalized groups they are studying. The rejection of evangelicals may merely be an extension of the logic such sociologists use to reject fundamentalists.

Since there is no inherent reason why Republicans, evangelicals, fundamentalists, or members of the NRA cannot perform the duties required by a college professor, scholars studying marginalized groups may be reacting out of an emotional process in rejecting such individuals or have cognitively decided that such individuals should not be granted the opportunity even tangentially to influence college students. In this way, sociologists studying marginalized groups may have negative images of these disfavored groups and thus seek to deny members of these groups a voice in their profession. Such a reaction is somewhat surprising given that these scholars consistently examine other groups that have been the victims of stereotyping or have had their voice stripped from influential places in society. Research in these areas may not have influenced these scholars to have a higher general level of tolerance than other scholars; rather, it

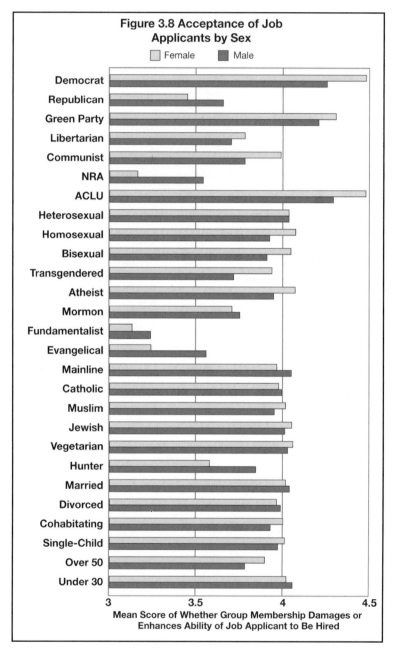

Figure 3.8 Acceptance of Job Applicants by Sex

may have more deeply ingrained a progressive in-group identity into such individuals, making them relatively likely to perceive religious and political conservatives as individuals who should be rejected. If this is true, then the effects of operating in a progressive subculture, and rejecting ideas that may threaten that subculture, are more powerful in determining the social biases of sociologists than an ideological adherence to religious tolerance.

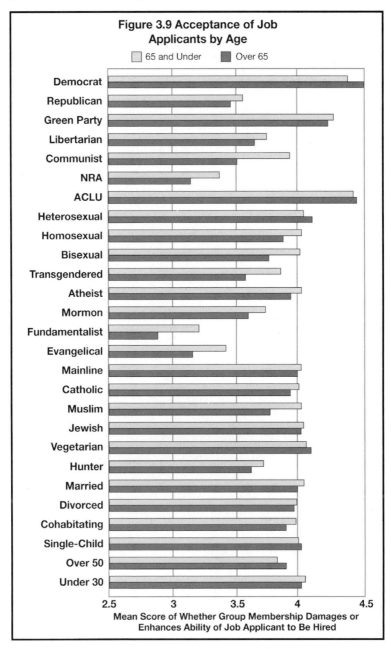

Finally, I also wanted to investigate other possible demographic determinants for the propensity of sociologists to use their social biases in determining whom they would hire. The means of the scores for the different social groups as grouped by the sex, age, and race of the sociologists can be seen in figures 3.8, 3.9, and 3.10. Figure 3.8 indicates sex effects worth noting. Women had more positive social biases toward Democrats, Communist Party members, ACLU members, cohabitators, homosexuals, bisexuals, the transgendered, atheists, and those over fifty than men. Male sociologists, on the other hand, had less negative social bias against Republicans, NRA members, evangelicals, mainline Protestants, hunters, and divorced individuals than women. Groups where there was a general positive social bias among sociologists were those in which women are more supportive than men, while men had less of a negative bias with groups where sociologists had a general negative bias. It is possible that the social groups that male sociologists were less likely to reject (e.g., hunters, NRA members) are the groups in which males are more likely to participate. Such participation can account for at least some of this gender effect. It is also notable that the groups likely to be rejected by sociologists, and thus more likely to be rejected by female sociologists, tend to be either politically or religiously conservative. Other research has suggested that women are generally more politically progressive than men (Bohm, 1998; Edlund & Pande, 2002; Seltzer, Newman, & Leighton, 1997), and such a tendency may persist even in a progressive subculture such as academia. The more progressive female sociologists may perceive a greater threat from disfavored conservative social groups than their male counterparts.

In figure 3.9, there is evidence that older sociologists are more likely to have negative social biases than younger sociologists. They were more likely than younger sociologists to reject Communist Party members, bisexuals, the transgendered, and Muslims. It is possible that older sociologists may be more set in their social outlooks and therefore less likely to alter their perspectives to accept a social environment that tolerates disfavored social groups. However, it is also possible that younger sociologists have been trained to recognize

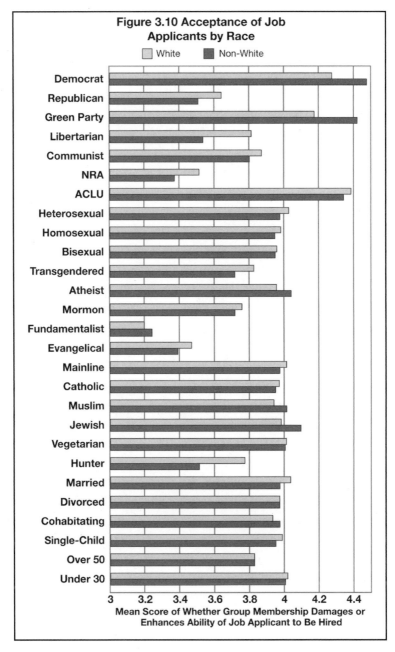

Figure 3.10 Acceptance of Job Applicants by Race

their biases and to keep those biases from turning into attitudes of unjustified intolerance. While older sociologists were less likely to accept those from disfavored groups, younger sociologists were not without their social biases. For example, sociologists under the age of sixty-five were still significantly more likely to favor candidates who identify themselves as Democrats over those who identify themselves as Republicans (4.394 versus 3.582: $p < .001$). On the one hand, this age effect suggests that while the propensity of sociologists to act out their social biases will not disappear, it possibly will grow less over time.[12] On the other hand, often older sociologists have more institutional power due to their higher rank in a given department and may be in a more advantageous position to enforce their social biases.

In figure 3.10, I have divided race into whites and nonwhites since none of the groups of color were large enough to warrant a statistically meaningful comparison.[13] White sociologists were less supportive of Democrats, but more supportive of Libertarians and hunters, than nonwhite sociologists. However, generally there was very little racial difference evident in these data. As it concerns conceptualizing social out-groups, the academic environment that sociologists work in may be more important than the racialized social reality in which they live. I am not arguing that racial identity is unimportant to scholars, but academia likely provides values that supersede the local racialized communities that sociologists come from.

This research indicates that some sociologists admit that their biases toward certain social groups make them more, or less, likely to favor members of those groups as potential job candidates and that this propensity is shaped by the characteristics of the sociologists themselves. Older female sociologists are more likely to have social biases that they use to discourage the candidacy of those from conservative religious and political groups. Without direct qualitative information, I cannot completely evaluate why these characteristics matter. However, future research may be able to document the accuracy or inaccuracy of the speculations I offer in this chapter. Despite these tendencies, all of the sociology groups adhered to the basic propensity of favoring religious and political progressives over conservatives. Even in the groups where these biases were less prominent (e.g., males, the young), they did not disappear.

Implications of Social Biases among Sociologists

Regardless of the characteristics influencing the degree to which sociologists are willing to act upon their social biases, the fact remains that some sociologists do penalize disfavored groups. The results of such penalties are multifaceted. Clearly religious and political conservatives suffer from the actions such biases create. Sociologists who come from the disfavored groups (admittedly there are likely to be relatively few individuals from these groups who are sociologists) have one of two unpleasant choices. They can be open about their membership in the disfavored group and, as this research illustrates, create a disadvantage toward obtaining a position in their chosen occupation. In this case, if they are hired, the individuals hiring them are at least aware of their position in the disfavored group and there is no need to hide this knowledge. Alternately, they can choose not to tell the members of the search committee of their religious and/or political conservatism and increase their chances of obtaining their position. Scholars seeking to hire them are not allowed to ask them about their religious or political affiliations, and thus such a deception may be easy to achieve. Yet we should not assume that such deceptions can always be easily achieved. A colleague once applied for a position at a school located in an area where Mormonism was the dominant religion. While at a social function during her interview, she was asked if she would like coffee or tea. Since Mormons are not allowed to drink caffeine, the question of beverage choice suggested that members of the search team were interested in whether or not she was a Mormon. We can see in this example how interviewers may discover the political or religious leanings of a candidate even though direct inquiry is illegal.

Costs to the members of disfavored groups do not stop in the attempt to obtain an academic position. If we were only concerned with the hiring process, then we would only need to instruct religious and political conservatives to hide their beliefs during the brief time they are being interviewed. To obtain and maintain an academic job as a sociologist, political and religious conservatives pay a nontrivial price for the social biases of other scholars. There is little reason to believe that the biases documented in this work are limited to interfering with the ability of members of disfavored groups to obtain an academic position. There are clearly other aspects of academic life likely to be affected by the social biases of sociologists. After a scholar has been hired, he or she must attempt to gain tenure. Tenure may be denied if that professor has not demonstrated a level of collegiality with senior professors. As we have seen, those who are Republicans, NRA members, evangelicals, and fundamentalists operate at a disadvantage with about half of their colleagues.

It is also vital to consider what these types of biases mean to scientific inquiry. To gain tenure at any type of research institution, a professor must be published in peer-reviewed journals. Professors often get insights about their research from influences within their own social networks. Academics may more highly prize insights gained from culturally progressive networks than those gained from culturally conservative networks. The ideas that a fundamentalist or evangelical picks up from religious associates, that a Republican picks up from political associations, and that an NRA member picks up from other NRA members are not likely to be well received by potential reviewers or editors who share some or all of the social biases illustrated in this work. On the other hand, ideas that Democrats or Green Party members pick up from their political associations or that ACLU members pick up from other ACLU members are more likely to be well received since these ideas likely feed into the positive social bias that resonates in the discipline. These ideas are not assessed only on their scientific accuracy since the social biases documented in this research likely influence the willingness of sociologists to accept ideas that violate their presuppositions. After all, if some sociologists are willing to allow their perceptions of the social groups to which job candidates belong influence whether they are willing to hire those candidates, then why would they not also consider giving more weight to research that fits those perceptions? It seems reasonable to speculate that this bias not only unduly influences who has an opportunity to succeed in academia but also limits the sort of ideas that are allowed to develop among sociologists.

Clearly the group facing the greatest level of rejection from sociologists is fundamentalists. In this it appears that some sociologists are part of the trend toward antifundamentalism documented by Bolce and De Maio (1999). However, we should also consider the implications of how some sociologists define fundamentalists. Some sociologists of religion have carefully thought of useable ways to distinguish fundamentalists from other Protestants. For example, Smith, Emerson, Gallagher, Kennedy, and Sikkink (1998) argue that fundamentalists tend to disengage themselves from the larger social world while evangelicals remained engaged. This disengagement makes it easier for fundamentalists to have viewpoints that are at variance with the rest of the society. However, it is not clear whether sociologists who do not study religion have made such a clear demarcation between fundamentalists and evangelicals.[14] There may be a tendency for such scholars to lump together all conservative Protestants together under a banner of "fundamentalists."[15] Such a lumping together is not unusual. For example, few individuals knowledgeable about Rick Warren, author of the bestselling book *The Purpose Driven Life*, would label him a fundamentalist. While conservative on social issues, he is also an advocate for more progressive political policies in dealing with issues of poverty and world hunger. Yet many progressive activists attempted to paint him as a right-wing fundamentalist when he was given the opportunity to do the invocation at President Obama's swearing-in ceremony. Likewise, many Protestants with fairly mainstream, but center-right, social or religious beliefs may be labeled as fundamentalists by scholars who are not well versed in the nuances of Protestant belief. It may not only be individuals accurately labeled as fundamentalists who suffer the effects of religious bias, for Protestants with more moderate religious perspectives may also be stigmatized if they are seen as fundamentalists.

Thus the field of sociology itself is deprived of the potential perspectives and insights religious and political conservatives may provide. In theory, scientific knowledge is advanced further and faster when there is healthy debate and different perspectives are allowed to be aired. Ideally such debates allow for a sharpening of ideas and furthering of our knowledge. Yet we can see that the perspectives of some individuals are not easily expressed. To the degree that religious and political conservatives offer solid academic sociological perspectives that can generate new avenues of research, the discipline is poorer due to the additional difficulty such individuals have entering the discipline. Some may argue, however, that such individuals do not have much to offer. They can contend that the ideas found within religious and political conservatism have already been refuted and that the science needs to move beyond those ideas. Given such an argument, social biases against these groups are justified, since such individuals may have less to offer to the field than adherents of progressive religious and political thought. Yet sociology has tended to be on the progressive edge of society. It is difficult to conceive of a time in which conservative religious or political ideology was the dominant ideological force among sociologists.[16] It does not seem likely that ideas emerging from religious and political conservatives have been exhausted by sociological inquiry. The barrier individuals from these subcultures may face is particularly vexing since we do not know how much they have to offer because members of such groups are discouraged from freely airing their sociological perspectives.

We should go beyond the debates within academia in order to factor in fully the costs of such social biases. For example, students often come from the disfavored social groups. If about half of all sociologists are willing to admit that they will look with disfavor at a fundamentalist job candidate, then what would we expect from these sociologists when a fundamentalist student takes their class? I would find it hard to believe that most sociologists would intentionally academically penalize such students since fairness is such an ingrained value among college teachers. However, there are many other ways professors can make life unpleasant for such students. They can treat comments from these students with disdain, make comments in their lectures that ridicule a disfavored group's beliefs, or be less willing to support the research endeavors of these students. Even if only a small percentage of sociologists act in these ways, they not only worsen the experience of these students as they attempt to obtain a college education but they send signals that such students are not welcome to pursue employment in this scientific field. This again potentially reinforces the social biases within the field by excluding potential future scholars who may have a disfavored religious belief.

It is also possible that these biases come out in how research is conducted when it includes members of the disfavored groups. As we will see in the following chapter, there is reason to believe that some sociologists have less of an ability to resist the tendency to believe negative information when it is directed at a member of a disfavored social group than when it is directed at a member of an approved social group. Approaches toward the study of progressive social groups are likely to be dramatically different than approaches toward the study of conservative social groups. Some sociologists may unconsciously weed out findings that produce a positive image of disfavored groups. This can result in work that paints a more pessimistic picture of disfavored groups than is warranted by those groups' behavior. It is beyond the scope of this work to tease out the different ways in which sociologists treat favored and disfavored groups with their research, but a careful analysis into the different types of assumptions and assertions sociologists bring into their research of favored and disfavored social groups is one that needs to be conducted.

Of course this is all speculation. The only thing I have demonstrated with this quantitative work is that membership in certain social groups negatively affects the chances one has of obtaining an academic position if that membership becomes known to the scholars in a search committee. Whether this bias also influences choices of academic research, the ability of certain individuals to gain promotion through the academic ranks, and how sociologists teach their classes is a question that can be better addressed with other empirical work. However, given that social bias is likely to transfer from one type of discrimination to another, the critics of my speculation have the burden to show that this bias is limited only to hiring decisions and to demonstrate why these likely are not generalizable effects. This documentation of the hiring bias, beyond unmasking an uncomfortable reality, can help us to under-stand the boundaries of acceptable scientific research and thus the limits of science itself.

Finally, we should also note that there were positive biases that came out of this research. Specifically, some sociologists were more likely to accept Democrats and members of the Green Party and the ACLU as colleagues than individuals from other social groups. The positive biases exhibited by sociologists tend to focus more on membership in political organizations than on any other social group category. It is also noteworthy that the positive bias exhibited by sociologists is not as strong as the negative bias. For example, the 3.379 score of NRA members is further below the midpoint of 4 than the 4.439 score of ACLU members is above the midpoint. The ACLU score reflects the strongest positive bias score any group received, and yet its distance from the 4.0 mid-point (4.439 − 4.0 = .439) is definitely shorter than the distances of the scores for fundamentalists (4.0 − 3.207 = .793) and evan-gelicals (4.0 − 3.423 = .577). As it concerns the effects of bias, it appears that sociologists are more likely to use their social per-spectives to reflect negatively upon disfavored social groups than to reflect positively on favored social groups.

Conclusion

Any notion we may have once had about the ability of sociologists to practice acceptance and tolerance equally toward all social groups is challenged by the evidence in this chapter. The scholars surveyed had little, if any, reason to reject any of the social groups they were asked about from teaching at a given college or university. Yet sub-stantial numbers of sociologists indicated a propensity to reject such individuals. This assertion is not based upon an isolated incident or two, but rather on a systematic pattern of social biases. Whether the social bias against members of these social groups is minor or substantial, these social biases can interfere with the ability of indi-viduals to obtain a position of employment. This fact should concern those who desire to limit the impact of intolerance on the accumu-lation of scientific knowledge. Even sociologists who indicate that membership in a disfavored social group slightly damages the candidacy of a potential colleague are creating a barrier for members of disfavored groups to participate in academia. Any such barrier will make it harder for members of disfavored groups to obtain an academic position and thus will reduce their ability to influence the scientific community.

It may be argued that the results of this chapter are merely due to individuals indicating the types of people they prefer to befriend. Such scholars may not intend to reject the ideas of political and social conservatives, but merely be indicating with whom they can develop friendly relationships. After all, this was sent out as a study of collegiality, and these scholars may merely be indicating the types of people with whom they are most likely to, or would most desire to, have collegial relations. But even if this is the case, the result of such desires is a limitation of scientific inquiry. The collegiality preferences of sociologists can act to limit the acceptance of members of disfavored groups, and thus certain perspectives about society will not be heard as members of disfavored groups are excluded from scientific inquiry. This work cannot document why sociologists tend to place members of disfavored groups at a disadvantage in the obtainment of a scholarly position, but it does document that this disadvantage exists, implying that the possible diversity of ideas that may emerge from sociologists has been compromised.

I do not believe that these results are merely due to scholars' personal preferences. Rather, these results emerge from real social biases that some sociologists have against religious and political conservatives. Some sociologists' perceptions of religious and political conservatives are so negative that it is difficult for a significant number of these scholars to envision working with them as colleagues. Such an assertion cannot be linked to the quantitative data used in this chapter. The quantitative work done in this chapter can provide us with some idea of how widespread these social biases are, but it does not tell us much about the nature of these biases or the personal ideas that may drive sociologists to have them. To this end, I have sought, and found, qualitative information that substantiates this argument. In the following chapter I present those data.

CHAPTER FOUR

Qualitative Explorations of Biases among Sociologists

The work in the previous chapter documents that fundamentalists, evangelicals, and Republicans face negative biases from some sociologists. But quantitative analysis cannot illustrate the nature of such bias, nor can it speculate about possible sources of this disfavor. To explore these issues, it is important to assess what sociologists say in their own words. This requires a qualitative examination of sociologists. In this chapter, I will use the online writings of sociologists to conduct such an examination. Doing so will allow me to assess the nature and intensity of bias sociologists have against Republicans and fundamentalists.

A nice side effect of studying sociologists, as opposed to most other academic professionals, is that they are the scholars most likely to examine societies and social groups scientifically. As we try to understand how individuals in academia conceptualize different social groups, it is the sociologists who should feel most equipped to write about those groups. They are the scientists who have been trained to make observations about society and the effects social groups may have in society. We would expect a sociologist to be more likely to write in his or her blog about the "religious right" than a chemist or even a philosopher. Given the similarity of the social background they share with other academics, the manner in which social biases influence their perception of different social groups is likely to differ in degree, but not in kind, from how those biases influence scholars in other scientific fields. However, the ability of sociologists to articulate those perceptions is likely higher than other scholars since they are more knowledgeable about the social dynamics that shape societies.

Assessing Sociologists' Attitudes

Asking academics directly about their attitudes toward certain social groups may not elicit frank and honest answers. Because of their desire to be seen as open and tolerant, academics can be unlikely to express their biases against certain social groups directly for fear of being perceived as intolerant. This is particularly the case with sociologists, who likely have an institutional value of cultural pluralism. For this reason I have chosen not to use an open-ended questionnaire to assess the attitudes of sociologists toward certain social groups. Rather, I will utilize an unobtrusive measure in which sociologists are able to discuss these groups in their own words, which is a more accurate way to determine what these scientists perceive about given social groups. Such a method will be particularly useful if these sociologists are speaking to audiences sympathetic to whatever views they express. For example, a sociologist teaching a class may not feel free to express all of his or her biases since many students may not support those perspectives and could complain to administrators. But one who has been given a format to attract and entertain individuals with similar perspectives can be more honest in his or her feelings toward certain social groups.

The challenge becomes finding such expressions from sociologists. The Internet provides a powerful tool with which such attitudes can be captured. The Internet allows individuals to find ideological communities in which they can be free to express social preferences and attitudes. One of the ways in which these communities communicate with each other is through the use of blogs. Often individuals start blogs as a way of expressing their social, religious, and political attitudes. These expressions take on certain ideological patterns, which then can act as a magnet to attract like-minded individuals, who often write comments supporting the ideas of the blog's author and provide the owner feedback for more support of those particular perspectives. Thus blogs express the social attitudes of their owners in an atmosphere of support.

Blogs can be a valuable way to assess the attitudes of members in a given social group. Thus, there is value in assessing blogs written by sociologists. Such writings may be especially attractive to social scientists who have been trained in written communication. Furthermore, since contemporary instructors work more with online innovations (such as Facebook or online courses) in an effort to keep up with their students, one would expect that many sociologists have become comfortable with the idea of starting a blog. Thus, finding blogs written by sociologists likely would provide a good indicator of the type of social attitudes prevalent among them. Nevertheless, there may be certain sociologists who are more likely to write blogs than others. Those at elite institutions may be less likely to work on blogs since there is institutional pressure for them to engage in more academic types of writing. Furthermore, blogs may tend to draw individuals who are very partisan in their views (Kahn & Kellner, 2004; Mowles, 2008; Scott, 2007), and thus the sociologists who author blogs may be more likely to engage in forms of political and social activism than other sociologists. Finally, older sociologists may not be comfortable with newer forms of electronic written expression. These limitations indicate that it is impossible to gather a random sample of the opinions of sociologists by locating their blogs. Clearly this will not be an accurate sample of all sociologists, but since this is qualitative research, the need for a probability sample is not evident. The larger patterns of bias were documented in the previous chapter. The information in these blogs will provide insight into how some sociologists tend to conceptualize certain social groups and the processes by which they formulate their opinions. Such insight will be helpful in allowing us to see how the social biases documented in the previous chapter can play themselves out among sociologists.

Finding Sociologists on the Internet

The challenge of locating blogs by sociologists seems daunting. The task is not merely to locate individuals who desire to discuss sociological topics, but to find those blogs that are authored by individuals who have received graduate-level academic training in sociology. I decided to limit myself to only those blogs written by scholars who have received a Ph.D. in sociology or by students who are currently in a sociology doctoral program. In this manner, I am able to explore the thoughts of those who are influencing, or are being influenced by, the larger academic discipline.

Fortunately, I was greatly aided by search engines that allowed me to search for Web sites that contained sociology blogs. I was also helped by the Web site at the American Sociological Association, which also contained a few blogs that were authored by sociologists. Once I found a few blogs, some of them included links to other blogs run by sociologists. Evidently some degree of community has developed among some of the sociologists who write blogs. Generally the blogs contained some basic personal information about the author, which allowed me to determine if the author met the criteria to be included in this study. If there was not a personal section, I used other information available to me, such as other Web sites with the author's name and academic position or the author's own blog comments, to determine if the author met the conditions for inclusion. Using this method of snowball sampling and search engines, I eventually found forty-two blogs on which to base my research.

Once I found the blogs, I had to determine what information to use to indicate the social atmosphere shared by sociologists. Some of the blogs concentrated on rather academic arguments about social reality. While those academic arguments did provide insight into the perspectives of a particular sociologist at times, I generally chose to ignore those arguments in my analysis since I could obtain academic arguments from sociologists without seeking out their blogs. I was more interested in the type of expressive and personal arguments these individuals laid out about how they perceived social reality and how they were able to conceptualize their attitudes toward certain social groups. The blogs generally had many individuals who posted comments in response to the arguments in them. Since I had no assurance that these comments came from social scientists, I did not include them in my analysis. I also found that many bloggers choose to link to other articles or Web sites to make their points. In fact, it was common for a large part of their blogs to be direct quotes from other articles or Web sites. I decided to exclude these other quotes from my analysis as well. As much as possible, I wanted to analyze the words of the actual blogger. It can be argued that the fact that a blogger chose to include parts of a given article or Web site can be insightful as to how the blogger approaches a particular topic. However, the information gained from this linking has to be carefully considered since it does not directly indicate the reasoning of the blogger. I chose to err in being cautious in what I would include in the analysis so that I did not make the mistake of including ideas not intended by the blogger.

I searched the blogs looking for the attitude of the blogger as it concerned the different social groups explored in the previous chapters. My general plan was to determine how and why the blogger legitimated the perceptions they indicated about these groups. As I went through each blog, I found that many of them had quite an extensive archive of former blogs. I decided to go back at least twenty posts if there were that many in a given blog so that I could get a real sense of the ideas that were promoted by the blogger.[1] I then read those posts, as well as any other posts the blogger made for the rest of 2008.[2] Some of the blogs contained internal search engines that allow a visitor to look for given words or terms in blogs from previous years. When I had the opportunity to use such search engines, I availed myself of that opportunity and searched for other posts that dealt with these particular social groups.

As I report on the content of these blogs I will also supply the URLs where they are located. The URLs were active at the time of my writing, but as anyone familiar with the Internet for any length of time is aware, some of them will have been removed by the time this book is published. I am unable to predict which blogs will persist over time, and for those instances, I apologize. I do not identify the blogs to place the blame of bias on these particular bloggers. My argument is not that these individuals are especially biased in comparison to other sociologists, but rather that they reflect the biases of the larger discipline.

General Findings of Sociologists' Blogs

Given the restrictions I placed on what material would be analyzed, it is not surprising that these blogs did not have an immense number of direct references to the social groups discussed in the previous chapter. When they were not directly citing other sources or engaging in academic analysis, often the sociologists in these blogs were discussing local politics, their own family and friends, or just general philosophical musings. However, there were those that made references to the social groups discussed in the last chapter. When sociologists were expressing their personal perspectives on these social groups, they generally discussed the groups that they disfavored rather than the groups they supported. It was clear that sociologist bloggers were more likely to use their blogs to criticize political and religious conservatives than they were to praise progressive social groups. This is in keeping with my observation in the previous chapter that negative bias is generally more powerfully expressed than positive bias.

When the topic on the blogs did come around to political and religious conservatives, the sociologists had no hesitation to express their animosity toward these groups.

> Any novel that exposes the hypocrisy of American fundamentalist evangelicals is guaranteed to have my vote![3]

> I personally think Rove is brilliant—evil—but brilliant.[4]

> Not surprising, but still infuriating. Impeachment is not sufficient. These bastards deserve imprisonment. As Dennis Kucinich said, "They are asking for four more years. In a just world, they'd get ten to twenty." (Only I think that life without parole would be more suitable.)[5]

This type of sentiment is not surprising given the findings of the previous chapter. The last chapter demonstrated that sociologists are less inclined to desire to have political and religious conservatives as potential colleagues than members of other social groups; therefore it is to be expected that these groups would be the subject of criticism in blogs written by sociologists. But it is important to dig deeper to see why this resentment has taken place. One would expect that these sociologists would be concerned about the incompetence and wrong decisions made by political conservatives. Indeed, some of the bloggers did support this image of Republicans.

> . . . conservatives like to see their leaders take action in line with their stated values, *regardless* of the consequences of those actions. liberals, on the other hand, seem to be more concerned with the actual outcomes (which makes way more sense to me).[6]

> Republicans resonate with agreeable, conscientious people to the extent that the Republicans offer an optimistic, *uncritical*, assessment of the country.[7]

> Barack Obama: "Science is the cornerstone of our prosperity and we must nurture the scientists and researchers of today if we hope to be competetive [*sic*] tomorrow."
> *** John McCain: "Grrrahhh! Fire BAD!"****
> ***Please note that all quotes are made-up though, really, entirely in character.[8]

But it is more than the fact that the Republicans are wrong. The bloggers perceived something more sinister than incompetence. Almost opposite of the idea that such individuals are naïve about the working of society is the idea that Republicans are manipulative and immoral. It is not merely a matter of the sociologists believing that these individuals are wrong in their assessments of reality. Several of the bloggers also question the motivations and personal character of members in disfavored groups. For example, the reasons political conservatives provided for their actions and attitudes were not generally taken at face value, but rather more disturbing motivations were often attributed to such individuals.

> Bush, et al are too cowardly to state what they are actually doing—torturing people; instead, they obfuscate by using the euphemisms (harsh interrogations, rough interrogations, etc.) to maintain the appearance of morality [. . .] bullshit. the very least that they could do is be honest about the fact that they intentionally harm people because they can and because they like to. as noted previously, torture doesn't work and they know this. why do they continue to do it then? because they are sadists, because they are vengeful, because no one has the power nor the will to stop them. it is the naked abuse of power, pure and simple.[9]

In short, the modern conservative movement's leaders consist of those who despise working people, those who proudly defend America's horrible racist legacy, the worst of the religious fanatics, and all those who wish to preserve America as an all-white, fundamentalist Christian patriarchy.

> On top of that is a group I can only call the New Imperialists, (the Neo-Conservatives) dedicated to imposing our "will" on every other nation on earth. And their methods of acquiring and keeping power have been so vicious and ugly as to shame any decent person.[10]

> Community service is a Republican priority but very low on the list of priorities. Sara [sic] Palin only used the word "service" once when she referred [to] military service.[11]

Thus the bloggers build on the notion that political conservatives are scheming and brilliantly evil. According to the bloggers, the Republicans intend to rule the country as a near-dictatorship. These bloggers build a perspective that political conservatives possess a degree of ignorance that is dangerous to society but that they also deviously manipulate whomever they can fool. Such a perspective makes sense if such individuals are competitors with sociologists for the role of legitimating societal morality. Sociologists can paint conservatives as incompetent competitors who do not offer much insight into morality and so must fool others into supporting them as moral and social leaders. Part of the frustration that some sociologists may have with political and religious conservatives is that they may believe that such individuals have obtained undue societal favor by illegitimate means and now use that favor to threaten the rightful place of reason and progressive ideology. This obviously makes them a force that must be stopped at all costs.

This assertion also has implications as it concerns the formation of scientific inquiry. Incompetence as moral agents can also indicate incompetence as potential researchers. Some sociologists may perceive political conservatives as not intellectually talented enough to conduct research about society. After all, if religious and political conservatives cannot make the societal observations so obvious to sociologists, it is not unreasonable to believe that they also would not be able to use adequately the tools of science to learn the subtle dynamics of society. Other sociologists may also question the motivations of such individuals. They may be hesitant to allow such individuals to spread their disfavored views to students and through research. As such, political conservatives would be seen as more likely to be unqualified for work in an academic position because of the perceptions put forth in such blogs. Such stereotypes provide a valuable indication of why political conservatives are seen as less likely to be quality candidates for academic positions.[12]

The bulk of the information from the blogs was collected in the fall of 2008. This was, of course, right in the middle of a presidential election. This may explain why the comments in the blogs centered so greatly on political, as opposed to religious, conservatives. Yet as we saw in the last chapter, sociologists generally directed their greatest level of rejection at religious fundamentalists. While there was less in the blogs about religious conservatives than political conservatives, when the discussion did come around to Christians, an interesting pattern began to emerge. To be sure, there were animosities directed at religious conservatives in general and at Christians in particular:

> To my activist friends on the left; please stop ridiculing and mocking people who act from principle. Sure, the principle might be corrupted beyond recognition by the most evil of evil people (I'm pretty sure that if there is a heaven and hell, Jerry

Fallwell [sic] went to the warm place; Jim Dobson, my guess is that you're next).[13]

The notion that millions of innocent children are being seduced into drug use by their serpentine friends (despite the best efforts of their omniscient makers) has always struck me more as a self-serving Judeo-Christian fantasy than a cogent sociological explanation.[14]

Self-righteous hypocrisy and the banner of Christianity have been staples of the ruling elite in the United States as they have led their followers on a 200 year spree of economic and geographic expansion at the expense of those unfortunate enough to stand in their way.[15]

I don't actually think it's ever a sign of love to go out of your way to tell others how they should live their lives. As such, I find evangelism of virtually all stripes distasteful.[16]

However, there was also a connecting of Christianity and political conservatism that came out in several of the comments provided by the sociologist bloggers. It was as if their animosity toward religious conservatives was due to the fact that they associated these individuals of faith with a far-right political ideology:

After seven years most Americans seem tired of Bush-bashing, but if President Bush's trips to Saudi Arabia and Africa are any indication, he does not want his comedic reputation to end. [. . .] The President's face was beaming with joy as he held the sword high in the air in the likeness of a crusading Christian.[17]

. . . pretty standard creationist fare with the [. . .] group from the 33% of America who still loves W.[18]

After the last election cycle, conservatism took on a whole new religious meaning. We think less of simply the "right" but more so of the "religious right."[19]

> What is somewhat frightening to me is that the neo-conservative voice which is so loud and clear in the Bush White House largely follows a path that seems appropriate to the zionist evangelical Christians.[20]

These quotes indicate that the bloggers blame the Bush presidency in part because of the number of religious conservatives who put him into office. Their perception of those religious conservatives is that they support the worst of the Bush presidency and are responsible for the wrong direction President Bush has taken the country. In this way sociologist bloggers link political and religious conservatism together. These bloggers articulate that to be Christian is to be a far-right political conservative. This may especially be the case if the Christian is seen as a fundamentalist or an evangelical. Because of that assertion, these individuals have developed a powerful antipathy toward certain kinds of Christians.

I speculate that it is not merely that many Christians are Republicans that angers sociologists, but that they are seen as being among the most conservative of Republicans. In the previous chapter it was the fundamentalists and evangelicals who were most likely to be rejected. Catholics and mainline Protestants were fairly accepted by most sociologists. While the bloggers did not often discuss these different variations of Christianity, it is reasonable to assert that Catholics and mainline Protestants are not as likely to be seen as highly conservative Republicans as are conservative Protestants. Catholics tend to be conservative on abortion, and possibly same-sex marriage, but also have a tradition of supporting progressive social programs. Mainline Protestants have a tradition of the social gospel that makes them more supportive of progressive political ideology than their evangelical or fundamentalist counterparts. Perception about the likelihood that a religious identity is tied to an adherence to certain political positions can help shape the bias that sociologists have toward certain religious groups.

The tie of fundamentalist/evangelical Christianity to political conservatism would also offer us insight as to why Muslims and Jews were not rejected as coworkers to the same degree as fundamentalists and evangelicals. Muslims and Jews in the United States are not typically associated with members of the religious right. Therefore, no matter how otherworldly such individuals may become, they fail to be the threat to potential progressive political desires that fundamentalists and evangelicals are. It is not merely the existence of supernatural faith that produces the type of animosity picked up from this research. It is supernatural faith buttressed by political conservatism that produces the motivation that a significant number of sociologists have to resist the inclusion of certain types of religious conservatives into the elite positions in academia.

Further evidence of this tendency to conflate conservative political ideology with Protestant conservatism can be seen in the treatment of Rick Warren. As I noted in the last chapter, many activists blasted Warren for his support of Proposition 8. They labeled Warren as an extremist despite his rather moderate overall political record. These activists felt that Warren's position on this single issue disqualified him from offering the invocation for President Obama. This pattern can be seen in the following blogs.

> So Obama his [sic] picked Rick Warren to give the invocation at the inauguration. For those of you who don't know him, Mr. Warren is the pastor of one of the largest mega-churches in the land. Depending on who you talk to, he's either been called the next Billy Graham, or a new James Dobson. Mr. Warren helped lead the charge on Proposition 8. He has compared gay marriage to pedophilia, incest, and plural marriage. And he has compared abortion to the holocaust. I knew this day would come. Just not so soon. Certainly not before the man was actually sworn in. There is no longer any change I can believe in.[21]

> One has to wonder what message President-Elect Barack Obama is sending with his selection of Rick Warren to give the inaugural prayer. Warren is the head of the evangelical Saddleback Church (comprised of four "campuses") in Lake Forest, California. Obama's selection of Warren is a slap in the face to those who support equality for gays, lesbians, bisexuals, and transgendered people, and recognition of same-sex relationships.[22]

I will not discuss here the merits of Proposition 8, but I point out these arguments for it to illustrate why conservative Protestants may be rejected by sociologists. As long as Warren deals with issues of poverty or other progressive causes, he is basically ignored by sociologist bloggers. However, when he chooses to depart from a progressive political position, he is vilified as not worthy to deliver a prayer. This line of reasoning stipulates that conservative Protestants who deviate from an acceptable progressive political position can be stigmatized. Once again fundamentalism and evangelicalism may symbolically represent this deviation, and we see why members of these groups can be rejected as potential colleagues. And as the example of Warren indicates, it does not take much to be rejected. Disagreement on one or two key political issues can lead to such stigmatization.

If Christian identity is tied to the most conservative wing in the Republican party, then we can understand why Republicans in general are seen as more acceptable than evangelicals and fundamentalists. A person who is a Republican may be a moderate Republican and thus may not be as damaging to the social order proposed by social scientists as more conservative Republicans. It is possible that a Republican may support progressive ideals on some cultural political issues such as abortion and stem cell research but remain Republican because of a conservative fiscal philosophy. Such a person may not be highly desirable but can be seen as someone that one can "agree to disagree" with on economic issues and as an ally on social and cultural concerns. But evangelicals and fundamentalists can be seen as representing the highly conservative wing of the Republican party and are seen as more of a threat to some of the social and cultural desires of some sociologists. They may represent ideas that are in near total disagreement with an overall progressive social and political philosophy. If this is the case, then there is little room for agreement between such individuals of faith and many sociologists.

Of course, many Christians are not highly conservative Republicans, and the notion of an identical identity between Christians and political conservatives is an inaccurate stereotype (Buell & Sigelman, 1985; Smith, 2000). Furthermore, there are issues, such as battling modern slavery, where conservative Christians have found allies with progressives (Hertzke, 2008). It is a misconception to think that fundamentalists and evangelicals must always be at odds with progressive social scientists. One would expect most educated individuals to be aware of the inaccuracy of this stereotype. This is especially likely to be the case with individuals who have an expertise in studying society and thus have a powerful ability to debunk inaccurate stereotypes. But little, if any, debunking of these stereotypes took place among sociologist bloggers.[23] Perpetuating stereotypes about evangelicals and fundamentalists allows sociologist bloggers to illustrate their animosity toward those in the religious right. Academic training is likely to give way to personal bias as it concerns understanding members of disfavored social groups. Rather than unpacking the stereotypes that feed into the cultural war, and possibly deflating some of the animosity that surrounds this conflict, there was a tendency to play up these stereotypes, as we have already seen in some of these early quotes. Later in this chapter, I will discuss a clearer illustration of this propensity as I look at myths that developed concerning Barack Obama and John McCain during the 2008 presidential election.

The highly conservative Republican/Christian fundamentalist and evangelical linkage also helps to put into perspective an observation I made as I went through the blogs. Generally the bloggers seemed more interested in attacking Sarah Palin than John McCain, who was seeking to be the top Republican standard-bearer. Furthermore, when they did address McCain they usually (with the notable exception illustrated later in the chapter) directly addressed his ideas while they often launched wide and unsubstantiated broadsides against Palin:

Sarah Palin was standing up for torture, and the Republicans cheered. It was then I finally realized: these people actually like torture.[24]

Writing at the LA Progressive, Charley James reports that Alaskan citizens who know Palin well say she is *"racist, sexist, vindictive, and mean.*" According to a James' [*sic*] interview with a local resident who served Palin breakfast shortly after an Obama victory over Hilary [*sic*] Rodham Clinton, Palin said: "So Sambo beat the bitch." Charming.[25]

Also notice that this blogger also takes aim at individuals who support Palin.

I wonder if any of the Palinistas realize that their chant derives from the black rioters of the sixties, people for whom they probably feel no kinship at all.[26]

The bloggers generally were quick to believe any negative attributes that were attached to Palin with little or no skepticism. This is unlikely to be an accident. Palin was clearly more overt in her religious and political conservatism than McCain. In many ways, Palin may represent the worst of all possible worlds to these bloggers. She represents the mixing of religious and political conservatism that they resent. And she does it as a female, which is an affront to notions of feminism the way most progressives understand that concept. In this way, Palin may be seen as objectionable in a way that McCain, who may be seen as merely being wrong, is able to escape. In fact, at times some of the bloggers talked about a respect for McCain that they had before his presidential run. I cannot remember any attempts at showing respect for Palin by any blogger.

To the degree that sociologists conflate religious and political conservatism, we have reasons why fundamentalists and evangelicals are not perceived as acceptable coworkers. Sociologists may see these "incompetent" individuals as threatening to invade the role that sociologists may seek to possess, the role of being the arbiters of how society should be constructed. In this way, sociologists seem to be staking out their position within the confines of the culture war. While these bloggers used the term *Christians* in their posts, it is reasonable to assert that they were likely not conceptualizing all Christians, but only fundamentalists and evangelicals, since those are the groups most likely to be seen as members of the religious right. If the culture war analogy is an accurate way to understand this social reality, then it is clear that having evangelicals and fundamentalists as coworkers is akin to bringing the enemy right into your command center.

However, Christianity could also be regarded with contempt even without this political connection. As I stated earlier, the bloggers occasionally commented on some of the grievances they have with Christians that are tied to the unique history and social positions of Christians in the United States. Consistently, the fears of a Christian-imposed political order seem to drive some of the animosity that sociologists expressed in their blogs. Further quotes from these blogs indicate that a fear of religious conservatives "taking over" the country plays a role in the anger that many of these bloggers expressed.

> With the backing of Diebold, Katherine Harris, the Supreme Court, and a heavily mobilized base of extremist Christians who stampeded to the polls to support Bush's eagerness to fulfill their apocryphal prophecies in the Holy Land, elect a degenerate individual many apparently believed was an Evangelical who manifested the virtues of Christ, and to empower a group willing to proclaim that Christianity is the official state religion, George Bush and his cronies blatantly subverted our Constitutional Republic by taking office twice without winning the electoral or the popular vote.[27]

> McCain's selection of Sarah Palin as his running mate was a naked play to garner the support of the so-called Republican base— narrow fundamentalist Christians. Let me be clear that NOT all Fundamentalist Christians (and not even the majority of them) are "radical" (meaning wanting to take over the government of the United States and reshape the country into a religious fiefdom). However, that is the base that McCain went after. It is the "base" that George Bush supposedly captured.[28]

Finally, it is important to take into consideration the timing of these blog entries. Most of these entries occurred right before or right after the election of President Obama.[29] That event can be seen as a potential watershed moment in the struggles linked to the idea of a culture war. Conservatives lost favored positions of power while cultural progressives took control of every arm of government. It is plausible that economic, more than cultural, issues fueled the win by Obama. But as my examples have shown, often it is the cultural issues that drive much of the ire that sociologists have developed against the religious right. The likelihood that economic issues drove Obama's victory does not stop sociologists who favor progressive cultural change from pushing for, and then celebrating, widespread victories of the Democratic Party. Thus it is not a surprise that a significant amount of energy exhibited through these blogs was used to weigh in on this election and to celebrate their victory over their cultural opponents—the religious right.

Favorable Groups and the Blogs of Sociologists

Just as there were bad groups that had to be confronted, sociologists also conceptualized good social groups that deserved support. However, sociologists who created blogs were more inclined to assess the problems of the social groups they possessed animosity toward than to compliment the social groups they favored. They were much quicker to condemn their enemies than to support their friends. Yet this does not mean that these sociologists were completely silent about groups they favored. We have already seen that sociologists do not have very many concerns about working with groups associated with progressive ideologies. There is evidence that these sociologists also are quite sympathetic to the challenges that these groups face:

> In that light, the current American animosity toward Jews, gays, Muslims, and women unearthed in the film is a grim reminder that we may not have changed as much as we'd like to think.[30]

> One of the latest countries confronting discrimination is Ireland. [. . .] Many Irish people do not accept the new immigrants, and this is especially true for Black immigrants, who come mostly from West African countries like Nigeria.[31]

It is common for people on the left to bemoan the particulars of the electoral system for why there is not a viable left third party in the United States. The bigger problem: unfortunately, the vast majority of Americans don't agree with us![32]

"The L-Word," *liberal*, recast as an insult by then-candidate George H. W. Bush in his campaign against Massachusetts governor Michael S. Dukakis. Bush successfully made Americans believe to be liberal was to be out of touch, perhaps even unpatriotic. He managed to do that even though most Americans then—as now—tell pollsters that they agree more with liberals than with conservatives on most issues! The L-word was particularly successful in that Bush never had to make the argument—it was the word that never needed to be spoken because everyone already knew what was to be said.[33]

So it would appear that the government, charged with the responsibility to protect U.S. citizens from each other is simply abdicating that responsibility when it comes to people of color, even though a study in 2002 found that 75% of U.S. citizens polled did **not** believe everyone in the U.S. is treated equally. [. . .] African-Americans, Latinos, Native Americans, and Asian-Americans want nothing more than what European-Americans want: safety, opportunity, respect.[34]

Yet even in these quotes we observe sociologists attacking their perceived social enemies even as they offer advice or comfort to their social allies. Entities like Trent Lott, Irish bigots, Americans with animosity toward progressives, and George W. Bush are seen as creating problems for certain progressive social groups. Generally the bloggers are not merely supportive of the groups they like. Usually there is criticism of another group embedded within their compliments of the acceptable social group. Whether this is a feature of the nature of blogging or sociologists remains to be seen.

Sometimes sociologists were supportive without being critical concerning the efforts of individuals. Heroes, when they were identified, were individuals who promoted progressive causes and ideologies. For example, one of the blogs spotlighted a particular activist, saying that she was

> exemplary of a new generation of brilliant young activists who are changing the direction of this nation. She was an organizer of the highly successful Liberty Parade that took place in Loring Park . . . [35]

I was at first unable to determine in what kind of activism the activist was engaged. However, as the blog described the account given by the activist, it became clear what sort of causes she was involved with:

> I decided to bring some treats to the ACLU office because I knew they were having a very busy week. I went to the office with cupcakes and blueberry muffins. They told me they were holding a press conference at 2:30 pm with Amy Goodman from Democracy Now!, and they asked if I'd come back from [sic] that. Would I come back? Amy is only one of my personal heroes. [36]

As we saw in the last chapter, the ACLU is heavily favored by sociologists. Democracy Now! is a news show that is part of Free Speech TV, which promotes radical and leftist political movements. Based on the results of the last chapter, I suspect that most sociologists who know of this organization think as highly of it as does this blogger. Thus it is clear that progressive activism is the type of activism promoted by this blogger.

It is not merely activism that is promoted by the sociologists. They also were supportive of attempts to understand progressive subcultures.

> . . . a Family Foundation policy analyst asked [. . .] how the research of Professor Kaila Story of the University of Louisville on "how the black male-bodied Drag Queen's presence within queer 'subcultures' disrupts mainstream notions of what is considered natural and fixed signifiers of black femininity and/or womanhood" moves Kentucky forward. The answer, as any anthropologist, sociologist or psychologist could tell him, is that it is only by examining the deviant [. . .] that we can understand "what is

considered natural and fixed signifiers of black femininity and/or womanhood."[37]

In this way sociologist bloggers would paint a picture of sociologists offering explanation to those who are not knowledgeable about these groups. The goal is to offer sympathy toward these groups and indirectly for progressive causes that these groups represent. Sociologists use their blogs as opportunities to bring into conversation societal innovations that support progressive groups, and in this way blogs are seen as tremendous opportunities for social progress. It is perhaps in these conversations that sociologists can be arbitrators of a progressive social morality that counters the traditional morality promoted by their opponents in the culture war. These bloggers clearly made it known which side they were fighting for in that war, and their blogs were tools to be used in that fight.

Evidence that sociologists' contributions to the culture war are affirming progressives as well as attacking conservatives can be seen in the reaction that many of the bloggers had to the passage of Proposition 8, which banned same-sex marriage in California. Some of them exhibited a great deal of sympathy for the opponents of the ban or used this as an opportunity to attack supporters of the ban.

> My joy at the news of last week's presidential election was quickly deflated as I learned about the passage of Proposition 8 in California and a number of other anti-gay measures around the nation.[38]

> "God says Homosexuality is wrong." It seems clear to me that what this eventually amounts to, when distilled to its most basic level, is an attempt to force one's religious beliefs on the rest of society.[39]

> . . . the "people," even if a simple majority, should never have the right to take away basic rights awarded to us in the Constitution. [. . .] For the "people" are a fickle bunch, and I don't want my basic rights to be decided by a majority of whoever decided to turn out and vote that day—that is really crazy.[40]

The information collected from these blogs confirms the general sense among sociologists that they are in the middle of the culture war. In that fight, the main purpose they serve is delegitimizing groups linked to orthodox values. To a lesser extent, they also work toward promoting understandings of progressive groups and the causes linked to them. Some of the bloggers promoted such ideologies with a more academic approach than the examples I have shown in this chapter, but their choice of which scholarly research to feature in the blogs clearly indicated their desire to support progressive groups and ideologies. This was an opportunity for them to apply the lessons learned in their sociological training in ways that promote ideas for cultural progressives. Their status as scientists provides them a role to play to support their perspectives in a societal disagreement on what our society should look like.

To be sure, not all sociologist bloggers invested a great deal of their writing toward promoting these goals. Some merely discussed their personal lives and reflected on the sociological imagination in nonpolitical ways. Others used their blogs to enunciate their perceptions about academia and the challenges of teaching or doing research. I want to make clear that in reading the blogs, I did not encounter a continual rant against religious and political conservatives. This also reflects the fact documented in the previous chapter that not all sociologists stated that they screened out traditional social groups. Thus, we have to be careful not to paint with too broad a stroke the propensity of some scholars to use their blogs to fight against conservative social institutions and individuals. However, the previous chapter also indicated that enough sociologists did screen out political and religious conservatives that it is likely that members of such groups face barriers against entrance into the field. Given the imagery of Palin promoted in the blogs, for instance, it is not unreasonable to think that some sociologists would question the mental faculties of a scholar who supported her and McCain, even though support of these Republicans says nothing about the ability of a sociology professor to perform his or her duties.

Most of the blog entries that dealt with the social groups analyzed in the previous chapter focused on negative assertions about disfavored groups rather than positive assertions about favored groups. However, enough bloggers did indicate support for accepted social groups that it is realistic to assert that there is a general social atmosphere that promotes politically progressive ideologies. Yet even here we can see this support as part of the effort to limit the influence of disfavored groups. The desire to promote progressive ideologies helps to explain why screens are applied on traditional social groups. A significant number, although probably not a majority, of sociologists likely perceive such groups as "enemies" to the progressive social order that they promote. To allow individuals from these groups into academia would be to allow them to share the social power that such sociologists hope to use to push forward progressive social ideologies.

Barack the Muslim versus McCain the Rude

Furthermore, these blogs indicated that the biases of sociologists are not limited to screening out job candidates from the disfavored groups. These biases also affect the ability of scholars to engage in critical thinking. For example, several bloggers defended Barack Obama from the charges that he was a Muslim and that he did not wear an American flag lapel. Usually the blogger noted that these were not good reasons not to vote for him even if true, but they also pointed out the falseness of those charges. The bloggers utilized their critical thinking skills to debunk such false charges and to show the irrelevancy of these claims.

> Fires are harder to put out than they are to start. The constant meme out of the McCain campaign has been that Obama is a Muslim, hates the United States, is a person to be afraid of, and now that he is a terrorist. [. . .] Starting with the meme that Obama was a Muslim schooled in madrassas [sic], the seed was planted that he was a "born and trained" terrorist. Even the long term relationship with Reverend Wright was not portrayed as proof of his Christianity, but was "proof" of his hatred of the United States. (Regardless that it **should** make no difference even if Obama **was** Muslim.)[41]

> Particularly emphasized are the comments that Barak [sic] Obama is (1) a terrorist, or (2) an Arab (or Muslim). I'm going to ignore the

former. Here's my issue with the latter: I get the political ramifications of this and that we all want to correct the facts. But I also
think something very dangerous is going on here when we just
correct the facts. [. . .] my issue with the rhetoric around this: the
response to, "he's an Arab" is, "No! He's a decent family man and
citizen"—as if the two were incompatible.[42]

However, these critical thinking skills failed them as it concerned falsehoods about John McCain. For example, there was a common video passed around the blogs after one of the Obama/McCain
debates that suggested that McCain refused to shake Obama's hand.
Some sociologists pushed forth this interpretation through their
blogs.

For example, at last night's presidential debate, John McCain
referred to Barack Obama as "that one" and at the close of the
debate refused to shake his hand.[43]

That bit was hard to miss, but I hadn't noticed the refusal of the
handshake. Ouch.[44]

However, the shot was taken out of context as McCain had earlier
shaken Obama's hand and was merely bringing Obama over to his
wife. All but one of the blogs that used the video did so to illustrate
the impoliteness of McCain. The one exception did accurately comment on the episode.

It [the video] was on YouTube minutes after the debate ended, and
liberal bloggers all over the Internet were linking to it. It appears
that McCain refuses to shake hands with Obama. [. . .] The clip is
misleading. It's taken out of context. The candidates had already
shaken hands, and McCain was trying to get Obama to shake
hands with Cindy as well, not instead of.[45]

The other entries of this blogger clearly indicated his support
was for Obama. This was not a defense put forth by a McCain sup-
porter. But the blogger had done the homework necessary to avoid
perpetuating a myth. For the other bloggers, this was clearly an
opportunity to imply that McCain was not a decent person. The care

that the sociology bloggers had put into debunking the falsehoods about Obama was abandoned with this chance to paint McCain in an unflattering manner. There likely were other misleading assertions by the bloggers about McCain that would have been cleared up had the bloggers taken the care in determining accurate information that scholars are supposed to use when they are seeking knowledge.

In a political campaign there are many falsehoods perpetuated by both political parties. I know of no reputable research that indicates that either Republicans or Democrats have more of an ability to tell the truth than their political rivals. Naturally individuals from both political parties accuse the other party of having less ability to tell the truth and of playing "dirty" politics. This comparison is not about whether it is worse for an American politician to be called a Muslim or rude. Both charges are clearly false in the contexts discussed in the previous paragraphs. A social scholar can clearly favor one party over the other and yet note the falsity of both charges. It is possible that those favoring Democrats may not learn of the video of McCain but have heard the false rumors about Obama. That should lead to blogs that talk about the false rumors about Obama but ignore the "hand-shake" incident. However, the blogs are often linked to each other, and so community knowledge about McCain's "rudeness" to Obama likely spread to most of the bloggers. Yet only one chose to clear the record. This illustrates that this was not merely a case of selective knowledge, but that scholars who should be trained in detecting social deception were fooled when they encountered rumors that met with their own political approval. The fact that bloggers accept distorted information to promote their political viewpoint is not new. But scholars trained to engage in critical thinking should be less likely to perpetuate such myths. Yet it may be the case that sociologist bloggers may be no more likely to weed out myths and stereotypes than other bloggers.

This comparison is enlightening because it suggests that the ability of scholars to investigate social reality may be compromised by their social biases. It is likely that this same inability to apply critical analysis to myths about disfavored groups applies when such groups are studied. If that is true, then social scientists who study religious and politically conservative social groups are susceptible to believing uncorroborated myths and stereotypes about disfavored groups while they are inclined to work at debunking such myths and stereotypes about groups they favor. This does not mean that all research that puts religious and political conservatives in a bad light is false, but it does mean that some sociologists are prone to produce such research without sufficiently thinking critically about the results accuracy. In the second chapter, I provided an example of how we might become convinced that auditors are mean individuals. This could lead us to develop a bias in which we highly value information that supports this stereotype and discount evidence that challenges the notion of the mean auditor. But over time, there is a pretty good chance that we will work with individuals who do not think auditors are mean and they will help us create the hypothesis that will assess the possible niceness of auditors. Yet this assumes that we allow for a variety of individuals to enter into research with us so that some of them do not have our presuppositions about auditors. But the evidence in the previous chapter suggests that there are few such checks and balances when it comes to challenging the negative perceptions of religious and political conservatives since members of these groups face higher barriers to entry into sociological study. Since sociologists are not immune from selectively seeking evidence that supports their social biases, this lack of dissenting opinion makes it even harder to discern what is true about these conservatives and what is rumor. In the view of these sociologists, Republicans and conservative Protestants are immoral individuals not only in their politics but even in their personal manners. This goes beyond whether one agrees with McCain or not to whether he is even a decent person. If other sociologists have the same perspectives as those that wrote these blogs, it is not surprising that sociologists are relatively hesitant to work with fundamentalist, evangelical, and Republican colleagues.

One may be tempted to argue that a blog is not intended to be a formal scientific statement and that we should expect sociologists with blogs to be less inclined to write with a great deal of sophistication. Yet many of these blogs clearly were written in an attempt to provide the reader with insights from a sociological perspective and included fairly sophisticated arguments and social analyses. Furthermore, we have seen from the evidence in chapter 3 that some sociologists are willing to allow their social biases to influence who may be hired into their workplaces, and we should not be surprised if the same biases in their arguments on their private blogs animate the logical assessments they may use while performing research. Finally, it should be noted that some of the bloggers did write in a more scholarly manner and attempted to persuade readers about their positions with academic arguments. I chose not to include these entries since they involved legitimate scientific debate rather than serving as a reflection of the social biases of sociologists. Yet even these entries tended to support the general sentiment of the other bloggers in that these sociologists used scholarly reasoning to support progressive initiatives and to debunk notions of religious and political conservatism. However, they relied on more sophisticated arguments than the polemic seen in most blogs. It is plausible that these scholars suffer from the same social biases as their more aggressive counterparts but utilized writing standards that make these biases less overt. Overall the information gathered in this assessment indicates that the social biases some sociologists possess likely affect their ability to conduct accurate sociological analysis.

Conclusion

The analysis of the output of these bloggers indicates that traditional social groups and ideologies are discredited while progressive groups and ideologies are held up as ideal. It is unrealistic to think that sociologists simply put these biases aside when they go to work and as they consider whom they will hire. The fact that members of certain traditional social groups are at a disadvantage when they seek employment in academic sociology indicates that such biases are not confined only to the online realm of these blogs. These tendencies indicate a phenomenon in which sociologists operate out of a need to screen out the traditional social groups discredited on these blogs to promote progressive ideologies. To a lesser degree, such sociologists may also help members of progressive social groups obtain academic positions, as these bloggers clearly indicated a certain degree of sympathy for those individuals.

The image of the culture war highly resonates with the results of this and the previous chapter. Wars polarize individuals into two groups: allies and enemies. Allies are to be supported at almost any cost since all soldiers, as allies, share the same goal. Likewise, enemies are to be defeated no matter what it takes. When religious and political conservatives are seen as enemies, it is acceptable to limit their access to academic positions. It is also acceptable to label them negatively and make it easier to stigmatize them, as we saw some sociologist bloggers do. The key is to get rid of the enemy, and in a culture war that means limiting whatever influence they may have. It is not my purpose to comment on the rightness of the causes promoted by many sociologists. Rather, I have observed that performing this central function of minimizing the enemy in a culture war does not serve sociologists well as it concerns developing information about society. These social biases must inevitably interfere with the objectivity of sociological study through an emphasis on promoting perceptions that aid progressive social groups and denigrate conservative social groups.

The general unit of analysis for sociologists is society. This is also true to a certain degree for other types of social scientists (e.g., anthropologists, political scientists). Therefore it is fairly simple to understand how social scientists perceive themselves as having a valued role in promoting a social vision in keeping with the values of the new class. Yet other scientific disciplines may not have such an inherent role in critiquing the larger society. If they do not have such a role, it is quite plausible that the need to screen out traditional social groups may not exist. Yet there may be other roles that scholars who do not study society play in the larger culture war. Such academics may seek to promote the use of scientific reason over traditional norms in issues that are not directly connected to social structure (such as in issues involving creationism). This means that it is vital to look at the attitudes of other academics. Exploring those attitudes will inform us whether the findings of this chapter are unique to sociologists or whether we can generalize these findings to the rest of academia. To this end, in the next chapter I will quantitatively explore those attitudes among non-sociologist scholars.

CHAPTER FIVE

Tolerance and Bias in Other Academic Disciplines

Focusing on the discipline of sociology has allowed me to dig deeply into the contours of social toleration in one particular field. But it is important also to see if we can generalize what we now know about sociologists to other academics. For this reason, there is great value in exploring the tolerance of social groups among non-sociologists. Doing so will help us to know if the findings among sociologists were due to unique features found within that discipline. Thus we will see how representative sociologists are of the rest of academia. These issues can only be addressed if we analyze other disciplines and compare the results of such analysis to the results discovered about sociologists. This chapter contains such an investigation. It will not be an exhaustive exploration that includes most academic fields, but it will include enough different academic disciplines to allow me to make general assertions about academia.

Differences in the Social Sciences, Humanities, and Physical Sciences

As noted in chapter 2, past research has indicated that scholars in the social sciences and the humanities are more likely to have progressive social attitudes than those in the physical and biological sciences

(Ladd & Lipset, 1975; Lazarsfeld & Thielens, 1958). To the extent that this is an accurate portrayal of academia, one might expect that the social biases in academia differ across disciplines. However, recent work has indicated that political and religious differences among the disciplines are less than originally imagined (Ecklund et al., 2008). The social biases common within sociology may be excellent predictors of the social biases in other academic disciplines.

Even if there are not powerful political and religious differences across the disciplines, there are still plausible reasons why social biases may be more intense in certain disciplines than others. To the degree that religious and political conservatives are perceived as a threat to scholars in certain disciplines, there should be higher levels of social bias against such groups. Conservative religious and political groups tend to promote ideas more threatening to the progressive ideals promoted within the social sciences and humanities than to those promoted in the physical sciences.[1] They also may be seen as competing with academics in the social sciences and humanities for being the arbitrators of social values and morals, while members of the physical sciences are granted areas of expertise that are not sufficiently challenged by cultural conservatives. If that is the case, then social biases against those groups should be more pronounced among academics in the social sciences and the humanities than among those in other academic endeavors.

Methodology

I have used much of the same methodology described in chapter 3 for this assessment of the different disciplines. The disciplines studied are anthropology, political science, history, language, philosophy, chemistry, experimental biology, and geophysics. I located faculty members in these disciplines at a variety of colleges and universities in the same manner in which I found sociologists—with directories of the discipline.[2] The only real difference in how I conducted the survey to non-sociologists is that I included fewer respondents for each discipline than the 1,500 sociologists who were surveyed. I did this because I did not need to determine the specializations of the scholars in each discipline as I did for sociologists. I found less of a need for a high number of respondents in the other disciplines since I was not going to assess the possible effects of different sub-specializations within those fields. As a sociologist, I am well acquainted with the sub-specializations that are part of my chosen discipline, but I am less confident that I can discuss the implications of different specializations in non-sociological disciplines. Thus it is reasonable that I drop the specialization question, without which there is no need for such a high number of respondents since I will only look at broad comparisons of the toleration of social groups among the distinct disciplines.

One can ask why I limited myself to only scientific disciplines and the humanities, to the exclusion of nonscientific specializations such as business and engineering. It is the case that professors in these disciplines do shape the social atmosphere on campuses.[3] However, I am interested in how social bias may shape the direction of science as much as, or more than, how it may influence the social atmosphere in academia. Scientists clearly affect this direction, and scholars in the humanities often provide some of the critical ideas that drive scientific inquiry. The assessment of the more applied disciplines would provide some of the answers to the latter question, but would not provide insight into the former one. The additional information I might gain from including such disciplines does not merit the extra time and effort needed to produce that information. Ideally, some future researcher will take up this question.

Findings

In chapter 3, I broke down the tendency of sociologists to engage in bias by looking at whether membership in a given social group greatly enhanced or damaged a person's candidacy for an academic position. I have used the same scale to investigate the willingness of scholars in eight other disciplines to hire members of the different groups. The measures on a seven-point scale produced mean scores that were positively related to the level of acceptance for each group. For convenience, I will not show the scores on the seven-point scale but will show the mean scores for each social group across the eight disciplines. These means can be seen in table 5.1.

The results indicate that the same general patterns found among sociologists are also found within the other disciplines. In all of the disciplines, fundamentalists were the group most likely to be rejected. Evangelicals and Mormons fared a little better, but still are groups that academics tend to reject. In chapter 3, it was evident that Mormons are more likely to be rejected than accepted by sociologists, but their level of rejection was not as high as it was for fundamentalists, evangelicals, or NRA members. But in this table we see evidence that the rejection of Mormons among scholars of other disciplines was greater than one would assume from the scores of sociologists. Mormons scored better than evangelicals in all groups except for physicists, but their scores are still low enough to suggest that they received a level of rejection similar to that received by evangelicals. It is possible that this is the result of a "Proposition 8" effect. Since most of the survey of sociologists was conducted before the November elections, the defeat of Proposition 8 in California could not have greatly affected the scores of sociologists.[4] After the election, there was a fair amount of speculation that part of the defeat of Proposition 8 was due to the influence of Mormons in the election (Garrison & Lin, 2008; Riccardi, 2008). This led to criticism of Mormons by progressives (Gorski, 2008; Kuruvila, 2008; McKay, 2009) that may have influenced the scores of the scientific groups assessed after the November elections.[5]

Fundamentalists scored the highest among experimental biologists with an average score of 3.481. But this score indicates that more than one-third of the experimental biologists stated that knowing that a person was a fundamentalist would damage their ability to support that person, and more than 13 percent of the experimental biologists indicated that this knowledge would at least moderately damage their support. Even among experimental biologists, the group where fundamentalists received the highest score, support was still lower than the score of the next lowest group, NRA members. Republicans and NRA members were unpopular, but in all groups they were still more likely to be accepted than fundamentalists, and in most groups they were more likely to be accepted than evangelicals. Among chemists, experimental biologists, historians,

Table 5.1. Comparison of Means Indicating Whether Belonging to Selected Social Groups Damages or Enhances Acceptance of Job Applicants by Discipline

	Political Science (n = 70)	Anthropology (n = 107)	History (n = 81)	Physics (n = 50)	Chemistry (n = 79)	Experimental Biology (n = 57)	Lang. English (n = 86)	Lang. Other (n = 34)	Philosophy (n = 160)
Democrat	4.215	4.444	4.275	4.08	4.247	4.185	4.5	4.133	4.248
Republican	3.723	3.556	3.725	4.0	3.822	3.87	3.654	3.767	3.699
Green Party	4.062	4.173	4.141	4.02	4.083	4.056	4.208	4.133	4.163
Libertarian	3.923	3.949	3.833	3.84	3.873	3.981	3.756	4.103	3.752
Communist Party	3.516	3.869	3.608	3.51	3.843	3.759	3.813	3.931	3.693
NRA	3.585	3.364	3.526	3.62	3.493	3.623	3.291	3.259	3.569
ACLU	4.2	4.36	4.127	4.102	4.333	4.255	4.342	4.333	4.197
Heterosexual	4.121	4.02	4.013	4.2	4.054	4.019	4.104	4.033	4.059
Homosexual	4.061	4.108	3.9	3.776	3.986	3.926	4.052	3.967	3.928
Bisexual	4.0	4.039	3.837	3.74	3.959	3.907	4.0	3.933	3.895
Transgendered	3.682	3.951	3.714	3.62	3.726	3.815	3.818	3.933	3.807
Atheist	3.833	4.139	3.913	4.0	4.219	3.981	4.026	4.067	3.993
Mormon	3.692	3.539	3.725	3.551	3.753	3.907	3.526	3.733	3.601
Fundamentalist	3.292	2.64	3.15	3.18	3.361	3.481	2.779	3.133	2.987
Evangelical	3.391	2.91	3.532	3.56	3.507	3.685	3.192	3.633	3.516
Mainline	4.046	3.941	4.037	4.14	3.973	4.0	4.0	3.867	3.993
Catholic	4.123	3.961	4.088	4.14	4.014	4.0	4.026	4.0	4.013
Muslim	3.938	4.03	4.05	3.82	3.973	3.963	4.013	4.033	3.941
Jewish	4.015	4.02	4.075	4.1	4.055	3.981	4.091	4.0	4.0
Vegetarian	4.03	4.0	3.975	4.08	4.041	3.981	4.104	4.0	4.099
Hunter	3.848	3.802	3.888	3.88	3.77	3.873	3.692	3.7	3.855
Married	4.076	4.04	4.076	4.3	4.0	4.056	4.091	4.0	4.065
Divorced	3.909	4.0	3.975	3.98	3.986	3.963	4.039	4.0	3.961
Cohabitating	3.924	4.0	3.888	3.88	3.986	3.963	3.974	4.0	3.838
Single-Child	3.97	4.039	4.0	3.92	4.0	3.944	4.013	4.0	4.006
Over 50	3.788	3.843	3.8	3.706	3.685	3.815	3.883	4.0	3.851
Under 30	4.06	3.961	4.037	4.137	4.069	3.944	4.117	4.034	3.994
% Not Matter*	31.7	23.9	18.1	22.2	30.6	43.8	13.0	40.0	28.3

*For any category.

and non-English language teachers, NRA members were less accepted than evangelicals. Republicans were more likely to be accepted than evangelicals in all of the disciplines. Thus we see more reinforcement of a type of negative hierarchy in which conservative religious groups are less acceptable to scholars than conservative political groups.

On the other hand, all of the disciplines indicated a positive bias toward Democrats and members of the ACLU. For the most part, the groups that were favored by sociologists were accepted by other academics while those that were disfavored by sociologists were rejected by other academics. Democrats were given the highest score by all of the groups except physicists, chemists, experimental biologists, and those who taught non-English languages. In those groups, the ACLU scored better than Democrats. In an anomaly, heterosexuals were the highest scoring group for physicists. Thus just as sociologists tended to provide their highest level of support for groups that were linked to progressive ideologies, so too did other scientific disciplines tend to display a positive bias toward such groups.

These academics generally did not show a tendency to reject individuals based on their sexual practices. There was an exception to this tendency as it concerned transgendered individuals within certain disciplines and homosexuality as it concerned physicists. The scores concerning transgendered individuals were below 3.8 within the disciplines of political science, history, physics, and chemistry. This indicates some degree of discomfort for transgendered individuals within these disciplines. For example, the score of 3.726 among chemists indicates that more than one out of every five chemists stated that knowing that someone was transgendered would damage that person's chances of gaining their support. Transgendered individuals received a distinctly lower level of support than other sexual groups. It may well be that scholars have more of an ability to accept individuals who have uncommon sexual practices as long as those practices are kept relatively hidden. However, the slightly negative image of transgendered individuals may be connected to fears that such colleagues might bring their practices into the public sphere. This would produce a level of concern among scholars that homosexuality and bisexuality fail to produce. However, we should not overemphasize the rejection of transgendered individuals. While they consistently scored below the 4.0 midpoint score, indicating that they were more likely to be rejected than accepted by scholars, their scores did not come close to the cellar-dwelling scores of fundamentalists, and only among physicists did they come close to the level of rejection experienced by evangelicals.[6]

The curious case of physicists deserves some attention. On the one hand, the group that received the highest score among physicists was heterosexuals, a group that was barely above the midpoint in other disciplines. Furthermore, physicists were the only group that had a score for homosexuals below 3.8 and thus low enough (3.776) to indicate that homosexuality may negatively impact a candidate's chances of being hired. Finally, their score of 3.62 for the transgendered was the lowest of the disciplines and rivaled the score of 3.56 for evangelicals. It is unclear why members of this discipline seem to have such an attachment, or nonattachment, to certain sexual groups. One possibility is that somehow a high percentage of physicists teach at religious schools that have rules concerning sexual morality. However, only 9.8 percent of the physicists in the sample teach at religious schools. Furthermore, part of the strong support of heterosexuals was driven by three respondents who stated that knowing that a candidate was heterosexual extremely enhanced their support of that candidate. Yet all three of these individuals teach at public nonreligious schools. It is possible that there is a subculture within this discipline that strongly supports notions of traditional morality and that this subculture helps to drive such results. But without a qualitative analysis of the reasons why members of this scientific discipline react differently than members of other scientific disciplines, it is difficult to substantiate this speculative assertion. Furthermore, because of the small sample size, these results may be driven by the outliers. This was one of the few times that the smaller sample size seriously interfered with my confidence in the results. Because of the general trend toward disdain for religious and political conservatives, it seems unlikely that physicists have a great love for members of those groups. But whether they also have mistrust of sexual nonconformists is a question that is not easily answered with these anomalous results. Research with a higher number of physicists would help to substantiate or refute these findings.

While the actual groups accepted or rejected did not greatly differ between disciplines, the degree to which the disciplines reacted to those various social groups did differ. For example, anthropologists and English language scholars were clearly the groups most antagonistic to evangelicals and most supportive of Democrats. Both of these groups scored below 2.8 as it concerned fundamentalists and above 4.4 as it concerned Democrats. None of the other groups had such low or high scores. To illustrate the level of rejection that these groups exhibited, in both cases more than two-thirds of the respondents indicated that knowing that a candidate was a fundamentalist would negatively influence whether they would hire that candidate. Among anthropologists, nearly half stated that it would at least moderately damage the candidate's chances. Imagine a known fundamentalist going to a job interview understanding that about half of the people in the search committee will be rooting against him or her even before the interview. However, more than a quarter of scholars in each group indicated that knowing that a candidate was a Democrat would enhance that person's chances of being hired. Thus the Democratic candidate has the advantage of knowing that about one-fourth of a search committee will be favorably disposed toward him or her. It is quite plausible that these two academic disciplines are more politicized than other disciplines, which may account for their more powerful tendency to engage in social bias. In the case of anthropology, it has been suggested that there are historical and institutionalized factors that may help to account for the level of animosity toward conservative Christians (Arnold, 2006; Priest, 2001). This may explain why anthropologists not only had a score below 3.0 for fundamentalists but for evangelicals as well.

On the other hand, groups such as the chemists and experimental biologists exhibited a much lower degree of range in scoring the different social groups. The chemists did not score much higher than any of the other disciplines, except for the physicists, as it concerned their admiration for Democrats, but they did provide a relatively high score for fundamentalists (3.361) and Mormons (3.753). The experimental biologists also exhibited a relatively small degree of range. ACLU members were the group with the highest score among experimental biologists, 4.255. This score was lower than the highest score for Democrats among anthropologists, historians, and English teachers. It was also lower than the high scores for the ACLU among chemists and teachers of non-English languages. Only political scientists, physicists, and philosophers had a lower "high score" than the experimental biologists. But their lowest score for fundamentalists (3.481) was clearly higher than the scores for fundamentalists in any of the other disciplines. Furthermore, more than two of five (43.8 percent) experimental biologists indicated in their assessments that none of the social groups would influence their evaluation of a job candidate. Experimental biologists were generally more immune to the effects of social bias than members of other disciplines. The general hierarchy of which groups were accepted did not differ between these groups and the other scientific disciplines; however, the degrees of acceptance and/or rejection do vary between the various disciplines. It is possible that this difference in degrees of acceptance/rejection was related to the fact that these are physical sciences, but non-English language teachers also showed a relatively low acceptance of Democrats (4.133) and relatively high acceptance of Mormons (3.733). Furthermore, it is worth noting that historians tended to have a relatively high degree of support for evangelicals (3.532), while philosophers had a relatively high degree of support for Mormons (3.601). Thus it is important to look more deeply into the possible divisions of the disciplines and to further test whether such divisions are predictive of the degree of social bias exhibited by academics.

To summarize, the basic findings in chapter 3 are reinforced with the non-sociological disciplines. While the degree of acceptance or rejection varies across disciplines, the patterns of who is accepted or rejected generally do not. There are two findings in this chapter that are somewhat different from the findings in chapter 3. First, there is more evidence for rejection of Mormons. Second, there is some indication that the relatively high level of acceptance that sociologists have for transgendered individuals is not replicated in all other academic disciplines. However, these two discrepancies do not negate the major findings of chapter 3 which show the low level of acceptance of religious conservatives, even relative to political conservatives, by scholars.

Differences in Types of Scientific Inquiry

Since there is evidence of a contrasting degree of acceptance and rejection of the various social groups, it is useful to look for reasons why such contrasts exist. A key distinction that has to be noted is the differences among the various types of academic inquiry. There are three divisions that can be seen among the disciplines used in this research. There are the social sciences, which are represented by the political scientists, historians, and anthropologists. There are the physical sciences, represented by physics, chemistry, and experimental biology. There are the humanities, represented by philosophy and language. Splitting the scholars into these three divisions allows us to see whether the type of scientific inquiry one engages in helps to shape one's potential to engage in social bias. The results of exploring this breakdown can be seen in figure 5.1.

There is very little difference between scholars in the social sciences and the humanities as it concerns social bias. Members of the humanities are significantly more likely to accept evangelicals and vegetarians than those in the social sciences. These differences are relatively minor, and for all practical purposes one can argue that the same social biases that are part of the social sciences are just as dominant in the humanities. Since so little distinguishes these two groups of sciences, we can assume them to be almost identical in the degree of social bias within their fields and in terms of which groups are more likely to experience the positive or negative effects of that bias.

However, the issue is different as it concerns the physical sciences. Scholars in the physical sciences are less supportive of Democrats and homosexuals, but they are more supportive of evangelicals than those in the social sciences. They are less supportive of members of the Green Party and individuals over fifty than scholars

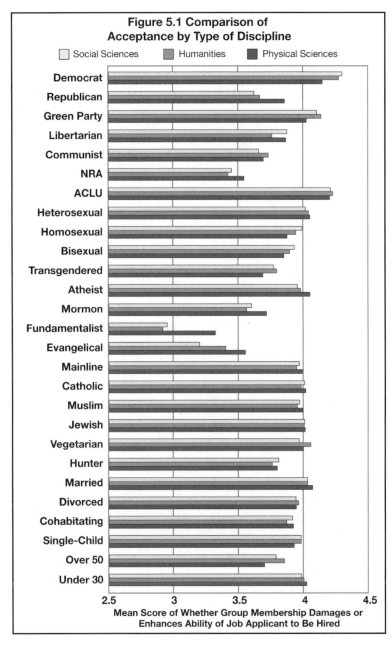

Figure 5.1 Comparison of Acceptance by Type of Discipline

Mean Score of Whether Group Membership Damages or Enhances Ability of Job Applicant to Be Hired

in the humanities. Physical science academics are more supportive of Republicans and fundamentalists than scholars of both groups. All of these results suggest a less progressive religious and political bias for scholars in the physical sciences. However, the general trend of favoring progressive social groups over conservative groups is maintained in these findings. For example, physical scientists are supportive of Democrats over Republicans (4.18 versus 3.888: $p < .001$) and atheists over evangelicals (4.085 versus 3.581: $p < .001$). However, the distance between the two groups is distinctly less than it is for academics in the social sciences or humanities.

The Nature of Academia versus the Nature of the Specific Discipline?

It should not be surprising that physical scientists are more supportive of conservative social groups than are social scientists and those in the humanities. After all, several studies have documented the higher levels of political progressiveness (Klein & Western, 2004–2005; Ladd & Lipset, 1975; Nieli, 2005) and irreligiosity (Lehman, 1972; Stark & Finke, 2000; Wuthnow, 1985) of those in the social sciences and humanities relative to those in the physical sciences. Even though some recent work suggests that this difference may no longer exist (Ecklund et al., 2008), the history of political progressiveness and hostility toward religion in the social sciences has perhaps created an atmosphere of social bias against religious and political conservatives that has not yet developed within the physical sciences. However, before we accept that the differences between these branches of academia are innately imbedded, it is worth our time to explore an alternative explanation. It is possible that these differences are as much due to demographic contrasts among the disciplines as they are to the distinctions within the different disciplines.

For example, in chapter 3 we observed that female sociologists were more likely to reject conservative religious and political groups than other sociologists. It may be the case that in the physical sciences there are a higher percentage of males compared to the other scientific disciplines. The contrasting tendencies of academics in the physical sciences to accept members of conservative groups may be linked to this demographic difference more than to the historical and institutional distinctions among the disciplines. To the degree that these differences are created by demographical variations among the disciplines, it is likely that the general atmosphere of academia accounts for these variations. In other words, there is a general hostility toward members of conservative religious and political social groups among academics in general, and the only reason that this hostility is not as strong in the physical sciences as it is in the social sciences is because academic men are less likely to have such a bias and are overrepresented in the physical sciences. Such a finding would reaffirm that there is a general academic culture that reinforces certain social biases even though certain members in academia are more likely to possess this bias than others.

Furthermore, there may be other variables that help to account for this difference. To see if this is the case, I combined the results of all of the non-sociology disciplines and performed regression analysis that controlled for age, gender, level of college or university at which the respondent works, the discipline of the scholar, and whether the scholar worked at a religious school.[7] The technical results can be seen and are more fully explained in table A in the appendix. But the general result of this work indicates that sex and attendance at a religious school are important factors shaping the tendency of scholars to engage in social bias. This is not surprising since in some religious schools, adherence to a given religious belief can be part of the requirements for obtaining a position. Indeed, the models where working at a religious school matter the most tend to deal either with religious (e.g., atheist, mainline) or sexual lifestyle (e.g., transgender, homosexuality) differences, which is what we would expect from those who teach in a traditional religious setting.

The regression models in table A in the appendix suggest that sex and working at a religious school are about as important as the differences in the disciplines when it comes to accounting for attitudes toward social groups. In fact, there are more models with significant effects for sex and/or working in a religious setting than models indicating possible effects according to discipline. This suggests that there is more evidence of a general academic culture effect than of a specific discipline effect in accounting for the emergence of these social biases. The basic findings are similar to the findings in chapter 3 and the examination of sociologists, although I did not replicate the findings concerning age. A series of cross-tabulation calculations in figure 5.2 will enable us to better understand these results.

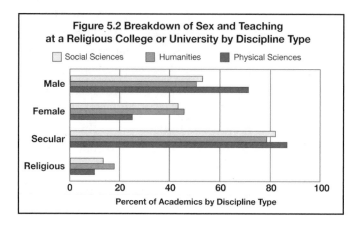

Figure 5.2 Breakdown of Sex and Teaching at a Religious College or University by Discipline Type

Because breaking these variables down into the individual disciplines creates some subcells with less than ten respondents, I will instead break this analysis down into type of discipline. Doing so does not change the basic result of the tables but does ensure that I have few, if any, subcells that are too small for meaningful analysis. The tables that indicate the results by the separate disciplines are given in supplemental table 5.3 in the supplemental material.

The results in figure 5.2 confirm our suspicion as it concerns male and female scholars. The percentage of males in the physical sciences is significantly higher than the percentage of males in either the social sciences or the humanities (73.1% versus 54.9%: $p < .001$; 73.1% versus 52.3%: $p < .001$). The results from supplemental table 5.1 in the supplemental material emerge in part because of the sex differences between the disciplines. However, there is less evidence that teaching at religious educational institutions helps to shape the disciplinary differences. Those from the physical sciences are slightly less likely to teach at a religious institution than other scholars (88.5% versus 80.4%: $p < .05$; 88.5% versus 83.8%: ns). However, because physical science scholars are less likely to teach at religious schools than other scholars, one would expect them to have more political and religious conservatism and not less.

It is plausible that while differences in teaching at a religious school may not explain the contrasts among the types of scientific inquiry, those differences may go a long way in explaining variations among disciplines within each of these distinct types of sciences. Likewise, we also have to account for the possibility that sex differences may have powerful effects within discipline types as well as across the different types of scientific disciplines. A comparison of male and female scholars for all non-sociology disciplines grouped by discipline type can be seen in figure 5.3.

Does the sex of the scholar matter within the discipline types? At times it does. For example, female scholars are significantly more supportive of transgendered candidates than male scholars across all three discipline types. They are less supportive of hunters and NRA members while being more supportive of cohabitators than male sociologists in all three disciplines as well, although the differences are not significant when it comes to those in the physical sciences. Furthermore, we see general trends of female scholars being more supportive of non-normative sexual practices than male scholars in all three discipline types, although the difference is not always significant. Generally speaking, sex predicts similar trends across the disciplines, although at times the prediction is not significant. There are a few effects that seem to be localized to discipline types, especially the physical sciences. Unlike females in the other two discipline types, female physical scientists actually show more acceptance of Republicans and less of Democrats than their male counterparts, although this difference is not significant. They show a much higher level of acceptance of evangelicals than do females in other disciplines. So while some overall trends can be explained by gender, some of the interdisciplinary differences may be shaped by the differences between female physical scientists and those in the social sciences and humanities.

The results in figure 5.3 show that sex does matter and must be taken into account as we attempt to understand these social biases. Females in all of the discipline types are generally more accepting of non-normative sexual practices and more hostile to conservative Christian groups. So even though female physical scientists

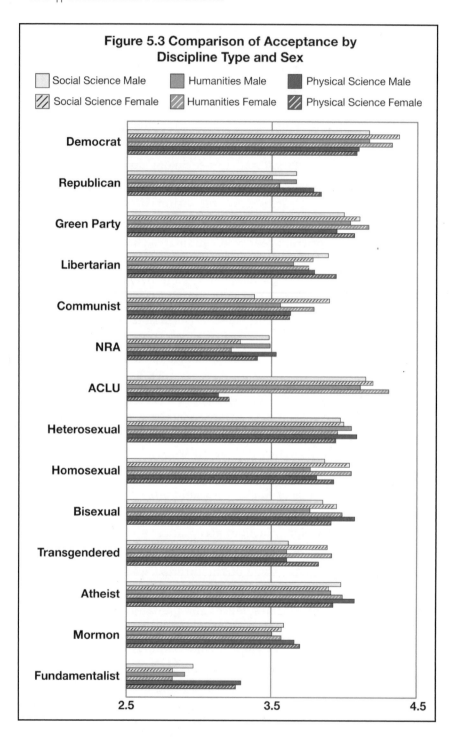

Figure 5.3 Comparison of Acceptance by Discipline Type and Sex

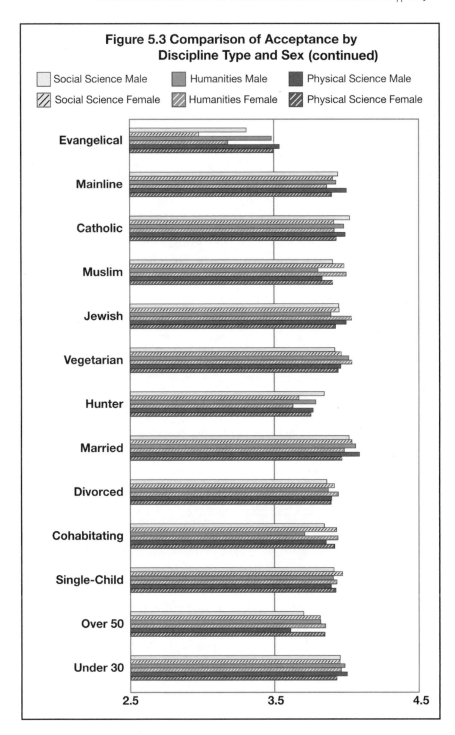

Figure 5.3 Comparison of Acceptance by Discipline Type and Sex (continued)

are less hostile to political conservatives than their counterparts in the social sciences and humanities, the fact that women make up less than a third of the physical scientists cannot be discounted as a reason why there is more powerful social bias in the social sciences and humanities relative to the physical sciences. My data do not allow me to learn why female scholars are generally more hostile to religious and political conservatives relative to male scholars. Of course there is work that documents the famous gender gap (Chaney, 1998; Edlund & Pande, 2002; Kaufmann & Petrocik, 1999; Studlar, McAllister, & Hayes, 1998) indicating that females in general are more likely to have progressive political attitudes than males. Earlier work of mine (Yancey, 1998) has illustrated that even within the politically progressive subculture of sociologists, females are more progressive than males. Female scholars may be more likely to possess political progressiveness, and those who are politically progressive may have a higher propensity to have positive social biases toward members of progressive social groups and negative biases toward members of conservative social groups.

Working at a religious campus was also found to be a significant predictor of the attitudes scholars have toward hiring new colleagues. Thus, it is also important to assess whether there may be effects due to whether certain academics work on religiously based campuses. The differences in the attitudes between the scholars who work at religious campuses and those who do not can be seen by discipline in figure 5.4.

In figure 5.4 it is clear that working on a religious campus is related to the types of social biases a scholar may have. This is most clearly seen when looking at issues of sexual lifestyle, religious preference, and family status. Across all three discipline types, scholars who work on religious campuses are less accepting of non-normative sexual lifestyles than other scholars. Only among physical scientists as it concerned the acceptance of heterosexuality was this trend not documented, and that result was insignificant compared to the results concerning homosexuals, bisexuals, and the transgendered. Acceptance of religious groups is a little more complex. Academics at religious campuses are less likely to accept atheists, but more likely to accept fundamentalists and evangelicals. Those in the social sciences and humanities also show a propensity to accept mainline Protestants, Catholics, and Jews, although the results are not always significant. Scholars in the social sciences and humanities at religious schools are also significantly more likely to reject divorced individuals and cohabitators than those at nonreligious schools. This effect is not found among those in the physical sciences. Thus there may be a localized effect of teaching at a religious school in that those teaching in the physical sciences are less likely to be affected by traditional norms, except when it concerns sexual lifestyle. However, generally there is a powerful effect of teaching at a religious school that is only somewhat moderated across disciplines.

As was the case when I explored gender, these data do not allow me to determine fully why scholars at religious schools have less powerful progressive biases than other scholars. I conceptualize them as less powerfully progressive, and not traditional, biases because these scholars still tend to favor progressive social groups over conservative social groups. For example, generally scholars on religious campuses are more favorably inclined to Democrats than to Republicans. Nevertheless, their level of progressive support is less than for those at secular campuses. There are two possible explanations for this. First, it may be the case that scholars who choose to work on religious campuses are less progressive than other scholars. Perhaps the academic biases I have discussed in this book have made secular campuses less comfortable for them. It is also possible that they choose, without any pressure, to be in an environment that matches their lower levels of progressiveness. They may have a religious faith that reduces their social and political progressiveness, and thus they are in a place that comports with their own political and religious beliefs.

However, there is an alternative possibility. Individuals at religious institutions may merely be adhering to the general rules on their campuses. On some of these campuses there may be rules about who may be hired in regard to religious beliefs and sexual lifestyle. The respondents may not have answered the questionnaire according to their own beliefs but according to their expectations about who they could actually hire on their campus. I have no way of knowing

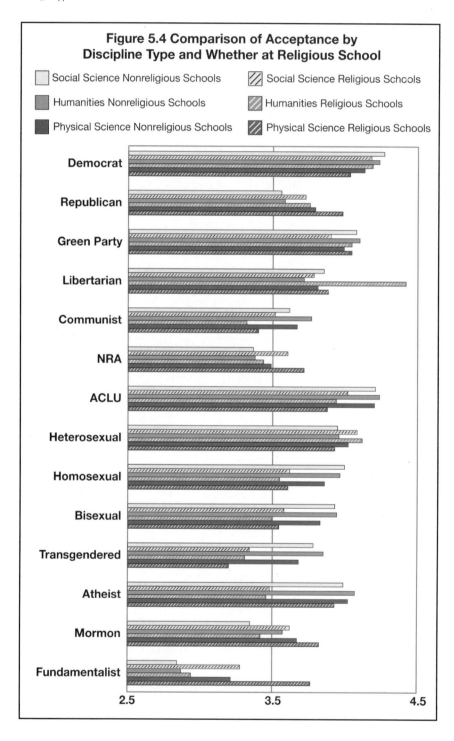

Figure 5.4 Comparison of Acceptance by
Discipline Type and Whether at Religious School

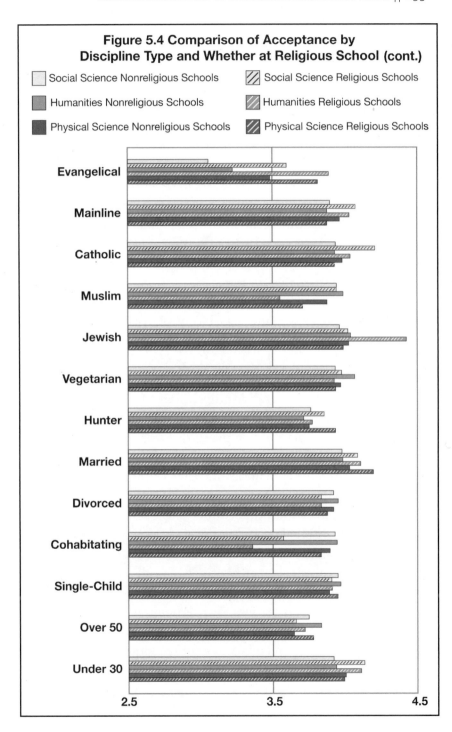

Figure 5.4 Comparison of Acceptance by Discipline Type and Whether at Religious School (cont.)

which of these explanations best explains the effect. However, clearly part of the source of the bias in academia is determined by the religious traditions of one's place of employment. To the degree that an institution is religiously oriented, the social biases documented in this work are likely less than they normally would be.

There is evidence that some of the differences among disciplines are due to demographic differences. Thus the fact that social scientists are more likely to be female than physical scientists can explain part of the tendency of social scientists to reject conservative social groups. This indicates that there is a general atmosphere in academia that has established the hierarchy of social groups that are seen as acceptable among scholars. Differences in the perception of these groups may arise due to demographic variations, but the ranking of acceptable groups remains the same.

Yet some effects of the different academic disciplines survive even after demographic and social controls have been applied. Disciplinary differences may not be as explanatory as sex and working at a religious college, but they still possess some explanatory power. Thus it is valuable to consider other reasons why different disciplines may have contrasting propensities to exhibit social bias. While I am not in a position to exhaust all possibilities, I do suggest that the role scholars play in the culture war offers one possible reason why there are disciplinary differences. It is plausible that the social sciences and the humanities are perceived as being more valuable than the physical sciences to promote ideas that further progressive aspirations within that culture war. These disciplines deal with arguments over values and norms and thus can more directly be utilized to challenge the presuppositions of social conservatives. Clearly the physical sciences can be utilized as well through a defense of evolution and the biological innateness of behaviors considered deviant to cultural conservatives, such as homosexuality. However, for progressives highly interested in issues surrounding the culture war, the social sciences and humanities offer more potential to gain an upper hand in their struggle.

If this speculation is accurate, then further insight may be gained about the academic culture that leads to these social biases. It is evident that there is a general social culture within academia that supports biases documented in this and previous chapters. However, it is also likely that this culture is fed by a desire to use science to promote the interests of progressives in the culture war. Scholars rarely would perceive this as the purpose for their work, and it may be that it is only when the work they produce operates against those progressive interests that it becomes clear how influential such interests are. I am not suggesting that there is some smoke-filled back room where academics are secretly planning their next move against religious and political conservatives. I am suggesting that over time, support of progressives in the culture war has become an unspoken request aimed at scholars. Social biases against religious and political conservatives who seek academic jobs can be an important way in which that request is fulfilled.

Is There Bias in Academia?

Before this chapter I had documented that social bias is a persistent feature among some sociologists. The information in this chapter indicates that sociologists are alone neither in their propensity to possess such a social bias nor in their propensity to use that bias in ways that harm disfavored groups. The degree to which such bias may be utilized differs among disciplines, but its existence can no longer be denied. I have also documented that this bias is stronger against religious conservatives than it is against political conservatives and that this tendency is true across the scientific disciplines. In chapter 4, I looked at the blogs of sociologists in an effort to speculate why religious conservatism is more objectionable to scholars than political conservatism. Whether those same dynamics accurately describe what occurs in other disciplines is unclear, but a future researcher might investigate such possibilities. The only definitive statement that can be made today is that while it is not good to be a political conservative in academia, in the eyes of many scholars it is even worse to be a religious conservative.

The implications of these findings are clear. If the respondents are being truthful in their assertions, then there are disciplines where there are tremendous barriers for the inclusion of those who are politically conservative, and these barriers are much higher for the religiously conservative. A conservative Protestant would do well to hide his or her religious beliefs if attempting to obtain a position in anthropology or English. The fact that several scholars deny that social bias is a problem in academia (Aby, 2007; Giroux, 2006; Krugman, 2005; Lazere, 2004; Lee, 2006) likely makes the situation of religious and political conservatives worse, as members on search committees possessing these biases are less likely to recognize this problem and may feel unrestrained to act upon those prejudices. In some disciplines, such as physics and chemistry, the effect of these biases appears to be a good deal less powerful. In fact, there is no evidence of any real bias against Republicans among physicists. Yet there is still enough bias that even in these relatively "tolerant" disciplines, religious conservatives face barriers to employment that nonreligious conservatives do not.

In chapter 3, I made the argument that there is no reason to assume that the biases documented in my question about the potential hiring of a colleague should be limited only to that decision in academia. I pointed out that decisions such as tenure, publishing, and how subjects are taught are also likely to be shaped by the social biases that academics may act upon. Likewise, the findings in this chapter should not automatically be relegated to only affecting potential hiring decisions. A religious fundamentalist who manages to get hired into an anthropology department may not indicate his or her religious beliefs at the time of the hiring. But after being in the department for a while, such an individual must either continue to hide those beliefs or face tenure in a department where perhaps about half of the individuals would have had serious reservations about hiring someone of his or her religious beliefs. One may also wonder about the sort of social climate created by English language teachers when two-thirds of them would penalize a religious conservative to some degree who sought a job in their department. Of course, anthropology and English are the two disciplines where the findings of potential bias were the most powerful. In all disciplines examined in this research, these same issues can be raised, but the degree of the resistance faced by religious and political conservatives in other disciplines may be less than the resistance faced by those who are anthropologists or English language scholars.

One may argue that I have happened to select the very disciplines that exhibit social bias in academia and have left out those that are relatively free of social bias. My decisions on the disciplines to include were based on availability of useable directories. There was no attempt on my part to seek out disciplines that have a reputation for social bias in order to gain a controversial result. Furthermore, the diversity in the different types of academic disciplines in this project makes it unlikely that these findings are anomalies within the larger academic institution. It is much more likely that scholarly disciplines where there is little, if any, social bias against religious and political conservatives are the exception rather than the rule. Nevertheless, there would be value in evaluating other academic disciplines, particularly in types of "applied" disciplines not represented here such as business, education, and engineering, and in the fine arts such as music or drama. Exploring these fields may not tell us as much about science and research, but it would provide insight into the type of overall atmosphere that is prevalent on college campuses.

The reality is that we do have a problem with social bias in academia. It is warranted to argue about the extent to which this bias exists, but this research provides evidence of its existence. To ignore this evidence is to put one's head in the sand and pretend that the problem does not exist.[8] We can no longer hide behind the argument that social bias is merely the unfounded charge of conservative religious and political opportunists. With this research, there is now empirical evidence documenting this bias.

Perhaps some individuals do not see the presence of these social biases as a problem. However, they should make such assertions with full knowledge that bias against certain social groups is present in academia and that such assertions help such bias continue to exist. For those of us who desire to address this problem, it is important to consider why social bias in academia is a serious problem. After considering the ways in which these biases impact our ability to conduct scientific inquiry, we will then be in a position to consider possible remedies to the problem of social bias in academia.

CHAPTER SIX

Social Bias and the Nature of Scientific Inquiry

Academics, like members of other occupational subcultures, have social biases that can shape their outlook and the work they do. This merely makes them human. What is important is what we do with our social biases. It is theoretically possible to have social biases and not allow them to shape our social actions, but most individuals are not able to accomplish that task. As this research suggests, scholars also have problems limiting themselves from operating out of their social biases.

I have examined the question of whom current scholars are willing to allow into academic research. I have used this question to investigate the presence of social biases among scholars. However, there are clearly other ways in which these social biases play themselves out. For example, there is research indicating that some academics are negatively biased against conservative Christians as it concerns how they are portrayed in textbooks (Hodge, Baughman, & Cummings, 2006), their entrance into graduate programs (Gartner, 1986), and how they are evaluated (Gartner, Harmatz, Hohmann, Larson, & Gartner, 1990; Neumann, Thompson, & Woolley, 1992). Furthermore, it is also possible that these social biases operate to reduce the ability of members of disfavored groups to obtain tenure, to gain academic publications, and to be promoted. Exploring how these biases may continue to operate in academia will help to inform us about the nature of scientific inquiry.

Some may be tempted to dismiss the presence of social bias in academia and to minimize the degree to which such a bias is perceived as a problem. But first we should ask what these social biases mean to the nature of academic study. There needs to be an exploration of the implications of these social biases on how scholarly data are collected. Perhaps there are vital issues not being addressed because of the way these social biases operate in academia. The purpose of this chapter is to explore these types of questions and to see how the nature of academia is altered through the social biases documented in this work. First I will address some of the possible criticisms that are likely to be leveled at the results of this work, and then I will more fully explore the possible implications of these findings.

Criticisms to the Idea of Scientific Bias

No research is beyond criticism. In all academic endeavors there are limits to our ability to conduct truly experimental research in our attempts to understand our social world. For example, a truly experimental design would have candidates with identical qualifications, except for their memberships in the relevant social groups, apply to the same colleges and universities to see who would receive a posted position. If the college or university was seeking a candidate for an actual position, we would have an opportunity to observe whether an individual's opportunity to obtain a given academic position is powerfully shaped by the potential social biases scholars have toward members of those groups. However, if it was an actual position, then it would be highly unethical to waste the precious time of a search committee so that we could run this experiment. Furthermore, exactly identical résumés, except for group membership, are likely to raise the suspicion of search committee members, who would possibly disqualify both of our candidates for suspicion of fraud. But if the résumés differed in any other way, then we would not know if the effects documented were due to those contrasts or to social group membership. Thus this hypothetical experimental research design is practically impossible.

Exploring this research design does bring to light one of the possible criticisms of this current research effort. I am asking what someone is seeking in a potential academic colleague. What they state they would do with this hypothetical position and what they actually do when they seek out a person for a real position may be different. Thus, how can I be sure that the results from this work truly reflect a potential bias that affects the occupational opportunities of favored and disfavored social groups? I contend that this work indicates the lower boundaries of social bias. The way individuals express their bias is likely more subtle than would be indicated on a survey. Many individuals who operate out of these biases may not even acknowledge that their social biases affect their decisions. Individuals who would use such criticism to dismiss these results have to answer an important question. Why would a person acknowledge that he or she would be less inclined to want to see a fundamentalist or NRA member hired on a survey and then not allow that social bias to have an impact in the actual situation? Is not the reverse situation, where a person does have bias against such a person but does not indicate it on a survey, more likely to take place? It is quite plausible that many scholars may find reasons that do not have to do with their religious or political status to eliminate individuals from disfavored groups, but subconsciously it may be religious or political membership that they are reacting against.[1] If this is the case, then an individual from a stigmatized social group would have to be a clearly superior candidate to convince individuals with unconscious hesitations that he or she should be hired.

Some might also dismiss the results of this work by stating that membership in the social groups placed in the survey actually does have an effect on the ability of individuals to conduct scientific inquiry. For example, some might argue that those who hold to a fundamentalist religious perspective are likely to rely heavily on a supernaturalist perspective about natural and social events. Such a perspective does not allow for them to accept the use of scientific methods that dismiss the importance of otherworldly perspectives. Yet I would argue that religious belief, in and of itself, does not disqualify an individual from engaging in scientific inquiry. Individuals have a tremendous capacity to compartmentalize their religious beliefs from their understanding of science or even to find creative ways to merge the two. For example, one might argue that Christian fundamentalists are unable to conduct research in biology since they are unable to accept evolution. Yet some Christians have developed the concept of theistic evolution, which argues that evolution did indeed occur but that it was directed by God. Whether otherworldly direction exists is a question outside the realm of science, and so adherence to supernatural beliefs can occur within an individual who still uses evolution as the major operating theory for his or her biological inquiry.[2] This example illustrates that religion and science tend to deal with different questions.[3] Science can investigate the processes that have created humans, but why humans were created, and if there is a purpose behind such a creation, is beyond the scope of science. Dealing with these types of issues is why religious and philosophical systems have developed. Those who argue that individuals with certain religious beliefs are disqualified from engaging in scientific inquiry are attempting to force academics to deal with questions outside of their scientific expertise.

I suspect that the resistance to the hiring of individuals from certain social groups is either due to animosity directed at them or to unfounded stereotypes perceived about them. I documented evidence of such stereotypes in chapter 4. These stereotypes, rather than actual incompetency from the members of the disfavored groups, form the basis for the belief that individuals with certain religious beliefs are unable to conduct scientific work. Furthermore, the idea that scientists are making an accurate assessment of the ability of individuals from certain social groups to conduct scientific work is damaged further when we consider that members of the NRA generally scored almost as low as evangelicals. There is no logical connection between belief in gun rights and the ability to conduct academic inquiry. As such, the only reason why members of the NRA would score so low is that scholars prefer not to be around individuals who support an extreme level of gun ownership.[4] Yet such preferences are not a logical basis for exclusion of members of the NRA from conducting scientific research.

Another potential critique is that I am overhyping these results. For example, it is true that nearly 50 percent of the sociologists who filled out the questionnaire indicated that a person being a fundamentalist made the sociologist less likely to want them as a colleague. However, half of those who made such a statement indicated that it would only slightly influence them. How such scholars define "slightly" is the key. These scholars might indicate that it provides them with a brief momentary concern which they quickly dismiss before going on to make a valid evaluation of the candidate's qualifications. In reality, it may be the case that we should be concerned with the 7.8 percent who stated that it would extremely damage their ability to hire such an individual, for clearly these sociologists are unlikely to provide a fair evaluation of such a candidate. But that reduces the odds of a person being hostile to fundamentalists to less than one in twelve and may not be a big concern even when the bias is at its worst.

I accept the premise that it is impossible to assess the degree of bias measured by these data, especially given the low response rates. We can assess whether members of certain social groups (e.g., Republicans, fundamentalists) face more social rejection than members of other social groups (e.g., Democrats, Jews), but we do not know how much more social rejection they face. But let us assume that those who stated that they were slightly less likely to support a candidate did not exhibit a great deal of bias. Does this truly lessen the importance of these findings? Let us imagine that instead of a fundamentalist, we are looking at a Jewish candidate. Would we be concerned if "only" a quarter of academics were slightly less likely to support that candidate because he or she is a Jew? What sort of justifiable uproar would develop from such a finding? This illustration clarifies what is at stake. Even such slight resistance would mean that anti-Semitism would influence whether or not an individual would obtain a position. That clearly is unacceptable. Should it not also be unacceptable that a person's Christian beliefs influence his or her ability to obtain an academic position, if the job is at a non-religious campus?

This assessment does not even take into account the one in twelve sociologists who openly stated that membership in the fundamentalist social group would extremely damage their ability to support a candidate. If this is true, then even this is not an inconsequential number. However, I suspect that it is probably a baseline estimate of the number of scholars who would have such reservations, since to make such a strong statement is difficult because of the desire not to be perceived as biased. Highly educated individuals desire to perceive themselves as tolerant, and it is quite likely that a number of these scholars are very hesitant to support a fundamentalist but shy away from the word *extremely* so that they can maintain a self-image of tolerance. Furthermore, I have been on enough search committees to know that the switch of support of one or two individuals is often enough to decide who gets a position. What this means is that between two evenly qualified candidates, one who is a fundamentalist is disadvantaged and less likely to gain the position.[5] For the fundamentalist candidate to gain the position, he or she has to be a superior candidate.

Of course, this is the worst-case scenario since we are looking at the group most likely to be rejected. This type of rejection is less likely to occur to Republicans and evangelicals, who are also disfavored groups. But the difference is only in degree, not in kind. Members of other disfavored groups must also prove themselves to be superior candidates to obtain an academic position. Furthermore, while the bias in sociology is stronger than the bias in some disciplines (e.g., biology, chemistry) it is less powerful than in others (e.g., philosophy, anthropology). Breakdowns of the actual percentages of scientists in the different disciplines by levels of enhancement or damage of their support of certain social groups can be found in supplemental table 5.1.

As such, these findings only serve to illustrate the larger problem of bias, and in certain disciplines this problem clearly is much worse than suggested by this analysis of sociologists.

There is a common criticism linked to work that has examined the religious and political construction of academia. Some have argued that the progressive nature of academia is due to the fact that conservatives are relatively unlikely to choose scientific inquiry as a profession (Ames et al., 2005; Lee, 2006). Self-selection likely does play a role in determining the religious and political makeup of individuals in academia. However, this work suggests that bias and discrimination play a role in establishing who gets to be a scholar as well. How much of a role social bias plays relative to self-selection cannot be determined by this current research, but it undoubtedly eliminates some religious and political conservatives. Future work can, and should, examine how much self-selection affects the religious and political composition of academia, but it is erroneous to assert that self-selection is the only factor that determines this composition.

There may be some who state that the results of this study are rigged. After all, I shoved a survey in the face of scholars and asked them what they thought about working with certain social groups. The mere act of asking them this question may have provided an implicit suggestion that it was all right to state that members of some groups are better to work with than others. The scholars might have only been acting on that presupposition and thus might have had no real social bias whatsoever. I argue that these well-educated men and women are not likely to have been so easily led. I intentionally provided them with the option that membership in these groups made no difference at all. In fact, 32.3 percent of sociologists, 25.0 percent of the other social scientists, 25.2 percent of those studying the humanities, and 31.3 percent of the physical scientists indicated that none of the social groups would influence their evaluation of a candidate. These individuals clearly had the option to indicate that they had no social bias, but most of them chose not to do so.[6]

Finally, some may criticize these findings because the results suggest that fundamentalists and Republicans are oppressed individuals. Yet such critics would rightly point out that membership in these groups is not generally linked to social disadvantage. Republicans are one of the two major political parties in the United States and thus cannot be considered a marginalized group. Social researchers have noted the power of religious fundamentalists in this party (Bednar & Hertzke, 1995; Knuckey, 1999; Oldfield, 1996) and would dispute any notion that these individuals are disadvantaged within American society. I agree with these general arguments. However, we are not discussing

the larger society, but an important subgroup in that society—
individuals in academia. It is within that subgroup that these individuals are marginalized and suffer effects of an unfair social bias. It is not
unique to acknowledge that a group with majority status in the larger
society can have minority status within a given subgroup. Christerson,
Edwards, and Emerson (2005) discuss a multiracial church where the
numerical dominant group is Filipinos. In that church whites, who
are clearly the majority group outside of the church, generally have
minority group status. Likewise fundamentalists, evangelicals, NRA
members, and Republicans can have a majority status outside of academia but can still be minority groups, as it concerns status and power,
within academia.

I would caution those who quickly dismiss the possibility that
religious and political conservatives suffer from social bias in academia to be careful with their assertions since often those who
make such arguments are not religious and political conservatives.
As such, it is easy for them to overlook the bias others must deal
with. As an African American, I have often been told by European
Americans that racism is not a big deal in the United States any-
more. It is easy for majority group members to make such assertions since they do not have to deal with the effects of that racism.
Furthermore, since we tend to have social networks that contain
individuals of our own race (Fetto, 2000; Joyner & Kao, 2000;
Korgen, 2002), it is likely that whites who make such assertions do
not have many friends of color sharing their experiences of racism
with them. Thus it is natural that these majority group members
easily dismiss the level of racism still in the United States even
though such an attitude can be quite insulting to people of color.
Likewise, religious and political progressives may easily dismiss the
concerns of religious and political conservatives in academia since
they have not directly suffered from the effects of that bias. Such
a dismissal may be particularly likely of those progressives who do
not have many religiously or politically conservative friends. This
does not mean that the bias is not real, but rather that those who
do not have to deal with intolerance among academics are the ones
who most quickly dismiss its poisonous effects.

Some criticisms of this work will doubtless come from scholars who honestly seek to point out its potential shortcomings. I welcome dialog with them. But because these results are critical of the very academics who might criticize them, we would be naïve not to appreciate also the socio-psychological motivations of many who might attack these results. Some of them may undoubtedly possess the biases documented in this work. This research has implications, which I will soon discuss, about the legitimacy of some scientific work and about who is allowed to have power in academia. Individuals who benefit from the status quo in academia are not likely to be willing to set into motion changes that threaten the status and position they possess in academia. For this reason, it is wise to be suspicious of criticisms that may have a motivation other than the advancement of scientific knowledge.

Exploring the effects of academic bias is vital if we are going to understand comprehensively its implications to scientific inquiry. While I am not certain as to how powerful these social biases are, this research strongly suggests that, even with the concerns raised above, they do exist. Dealing with these biases is not only important for individuals from disfavored groups, but also for those of us who want to see scientific inquiry reach its full potential. For this reason, I will now more fully explore the implications of social bias among scholars.

The Effects of Social Bias in Academia

This work has indicated that scholars do not leave their social biases at home when they enter the research field. In chapter 3, I pointed out that it is likely that the biases exhibited toward potential job applicants likely show up in a variety of other ways. For example, I argued that such biases also likely influence decisions concerning tenure, publication of articles, and research topics. The search for scientific reality is easily corrupted by biases that promulgate certain social and political perspectives. Such influences are clearer as it concerns the social sciences and humanities, yet it is also likely that such biases influence the physical sciences; indeed, much of the original science/religion debate developed within the physical science fields.

Even if the only significant effect of social bias is the limitation of religious and political conservatives from initial participation in academic research, that limitation alone is powerful enough to damage greatly the ability of academia to pursue scientific knowledge. Such limitations reduce the number of religious and political conservatives who conduct scientific research and naturally create a social environment where there is a taken-for-granted reality based upon progressive political and religious ideas. The removal of consideration of conservative religious and political ideals reduces resistance to the advancement of progressive social thought. It has been argued that in environments where progressive social thought is not challenged, there is a tendency for extreme progressive ideas to become dominant since there is little to prevent individuals with progressive ideas from taking those ideas to an exaggerated degree (Nieli, 2005). In chapter 4, we saw evidence of this tendency with sociologists feeling a freedom in their blogs to denigrate religious and political conservatives in ways that would not be acceptable if they were writing about religious and political progressives. Thus, expressions of ideas that do not fit into a progressive framework are subject to sanctions because of the predominance of religious and political progressives in academia.[7]

The scholars who have these biases are not bad individuals, but the effects of these biases have potentially devastating consequences on the power of scientific inquiry and on those who are in disfavored social groups. Niebuhr's (1949) classic work contends that moral and selfless individuals often develop ideologies within groups that disregard the concerns of those outside of their group. He argues that groups need to develop an ideology powerful enough to maintain the group's cohesion. This ideology often inspires members of a group to act in selfless ways to aid others in the group. Loyalty to the group is prized and can lead to benevolent actions in behalf of in-group members. Yet this same propensity to find in-group motivation that allows individuals to provide for others within their groups also limits the desires of in-group members to become concerned about the struggles of those outside their group. In-group loyalty leading to selfless actions in behalf of members in the in-group also produces a group selfishness that neglects the interests of members not in one's group.

A group often can clearly see the effects of prejudice and dis-crimination against its own members. This leads to struggles to overcome the biases directed toward them. But groups generally develop new standards that are often just as exclusionary as previ-ous standards. Coercion is often used to maintain these standards, and group members are socialized to put the interests of their group over the interests of all others. Because members of the in-group often do not know many members of out-groups, they become less sympathetic to those out-group members and thus it is easy to allow this coercion to foster an uncaring attitude toward those out-groups. This attitude becomes a natural extension of the in-group loyalty that has developed and is not based on the morality of a given per-son. Thus, even good, moral people put the interests of their family, community, and nation above the interests of those outside their family, community, and nation.

Ironically, one of the examples that Niebuhr provides is that social scientists often complain about the particularistic nature of other groups while they forget about their own middle-class preju-dices. While he addresses issues of class, the literature on the culture war suggests that today's scholars may use adherence to progressive cultures as the basis for developing their in-group concerns. Members of social groups connected with a progressive ideology are accorded little or no hostility from academics. However, there is little sympa-thy given to individuals who are identified as being part of conser-vative traditional culture. Their voices are not important to those in academia, so scholars have little, if any, inhibition against dis-criminating against them. It would be unthinkable for most scholars to discriminate against a potential Jewish scholar based on his or her religion, but it may be acceptable to endorse such discrimination against a potential fundamentalist scholar. Caring and compassion-ate academics may have few friends from these traditional groups and thus have little understanding about the concerns traditional individuals have. This creates a science where certain religious and political perspectives are not allowed to influence the conclusions that scientists develop, while other religious and political perspec-tives must be taken into account.

The potential effects of these social biases are sobering and should prompt us to consider whether or not we can utilize scientific inquiry to gain an accurate perception of social and natural reality. Scientific knowledge that promotes the interests of favored social groups, such as the ACLU and the Democratic Party, may be encouraged as the needs and interests of members of these groups gain special favor among scholars. On the other hand, academics may possess little interest in addressing the interests or concerns of disfavored groups. The members of those groups are unlikely to find scholars sympathetic to issues that trouble them. This bias is intensified as scholars surround themselves with individuals who have similar levels of progressive social ideas. With few religious or political conservatives in their social network, there is little feedback that scholars may receive to check their urges to ignore the concerns of these groups.[8] This tendency can shape scientific inquiry in a way so that the interests of religious and political progressives are promoted at the expense of political and religious conservatives.

It is reasonable to question whether this has not always been the case. I documented in chapter 2 that since the inception of science, academics generally have been more politically progressive and less religious than the rest of the population. It can be asserted that we have survived just fine with the way scientific inquiry has been conducted. The answer to this assertion is twofold. First, it is not completely clear whether we have done as well as we could have with scientific inquiry over the years. Because of the embedded biases within the scientific fields, it is quite likely that intolerance has damaged our ability to accumulate scientific knowledge for some time now, but that we have not yet recognized its effects. To be sure, there have been those who have criticized the religious and political biases of the sciences (Coulter, 2004; D'Souza, 1991; Horowitz, 2006; Sykes, 1990), but those individuals have tended not to be scholars themselves but activists connected to the disfavored social groups. As one might imagine, their critiques have been met with a quite skeptical response and have been easily dismissed by most academics. However, the results of this research leave little doubt that such critics have some basis for their concerns.

Second, we have to consider the social and cultural context we currently have. Even if scientific inquiry has not been unduly influenced by social intolerance in the past, the emergence of the culture war has multiplied the potential rewards that scholars may gain by acting on their biases. Hunter (1991) points out that we have had culture wars in the past, but usually they were based on conflict between different religious perspectives. The current war between those who find religion to be extremely important and those who want to minimize the potential effects of religion naturally raises issues of scientific inquiry. For some scholars, doing science has purposes that go beyond learning about our social and natural world. It also is a valuable way to reduce the social power of the traditionalists in a culture war (Hunter, 1994; Howard, 2003; Lincoln and Cannella, 2004; Sharfstein, 2006). Academics who conduct research that achieves this goal are likely to receive at least informal positive reinforcement from their peers. Any who produce work that retards a progressive cultural agenda may face informal negative sanctions, and if they are early in their academic careers, they may face official negative costs that inhibit their ability to go much further in their academic pursuits.

What Is Diversity in Academia?

Those who deal with issues of diversity tend to conceptualize those issues in terms of race, gender, and sexuality. There is still evidence of racial (Astin, Antonio, Cress, & Astin, 1997; Beutel & Nelson, 2006; Turner & Myers, 2000) and gender (Beutel & Nelson, 2006; Xu, 2008) underrepresentation in some academic disciplines. Scholars have argued that this underrepresentation has led to the perspectives of women and people of color being less likely to be taken into account (Patton, 2004; Smith, Altbach, & Lomotey, 2002; Statham, Richardson, & Cook, 1991). This has facilitated a desire to find measures that increase the number of individuals from these disadvantaged populations in academia (Clayton-Pedersen, Parker, Smith, Morena, & Teraguchi, 2007; Finke, 2005; Hurtado, Milem, Clayton-Pedersen, & Allen, 1998; Mayhew, Grunwald, & Dey, 2005). I support such efforts since having diverse ideas is better than limiting ourselves to a few selected perspectives. But previous work has clearly documented that religious and political conservatives are also underrepresented in academia (Ecklund et al., 2008; Klein & Western, 2004–2005; Larson & Witham, 1998; Zipp & Fenwick, 2006). This underrepresentation may have more pronounced effects than the underrepresentation of gender and race. Efforts to increase the number of women and individuals of color in academia suggest that women and race minority group members are desired in academia. Yet we clearly see that religious and political conservatives are unwanted by a significant number of academics.

As a result of the undesirability of religious and political conservatives in academia relative to women and individuals of color, there are important differences between the underrepresentation of the former groups and the underrepresentation of the latter. While there are efforts in the social sciences and humanities to include the perspectives of women and individuals of color, there are few such efforts to include the perspectives of religious and political conservatives. At times some white scholars attempt to support the interests of people of color (Feagin, 2006; McIntosh, 2002), and some male scholars attempt to support the interests of women (Johnson, 1997; Kimmel & Mosmiller, 1992). But the underrepresentation of religious and political conservatives may be even more powerful in its potential impact since few irreligious or political non-conservative scholars likely support the interests of religious and political conservatives. Religious and political conservatives are marginalized groups with few academic allies.[9] Academics likely have more freedom to create a hostile social atmosphere for religious and political conservatives than for women and people of color. My search of the sociologists' blogs found no instances of overtly derogatory statements being made about women and people of color, but I documented several such statements about religious and political conservatives. Unlike women and people of color, religious and political conservatives may have to work with those who freely engage in prejudice against them.

If science is an endeavor into which we desire to bring those with diverse perspectives, then clearly religious and political conservatives can provide ideological diversity. Scholars would do well to consider how to produce an atmosphere more conducive to attracting individuals from conservative religious and political groups, even if they disagree with those individuals' religious and political beliefs. Academics should not be hired solely for their different religious and political perspectives, as they need to demonstrate that they are engaging in solid academic research and are effective teachers. But their diverse perspectives are of great potential value to the scientific community. We will enhance our ability to conduct sound scholarly work if we recognize the problems created by these social biases so that we can be motivated to lessen the power they have over academics.

The Hidden Costs of Social Biases and Intolerance

The real power of social biases comes from their hidden nature. The results of this work do not indicate that academia is made up of immoral individuals. Rather, many of these individuals highly value tolerance and honestly attempt to live it out. However, the context of academic work generates negative social biases against religious and political conservatives or supports the negative biases that already exist. Scholars who operate in that context may be unable to appreciate these biases because such biases are so universally accepted in academic culture.

An example from my personal experience may suffice to illustrate this point. When I was an adjunct professor, I requested a semester in which I could teach sociology of religion. Much to my delight, I was allowed to teach that class. In the middle of the semester, I heard through a friend that some individuals questioned whether I should have been allowed to teach it. I had been quite open about my Christian beliefs, and some professors worried that I would not be unbiased in my teaching. I had to wonder whether such individuals would have had such doubts if I was an atheist. After all, everyone has beliefs about religion regardless if that person is a Christian or an atheist, so the challenge of presenting the material in an objective and fair manner should apply to all. It is possible that these professors were concerned because of what they heard from students or because I have a teaching style that lends itself to presenting material in a biased manner. Yet I doubt that was the case. In that same semester, I also taught sociology of race and ethnicity. But no one questioned whether I should have been able to teach that class because I am black. It was only in regard to my faith, and not to my race, where professors showed a concern about my bias.

The scholars believed that a Christian would struggle to stay objective in teaching about religion, but not that a black would struggle to stay objective in teaching about race and ethnicity. I have no way of getting into the thought processes of my colleagues, but it is likely that unseen perspectives and biases these scholars have toward religious conservatives inform these beliefs. The scholars did not stop me from teaching sociology of religion, but as you may imagine, I felt more pressure from them as I taught that class than as I taught my race and ethnicity course. The unspoken biases that emerged from that situation shaped the academic environment in which I taught. I speculate that every day, many other academic situations are shaped by unspoken biases that scholars do not even realize they have. The prejudices and intolerances documented in this work are often unrealized, which can make them even more potent in interfering with scientific inquiry.

The Purpose of Science

Scientific inquiry is important for allowing us to understand our social and physical worlds. It provides a way we can systematically gather knowledge that relies upon rationality and logic. The ideal of science is a rational and objective assessment of reality. We may not always be able to overcome our barriers to rationality, but the pursuit of using logic to acquire knowledge is the underlying value of science. Accordingly, many scholars use some form of the scientific method, which allows them to create predictions about our world and tests to see if these predictions are accurate.

When science is done correctly, we are in a position to assess our social and physical worlds. Science builds up a body of knowledge so that we can, with some degree of confidence, accurately evaluate social and physical reality. It is not the case that science is the only way to accumulate knowledge. There are some questions that are not well suited for scientific exploration. Questions of ultimate meaning are better handled by the various religious and philosophical systems that have arisen to deal with them. We also use previous experiences to answer questions about ourselves not well suited for scientific inquiry. Science generally requires that we have testable predictions, and when we have questions that do not lend themselves to such testing, science is not always the best mechanism to be used. But there is much we can learn about our world through the process of scientific testing and the application of rationality.

The fruits of scientific inquiry constantly pay dividends in our society. Who can doubt the use of science in the construction of many of the inventions that make our lives easier? Engineers constantly apply scientific knowledge in their endeavors to create innovative mechanisms that solve important problems. The social sciences and humanities provide for us ways in which we can understand our social tendencies. Principles that emerge from this work, such as groupthink theory or the power of ethnocentrism, enable us to organize our society better and to create a culture that is better positioned to serve the highest number of individuals possible. Additionally, there is theoretical science, which is important for helping us to understand larger social and physical processes. While theoretical scientific endeavors do not always directly lead to the development of practical societal solutions, they often shape the ideas in a discipline and thus contribute overarching themes about social and physical reality.

When we have confidence in the scientific knowledge that has been accumulated, we have confidence that valuable efforts have been made to improve our society. Individuals may understand that scientific knowledge is not appropriate for dealing with every important question, but it is valuable in helping us understand the physical and social environments in which we dwell. Modern societies have sought to support scientific pursuits because of the social and physical benefits that science offers us. In fact, it is reasonable to argue that part of the reason that societies have modernized is that we have learned to rely upon rational and logical acquisition of knowledge and in doing so have been able to technologically and socially develop our societies more completely.

A Desire for Better Science

These biases and their effects in academia should trouble any of us who care about the accumulation of scientific knowledge. The boundaries of scientific knowledge are shaped by the topics open for exploration. The early development of science met with resistance from traditional religious forces that limited what was acceptable for individuals to study. Galileo's failure to abide by such restrictions led to his excommunication. Scientists of that era rightly perceived such actions as the suppression of scientific knowledge and fought against those who sought to impose these restrictions. Any attempt based upon nonrational motivations to suppress potential scientific theory must be fought against. Only by struggling against these efforts at suppression can we develop academic research that is free to investigate all possible avenues of scientific inquiry.

But today scientific suppression does not originate from traditional religious or political forces that reside outside of academia. To be sure, there are conservative social efforts that seek to limit the scope of scientific inquiry (Giroux, 2006; Kimura-Walsh, 2008; Lazere, 2004; Lechuga, 2005), and these attempts can at times influence the funding of science. The most notable example of this is unwillingness, until recently, of the federal government to fund embryonic stem cell research. Yet the culture war has given scientists cover, and while some funding may be affected by political and religious conservatives, the actual choice of what scientists study is largely unaffected by conservatives. If these conservatives had power to alter scientists' choice of research topics, then one would expect that work in areas such as biological evolution and queer theory would not have developed to the extent it has today. These conservatives can influence some scientific work at the margins, but they are not able to influence the fundamental direction of science.

Today the more potent barriers to free inquiry come from within science itself. They come from the progressive social biases of the scholars. This research indicates that political and religious conservatives have a likelihood of being rejected, and thus it follows that their potential scientific perspectives may be rejected as well. This type of suppression is difficult to deal with because it is not as clearly documented as fights over funding, and the hidden characteristics of this suppression make it all the more powerful. Everyday decisions on hiring, tenure, and selection of articles in academic journals undoubtedly help to influence the direction of scientific work. Individuals are likely to be socialized to reinforce the social biases documented in this work. Those who violate these biases quickly face formal or informal sanctions. I have documented one possible sanction in that violators of these biases find it harder to obtain an academic position. Such sanctions help to keep academics who disagree with the political and religious progressiveness in the discipline from expressing their disagreement. In this way, ideas tied to conservative religious and political perspectives are suppressed in subtle ways that are not as public as fights over embryonic stem cell research but are more potent in limiting scientific inquiry than those funding wars.

Several authors have complained about the interference of religious and political conservatives in scientific inquiry (Bergman, 2001; Dawkins, 2006; Giroux, 2006; Kimura-Walsh, 2008; Lazere, 2004; Lechuga, 2005; White, 2004). These individuals argue that scientists should be free to engage in whatever inquiry their imaginations suggest to them. Yet these arguments fail to acknowledge that internal social pressures have more potency for limiting the imaginations of contemporary scientists than interference of religious and political conservatives. If these individuals are correct in their arguments that stifling the freedom of scientists to engage in the work they desire to do is a threat to science, and I believe their basic argument is correct, then the effects of these social biases are a threat to the basic nature of what science is. Science should be the open search for knowledge. Ideas should be tested by rational examination. Those ideas should be accepted or rejected based upon this examination. Social biases that interrupt this examination force the rejection of ideas before they have been fully vetted. They are rejected not because they are scientifically unsound but because of the social biases of academics.

Scholars play an important, but generally unrecognized, role in the culture war. If progressive scholars are to play such a role, they must neutralize dissenting opinions even as they argue that conservative forces are the major threat against free inquiry. Informal bias against those opinions can be an effective way to deal with them. Science is still being used to accumulate knowledge. However, I speculate that another purpose in scientific inquiry is the promotion of progressives in the culture war. Such a promotion can often lead scholars to engage in actions that are decidedly "unscientific." Perhaps a valuable example of this can be seen in the fate of Lawrence Summers when he was president of Harvard University.

What the Fate of Lawrence Summers Tells Us about Science

I have talked about the possibility that research that originates from the ideologies of religious and political conservatives may be discouraged by the social biases documented in this work. Yet I have not provided an example of possible research questions that have been suppressed by these biases. One could argue that while there may be biases against certain individuals going into academia, once individuals are in academia all legitimate scientific questions are freely pursued. Yet anecdotal evidence indicates that the biases documented in the early chapters also influence choices of scientific topics. Perhaps one of the best examples of how these biases inhibit the ability of scientists to search out alternative theories and the effect they have on the general public can be seen in the case of Lawrence Summers. Although he is neither a religious nor a political conservative, he introduced ideas that violated some of the principles held by social progressives. I have chosen this case not only because it illustrates the dynamics that this work addresses, but also because it became a well-known case for those who are critical of science. It became the poster child for those who wanted to illustrate that science is not an objective search for an understanding of reality, but rather that it is merely an instrument by which individuals from certain subcultures are able to push their own political agendas.

Summers, an economist, was president of Harvard University in 2005 when he was asked to address an academic conference dealing with diversifying the sciences and engineering professions. He suggested that a possible factor in the lack of females in these professions may be linked to potential biological distinctions between men and women. In his speech, he argued that small variations in innate ability between the sexes can potentially lead to huge differences when one tries to understand the sex composition of elite scientists. He acknowledged that discrimination plays a role and should not be ignored. However, he argued that it would be a mistake to automatically link all of the differences to discrimination. He contended that there should be solid research that attempts to investigate the viability of biological sources of sex differences. He ended his speech with several possible scientific projects that could begin to address this research question.

The reaction to Summers' speech was decisive. His comments were labeled sexist. He received a vote of no confidence from the Harvard Faculty of Arts and Sciences. Pressures to resign were placed upon him for this, and other, issues that the faculty was dissatisfied about. Consequently, in 2006 Summers resigned from his post as president. While this was not the only issue that created controversy for Summers, the reaction of members in academia was noteworthy. The research questions that he attempted to bring up were roundly dismissed. He was accused of ignoring gender discrimination in an attempt to justify the current patriarchal status quo. It was not that scientific evidence was brought to bear illustrating that Summers' ideas were incorrect. Rather, these critics did not believe that the question of possible biological differences accounting for some of the sex differences in the sciences was even a topic worthy of discussion. Scientific questions were not dismissed because of a lack of scientific evidence, significance, or relevance, but merely because those questions violated the social biases among scholars who refused to allow these questions to be pursued.[10]

Not all academics interpreted Summers' challenges as merely an extension of sexism. Steven Pinker ("Psychoanalysis Q and A," 2005), a prominent psychology professor, commented,

> Look, the truth cannot be offensive. Perhaps the hypothesis is wrong, but how would we ever find out whether it is wrong if it is "offensive" even to consider it? People who storm out of a

meeting at the mention of a hypothesis, or declare it taboo or offensive without providing arguments or evidence, don't get the concept of a university or free inquiry.

His observation is instructive in that he perceives the threat that the rancor over Summers' resignation can create. This rancor removes from us the ability to use rationality and logic as ways to direct scientific research. Summers is a nationally renowned economist and was president of one of the most prestigious universities in the nation. If he is not free from experiencing the effects of asking the "wrong" scientific questions, then we should not expect academics that are in more vulnerable occupational positions to have the courage to address those questions. The biases of academics lead to an intolerance of certain views that is not appropriate for scientists. It may be appropriate for faith, experience, or some other way of gathering knowledge, but not for scientific inquiry.

When nonscientists are hesitant to accept the ability of academics to assess social and physical reality, it is episodes such as what happened to Summers that provide them with evidence that supports their doubts. Conservative commentators (Davis, 2005; McElroy, 2006; Paglia, 2006; Thernstrom, 2005) have used this specific event to illustrate their hesitation to accept the accuracy of scientific work. For many such critics, the question is not whether there are biological differences between men and women that may account for some of the occupational differences between them in the sciences. The real question is why scientists are not willing to honestly investigate that question. These critics suspect that scientific attempts to investigate possible sex differences would be accepted only if they discovered that those differences do not matter. The critics fail to see a fair investigation of truth, which leads them to question whether science, in the way it is done today, is an open search for truth or if a predetermined outcome is the normal state of scientific affairs. Thus an unfortunate result of events such as Summers' resignation is the loss of legitimacy of science and scientists in the nonacademic world.

If all we had was Summers' situation and a few other anecdotal cases, we could ask whether such biases are a common feature of scientific work. However, the research in the earlier chapters provided evidence of systematic social biases within academia. This is not the result of a few extreme individuals or a rogue department or two. What happened at Harvard can happen at most other colleges and universities. The Summers case merely illustrates that the problem is not merely one of selective hiring, but that social bias affects other areas of academic inquiry. This case is useful since the decision to pressure a president out of office is a public one and can be documented. Other decisions, such as votes for tenure and whether to publish a given piece of research, are private. Those decisions cannot be easily documented, but they may also be deeply influenced by biases against disfavored groups.

These types of bias threaten science as they cast doubt upon the accuracy of scientific work. Scientific research that supports progressive social ideals is seen with suspicion by moderates and conservatives. Those individuals perceive that ideas comporting with their view of reality do not get adequate respect from scholars. We see consistent evidence of this suspicion of science. For example, many individuals refuse to accept evolutionary theory because they believe that it offers a challenge to a supernaturalist perspective about the beginning of life. They suspect that alternatives to evolution are not taken seriously by biologists. Without making any assertions about the accuracy of evolutionary theory, one can understand why such doubts exist. These individuals perceive social biases among scientists. These biases feed their suspicion of scientists, and thus no amount of scientific evidence will engender their trust. A scientific community less connected to bias against religious conservatives could provide a more convincing case for evolution to a doubting general public.

Losing Science

There are two distinctive costs that the social biases in academia impose upon scientific inquiry. These costs threaten the essential nature of science. The work in this book and situations such as what happened to Lawrence Summers suggest that we have already lost part of what science should be. Whether we can ever completely neutralize the power of social biases in academia is questionable. But it is likely that we can minimize their effects with some effort.

The first clear cost to scientific inquiry is that the effects of these social biases deeply threaten the free nature of scientific exploration. Scientists are not free to investigate any question that may be relevant to their field of inquiry. There are litmus tests that must be passed before a given question can be seen as worthy of study. Questions that challenge the religiously and politically progressive core beliefs of most academics are often deemed out of bounds. Those who pursue those topics may be attacked for their moral values (with titles such as racist, classist, sexist, or homophobic) instead of for their methodology, theory construction, or some other viable scientific criteria. Thus we shrink science by limiting ourselves to comparatively few viable research questions.

Academic communities that allow for competing ideas and do not unduly penalize those without the "correct" political and religious ideals obviously gain an opportunity to include non-progressive perspectives. It may be case that most, or even all, of these non-progressive perspectives fail to pan out. But if they are never truly tested, then they have never been truly ruled out. Given the biases documented by this work, can we have any confidence that non-progressive alternatives have been sufficiently tested? There is a faith in progressive ideas that has developed at the expense of scientific inquiry. There is nothing wrong with having faith. I have already admitted that I have religious faith myself. But religion is not science. They are not intended to address the same questions. When we replace scientific rigor with a "religious" faith in progressive ideals, we investigate scientific questions with inappropriate mechanisms. Those who do not adhere to the proper faith are "excommunicated" from the scientific community, and we are all the poorer for having lost their input.

The second cost of these social biases is that nonscientists stop looking toward academia and academics to understand scientific truth. Thus scholars lose respect from the general public to such a degree that they no longer are seen as the source of scientific knowledge. If scientific inquiry is going to help us to develop our society further, then it will do so only if individuals are willing to accept the results of that inquiry. If they do not offer such acceptance, science will dramatically lose much of its place in our larger society and its irrelevancy will make it harder for scientists to contribute to that society.

If individuals stop believing in the legitimacy of scientific knowledge, they will also stop accepting the fruits that come from that inquiry and might question the very need for scientific work. The controversy over embryonic stem cell research illustrates such a problem. Many of the critics of this research argue that it is not necessary and that there may be better ways to conduct this type of research (Doerflinger, 1999; Heinemann & Honnefelder, 2002; Ruiz-Canela, 2002). With my very limited biological knowledge, I am in no position to weigh in on this scientific argument, but the biases documented in this work indicate a reason why some individuals dismiss the argument that such work is necessary. Fairly or unfairly, the debate of embryonic stem cell research has been connected to the debate about when life begins and therefore has implicated the issue of abortion. Undoubtedly many of the opponents of embryonic stem cell work believe that some of its proponents operate out of a progressive political agenda more than out of scientific reasoning. They see the use of such research as a way to critique a conservative perspective on life before birth, and thus to give progressives an upper hand in the culture war, rather than as a way to promote medical research (Novak, 2006; Colson, 2007; Railey, 2009). The results of my current research indicate the power of the progressive bias, which provides ammunition to such fears. Scientists have failed to be fully supported in their endeavors because of the social biases that are part of academia. As long as nonscientists see evidence of those biases, as they saw in Summers' case, such limited support is likely to continue and issues such as embryonic stem cell research will remain controversial.

These biases threaten the very nature of what science is. All who want to see the full potential of science should be disturbed by the manner in which these social biases disrupt that potential.

Science is meant to be a tool by which we can gain an understanding of social and physical reality with logical and rational assessment. These social biases not only limit the ability of scholars to comprehend new possibilities, but they also indicate to nonscientists that scientific findings are not based only on rational assessment. In a knowledge-based society with so much available information, scientists are not going to be able to hide the reality of social bias behind some veil of secrecy. Instead, scholars are going to have to face their social biases directly, or they will find a society that becomes less and less likely to accept their work.

Conclusion

In the first chapter, I indicated that I have my own personal bias as an evangelical Christian and a political independent. Because I occupy those religious and political positions, it is right to wonder how much these results are due to my own biases. Indeed, I am not immune from shaping my findings based on my own social preferences. It is because I am aware of that tendency that I worked at finding a research design that would limit my ability to shape the quantitative results of my work. My interpretation of the data is straightforward, and the conclusion that there is bias among scholars against religious and political conservatives is inescapable. This is not to state that my own religious and political beliefs were irrelevant as I conducted this research. The very fact that I chose this topic is likely tied to those beliefs. However, I have not done this research to push a given religious or political agenda. Rather, I am concerned that others pushing certain religious or political agendas may be distorting our ability to engage in academic work.

This work has been years in the making. Because I do not have the types of social bias documented in most other academics, it has been easier for me to see the power of these biases and the way they affect the work of scholars than it would have been for those with more powerful progressive outlooks. This has motivated me to investigate more fully the extent to which such biases are a part of the perspectives of scholars. I grew up with the image of science being an endeavor where there was an objective and rational search for the truth. I now know that such complete objectivity is not possible, but that we can do a better job of limiting the impact of our social biases on how we conduct scientific work. To this end, I desire to see a stronger scientific dimension where ideas can freely be debated and individuals from all walks of life are invited to participate in that debate. We are certainly far from such a reality at this current point in science, but hopefully moving toward such a position will become something that most of us who appreciate a rational approach toward acquiring information will begin to value.

To reach that position, we will have to make a proactive effort to combat the social biases this work documents. As an instructor of race and ethnicity, I know that many of the problems connected to racial issues are due to social structures that perpetuate our racial divisions. Contemporary racialized structures do not exist because whites have a high level of animosity toward people of color, but because society has not been introspective about the quiet and subtle ways in which racial advantage helps majority group members relative to minority group members.[11] I refuse to believe that the vast majority of scholars desire and intend to marginalize those from whom they differ religiously and politically. But only proactive and intentional attempts to confront this bias will succeed in loosing its hold on the scientific community. In the final chapter, I will speculate about some of these proactive steps.

CHAPTER SEVEN

What Can Be Done to Deal with Social Bias in Academia

I have conducted this work because of my love for scientific thinking and my desire to support it. I have been dismayed by the results of this work, but unfortunately I have not been surprised by them. My experiences, and conversations I have had with other scholars, have confirmed that certain individuals are not encouraged to engage freely in research. It may not be possible to end problems connected to social bias completely, but there are likely ways we can reduce its effects. Those who want to see a science that is more respected in the larger society and engage in a more free, open search for information should look toward taking steps to deal with the problems such bias creates.

Some individuals may not perceive the social biases documented in this work as a problem. Those who support progressive ideologies may conceptualize such biases as desirable. Those deeply embedded in supporting the progressive forces in the culture war would naturally appreciate the intellectual resources provided by academics. Others may not have progressive proclivities, yet they may consider social biases as just a natural part of society and thus not perceive a problem in the sciences. I obviously disagree with such assessments. The issues outlined in the previous chapter indicate that it is important to address these social biases. A failure to address the tendency of academics to support certain social groups over others leaves us with a weaker scholarly atmosphere.

In this chapter, I operate on the assumption that it is important to deal with these social biases. To this end, I speculate about the sort of steps scientific institutions and academics need to make to reduce the effects of these social biases on the discovery of scientific knowledge. As much as possible I will be specific about these reforms. To this end, I will draw on the work done combating biases against people of color and women in order to speculate about likely solutions to deal with religious and political biases. Then I will look at possible extensions to this work and suggest where we need to go to further improve our ability to obtain scientific knowledge. Finally, I will close with a brief discussion about power in academia and the challenges that await cultural progressives.

Measures to Create a More Accepting Atmosphere

The United States is a society that is formally and informally segregated in many different ways. Despite the election of President Obama, African Americans are still underrepresented in many professional occupations (Grumbach, Coffman, Rosenoff, & Munoz, 2001; Mervis, 2001). Women have also been unable to crack the glass ceiling completely (Corsun & Costen, 2001; Cotter, Hermsen, Ovadia, & Vanneman, 2001; Rosser, 2004). Other marginalized groups based on issues such as adhering to a rejected religious belief (Harper, 2007; Maira, 2004) or sexuality (Keller, 2002; Pengree, 2006) also may suffer because of an inhospitable atmosphere in social institutions. The lack of diversity in these areas is obviously problematic for marginalized groups, as they lose opportunities to experience a fair chance to enjoy all our society has to offer. But it is also troublesome for organizations that fail to take full advantage of the talents of individuals in those groups. We have not achieved all that is desirable in producing racial and sexual equality, but we at least recognize that problems exist and are closer to dealing with them than we have been in the past.

However, the academy is an institution in which certain disfavored groups have been marginalized. These disfavored groups are quite different than the racial and sexual categories we generally use when thinking of marginalized groups in academic institutions. It is reasonable to contend that the Republicans and conservative Protestants who suffer in academia possess advantages in other areas of society. Yet the fact that these groups are not disproportionately rejected in other social places does not nullify the alienation members of these groups face in academia. If we want scientific endeavors open to multiple pathways, then we must create an academic atmosphere inclusive of groups that are currently rejected. Recognizing the importance of dealing with the biases of academics is the first important step to be taken if we are to overcome the problems that have been pointed out in this work.

Of course, this leaves the question of what actually can be done to create that inclusive atmosphere. Since there is not any previous program geared at ameliorating religious and political bias in academia, there may be value in exploring the previous attempts at dealing with the underrepresentation of racial minorities and women. It should not be our goal to manufacture some artificial quota of religious and political conservatives. But we should seek an inclusive social atmosphere that would undoubtedly increase the current low percentages of such individuals in the academy. It is important to see if these efforts at inclusion help to minimize the social bias and intolerance that is embedded within academic circles. It is with that in mind that I will look at previous work about programs dealing with racial and sexual inequality so that reasonable suggestions may be put forth for dealing with the biases against religious and political minorities in academia.

I should make one final caveat before I look at these various approaches that have been taken for dealing with bias in social institutions. My exploration is tilted toward examples from the field of race and ethnicity. One obvious explanation for this is that my previous scholarly worked has focused heavily on the study of race and ethnicity. It is the field I know the best and thus the one I am most likely to draw examples from. I did look at research in sex differences to see if solutions were offered there by those that deal with sexual, but not racial, discrimination that would fit into this analysis. I found that many of those solutions tended to focus on issues of macrolevel societal change, socialization, and pay equity, although that is clearly not an exhaustive list of possible solutions. Educational institutions play a role but are not solely responsible, or able, to create a macrolevel change in our society. Addressing how individuals may be socialized to mistrust religious and political conservatives is an important topic, but there seems to be little that academic institutions of higher education can do to alter how scholars are socialized in their families of origin. Furthermore, this current study does not document any income differentials between religious and political conservatives and other scholars. Until there is a systematic study that does document such a difference, it is inappropriate to address issues of pay equity. Thus it is possible that issues surrounding the acceptance of racial and ethnic minorities may shed more light on how to deal with social bias than issues surrounding institutional alterations that promote sex equality.

Diversity Management Programs

One of the most common ways organizations have attempted to deal with underrepresentation of marginalized groups is through the development of diversity management programs. According to Farley (2010, 442) the objective of these programs is to "empower all employees, particularly women and people of color, to work, produce, and advance in the organization to their full potential." Since the goal is not merely to obtain some preset quota of marginalized groups in the academy, but rather to create an atmosphere that maximizes the productivity and contributions of marginalized groups, these are the types of programs that should be helpful in dealing with the social biases that disfavored groups are likely to encounter in academia.

These programs are designed in a number of different ways. Some programs focus on the behaviors of individuals instead of attempting to change their attitudes (Caudron & Hayes, 1997; Hemphill & Haines, 1997). However, if intolerance is the main contributor to the inhospitable social atmosphere marginalized groups face, then it is important to alter social attitudes as well. Ashmore (2008) argues that whites must recognize the advantages they enjoy in society because of their racial status for such programs to be successful. Helping members who enjoy majority group status understand the results of their attitudes and actions can play an important role in creating an effective diversity management program. Ideally, such programs would address both the actions and the attitudes of those in the majority. Doing so should maximize the effectiveness of these programs. Farley (2010) suggests that other factors are important in successful diversity management programs. He indicates that characteristics of successful programs are that they generally begin with an assessment, deal with issues promptly, use case studies in training, have goals and objectives, include accountability, and address the concerns of the majority. His arguments are based on current research on diversity management programs and may be updated with future research. But his assertions clearly indicate that some diversity management programs have a higher likelihood of success than others.

Given that we now have some research as to how these diversity management programs can be successful in addressing issues of race, gender, sexuality, and ability in a nonacademic setting, it is valuable to consider how they may be useful in academia. Since academics tend to be religiously and politically progressive, many of them likely already support the use of such programs to deal with the exclusion of race, gender, and sex minority groups. Thus they may be open to learning from programs that deal with the exclusion of religious and political conservatives. The principles discussed above indicate that such programs likely should address the attitudes of academics as well as whatever actions they may take that create bias against disfavored social groups. Speakers may be brought in or academics may be encouraged to take self-assessment tests with the goal of locating social bias among scholars and then taking steps to combat that bias. The use of assessments in the current academic environment, accountability, goals and objectives, and addressing the concerns of members of favored groups would also be useful elements to include in such programs.

Even the attempt to implement programs that would help scholars to recognize and combat their own social biases would be helpful for signaling to disfavored social groups that their concerns are being addressed. This may enable more members from these disfavored groups to seek out academic positions and increase the levels of ideological diversity in scholarly institutions today. Since there are few, if any, such programs today, there is likely to be early resistance to the implementation of such efforts. But it is important to attempt to create diversity programs aimed at creating a more accepting atmosphere for religious and political conservatives, even if the first few attempts at such programs are not well received by academics in general.

Bias Speech

Another way individuals have attempted to deal with the inhospitable atmospheres that marginalized individuals have faced is by addressing racist, sexist, homophobic, classist, ableist, and anti-Semitic speech. The general argument is that demeaning speech about members of minority groups naturally creates a social atmosphere that discourages the participation of such individuals in the institutions or organizations that allow such speech to take place (Calvert, 2006; Grey, 1991; Nielsen, 2002). Some have gone as far as to suggest that such speech can be considered a form of violence (Lawrence, 1993; Matsuda & Lawrence, 1993; Mildorf, 2005). Feminists (Kann, 1998; Mildorf, 2005; Mills, 2008; Swim, Mallett, & Stangor, 2004) in particular have been quick to point out that the gendered nature of our language often can be used to trivialize women. Therefore, it is not only the right of institutions to limit hateful speech but their obligation as well. Failure to make an attempt in good faith to limit the use of hateful speech can lead to legal peril for an organization.

The desire to control hateful speech has to be balanced by the right to free speech. Because of constitutional concerns, there are few overt speech codes in most formal organizations. Instead of actual phrases or words that individuals are not allowed to use, there is a general societal understanding of acceptable speech. The contexts in which certain statements are made have to be taken into consideration, as does the intent of the speaker, as far as it can be determined. There are powerful informal sanctions for those who violate these speech norms. Such individuals quickly learn that they will be ostracized and condemned for comments indicating that they may be sexist, racist, homophobic, classist, ableist, or anti-Semitic. In this way, informal pressure, rather than formal rules, often is conceived as the best way to police impolite and crude speech.

Hostile speech can create an intolerant atmosphere for religious and political conservatives in academic settings. The professor who spends his or her time perpetuating stereotypes about these social groups in class is unlikely to inspire any students from these groups to consider academia a worthy future occupation. Religiously and politically conservative colleagues of such individuals may also have to endure a level of discomfort that will negatively affect their opportunities to develop collegial relations with such faculty members. Just as formal speech codes contain problems in regulating speech that is directed at people of color, so too do they have problems dealing with comments that are directed at fundamentalists or Republicans. However, the development of a social atmosphere where religious bigotry is seen as distasteful, whether it is directed at Jews or fundamentalists, is an achievable goal. Encouraging informal sanctions that can discourage unfair expressions of rejection of religious and political minorities should be the goal of those that desire to limit the damage of hateful speech.

Anti-Racism

Recently some activists and scholars have promoted an idea known as "anti-racism." This concept refers to individuals who take a powerful proactive approach to ending racial bias. It is a reaction to the push toward conservative arguments for ignoring the racialized nature of the United States. Advocates of anti-racism contend that it is not enough to attempt to live in a colorblind manner (Aveling, 2002; Feagin & Vera, 2002; Katz, 2003). We must also seek out how racism has continued to plague our society and find ways to overcome its effects. Thus anti-racism is a reaction against attempts to

174 || COMPROMISING SCHOLARSHIP

take a passive approach toward ending racism and actively seeks ways to eliminate problems created by racial bias.

For example, McIntosh (2002) has enunciated many ways in which whites have hidden advantages in our society. She notes that whites are able to experience negative social encounters without worrying about them being attributed to racism, they can more easily find cultural representations of their group, and they are unlikely to have to overcome racial stereotypes relative to people of color. These advantages are not obvious, but they are real nonetheless. She labels these advantages "white privileges." Many individuals who take a colorblind approach to racial issues may not see the effects of these privileges and exhort us to ignore racial issues. But anti-racism is a philosophy that recognizes such advantages, and with this recognition we can attempt to find solutions that will create more racial equality.[1] By training individuals to recognize the racialized effects that are still prevalent in our society, anti-racism operates on the hope that many majority group members will become allies with people of color as they struggle to overcome the racial disadvantages they face rather than create additional barriers against racial equality.

What anti-racism brings to this discussion is the need to be proactive in dealing with bias and inequality in our society. Just as the racialized nature of our society is maintained in part by attempts of some individuals to ignore racial issues, so too can the bias against religious and political conservatives be supported by silence concerning that bias. In this way, even those who did not indicate bias against religious and political conservatives in the research may perpetuate this bias by their inaction against it. This research documents the degree of bias present in different scientific disciplines. But there is a need for academics to understand the consequences of this bias, that the attitudes of religious and political progressives may unfairly hinder opportunities for religious and political conservatives. Some of those conservatives may need to share their own experiences to emphasize this point. Understanding the full effects of this bias and making proactive efforts to deal with them is critical if the academy is to be able to undercut the powerful effects of religious and political bias. If more religious and political progressives speak out against unfair attitudes toward religious and political conservatives, then these powerful effects can be greatly reduced, as it will no longer be seen as socially acceptable to express such biases.

To this end, it is important that academic departments work at overcoming the powerful effects of bias with training that highlights the difficulties that religiously and politically conservative students and colleagues may face. To be specific, there is a need for more research that documents such disadvantages so that progressive scholars can have a better understanding of the types of problems that bias among scholars has created. Much of the efforts of anti-racism are aimed at majority group members, as those individuals are less likely than members of racial minorities to understand how they have advantages in our society. Likewise, it may well be religious and political progressives who are in most need of instruction about the disadvantages that their conservative counterparts face, as they are likely to be ignorant of those disadvantages. This type of training may differ from the diversity training discussed in the earlier section, as it does not necessarily seek to address the bias that the individual scholar may have but rather attempts to help that scholar understand the difficulties that his or her colleagues may face. There is a proactive element in anti-racism that is not always present in diversity programs, and it is that element that we may need to add to efforts to confront religious and political bias in academia. Ideally, once the problems generated by bias are fully understood, there is a chance that religiously and politically conservative academics may gain allies who help them to deal with these biases.

Addressing Systemic Issues

The framework of social justice has been used in attempts to assess the institutional factors that work to the disadvantage of women and people of color (Benokraitis, 1997; Bonilla-Silva, 2003; Capeheart & Milovanovic, 2007; Feagin & Feagin, 1986; Goodman, 2000). These efforts call attention to the idea that bias is not merely an individualistic phenomenon but that it is also fed by social structures that reinforce the damage it can do. In contemporary society few individuals are willing to admit to a bias against women and people of color, but many participate in social structures and practices that nonetheless work to the disadvantage of these groups. For example, racial residential segregation has been clearly documented as producing an institutional disadvantage for people of color (Massey & Denton, 1996), while use of sexist language has been shown to produce a disadvantage for women (Mills, 2008; Swim et al., 2004).

Such analysis would also be important for assessing whether there are institutional structures within academia that work against the ability of religious and political conservatives to make their potential scholarly contributions. Discovering such potential institutional factors will not occur immediately. Just as it has taken a long time to understand fully how social structures and practices impact women and people of color, so too will it take time and effort to explore how religious and political conservatives may be restricted by certain systemic elements within our colleges and universities. Scholars have put forth a great deal of effort to learn about the possible institutional ways in which sexism and racism are perpetrated in our society. Likewise, there is a need for scholarly work that investigates how social structures within academia also perpetuate intolerance against religious and political conservatives.

For example, academic departments may want to consider political activism among their faculty members while they are on campus. What faculty members do on their own time is, of course, their own business. But a department that allows, or even encourages, faculty members to advertise their political activism may be creating an atmosphere where those with a minority political opinion feel excluded or marginalized. This activism is more often than not focused on progressive causes, and scholars who are not political progressives may perceive undue pressure to support such causes. If activism is allowed, it may be insightful to consider what types of activism create an uncomfortable work environment. It may be that only certain types of activism need to be curtailed. It may be that these types of institutional pressures discourage work challenging the progressive paradigm in sociological research and help to create an atmosphere whereby about a third of all sociologists are willing to disfavor a job candidate because of their allegiance to the Republican party.

What Is the Role of Those from Disfavored Groups?

Much of the work in this book has illustrated that there is a problem of social bias among scholars that unduly punishes those from disfavored social groups. While those from disfavored groups do not have as much social power as those from favored groups, this does not mean that they are blameless about the current situation. The social bias that has developed within academia cannot maintain itself unless individuals from disfavored groups fail to challenge it. Challenging social biases lodged against them will help religious and political conservatives demonstrate to their progressive counterparts the need to eliminate such bias. Once those progressives have been shown how their actions or attitudes unfairly penalize or stigmatize out-group members, it will be the responsibility of the progressives to help produce changes. But one cannot expect to see any changes until offensive actions and practices have been brought to their attention.

However, rather than being open with their perspectives, often religious and political conservatives hide their ideas to escape ridicule. This is to be expected, for students and professors wield a great deal of social power over them. Furthermore, individuals on the job market or who are junior faculty may desire to be careful, as there can be occupational repercussions to openly belonging to a disfavored social group, as seen in this research. Thus it must be the responsibility of senior professors who are religious and political conservatives to point out the harmful ways that scholars may inadvertently discourage members from disfavored groups. Often these individuals have spent years hiding their perceptions and are uncomfortable coming out with their ideas toward the end of their career.[2] But such habits have to be broken if we are to expect other scholars to work toward developing a more inclusive science.

In that spirit, I will document one situation that I, as a Christian, have witnessed and with which I believe we can deal. There are certain terms that are derogatory in their intent when directed at evangelicals and fundamentalists.[3] One of those terms is "bible thumper." This offensive term has been used to create an image of an ignorant, rude individual who consistently pushes his or her ideas upon others at inappropriate times. It is clearly an insult, and I have heard professors use it in their classrooms in front of students and in the hallways with other colleagues. This is an example of the lack of sensitivity that keeps academia from being a place that welcomes all individuals and promises that their ideas will be evaluated for their own merit and not according to some gross stereotype.

To illustrate why "bible thumper" is a derogatory term, consider a similar term for a religious group that is not as highly disfavored by academics. The term "raghead" is parallel to "bible thumper" except that it is a term that is used to stigmatize Muslims. Both are terms that generate unfavorable images of a particular religious group. They promote gross and unfair stereotypes of these groups. I dare say that few scholars would use the term "raghead" in describing Muslims in their classes and in the hallways of their campuses. If they chose to do so, they would likely hear from Muslim groups who would rightly resist such objectification. Because these groups would find some allies within academia, the guilty scholar would have a problematic time retaining his or her position. I would agree with the Muslim groups about questioning the wisdom of retaining a scholar who so willingly insults a significant proportion of the population. Yet I suspect that some of the academics reading this book can recall times when they have heard (perhaps even from their own mouths) the term "bible thumper." I would ask that such scholars rethink the advisability of using, or supporting the use of, either term in public discourse.

In time, it is my hope that members of disfavored groups will be able to respectfully speak out against some of the demeaning ways in which scholars treat them and in doing so will help us to create a truly inclusive subculture within academia. It is that sort of subculture where we have the best opportunity to conduct solid scientific research. Without an environment that encourages those of different social groups to express their perspectives, scientific endeavor will be limited in its potential to conduct open inquiry. While scholars from favored social groups have a responsibility to defend those from disfavored groups, scholars from disfavored groups, especially those that possess the protection of tenure, cannot shirk their responsibility either. They should become involved, not merely for the sake of scholars from disfavored groups, but also as a way to help produce an academic atmosphere that allows for a maximum level of scientific freedom. It is in that spirit that I have written this book.

Future Research Ideas

This research is not the first endeavor to document the social and religious differences between scientists and others in our society. But it is the first systematic attempt to illustrate that these differences have led to a dysfunctional academic social environment that punishes those who do not adhere to proper, which is to say progressive, religious and political values. As such, there is more work that needs to be done. I have based my assertions on a question about the possibility of hiring individuals who have made certain political, religious, and lifestyle choices. From the results of that question, I have speculated on how other aspects of one's academic career may be affected by being a member of a disfavored social group. It would strengthen this work if we could document how social bias and intolerance among scholars influence other decisions that may affect an academic's occupational life. Documenting whether choices about tenure, acceptance of articles, research topics, or teaching material are influenced by these social biases would add to our knowledge about how powerful these biases are. Such work would also eliminate or lessen the need to engage in speculation.

This work is also important as it documents prejudice against targets less likely to experience prejudice outside of academia. Since Christianity is a majority religion in our society, and Republicans are a major political party, it is unlikely that members of these social groups face the same degree of prejudice outside of academia that they do inside of it.[4] This should not be an excuse for scholars to minimize the potential discrimination and prejudice these groups do face in academia. The stigma religious and political conservatives face in academia is likely just as real to them as the stigma minority groups face in nonacademic communities.[5] However, it may be of interest to document how these cultural conservatives handle the pressures they face in academia since they might not have much of an opportunity to deal with such pressures outside of the academy.

The suggestions given earlier in the chapter can also benefit from additional research. It is quite possible that programs designed to produce more tolerant attitudes among individuals with an average level of educational attainment may not be effective when dealing with scholars who have an extraordinary level of educational attainment. Their educational experiences may make them more accepting of the correction they receive from program leaders or it may harden their resolve against new information about their own social biases. Only future research can fully investigate which efforts at diversity are effective in influencing a highly educated group and which ones are less effective because of the educational training of the scholars.

Furthermore, there may be valuable information to be gained by conducting a qualitative exploration into how prejudice develops and is sustained among academics. The willingness of academics to engage in bias seems to be at odds with their stated values of open inquiry and tolerance. Of particular interest is that the disciplines that most emphasize acceptance of those in different cultures (i.e., anthropology and language) are the ones that are most likely to screen out disfavored social groups. How do academics deal with these seemingly contradictory strains in their values? In-depth qualitative research may be able to obtain answers to such questions. Such work could include interviews and focus groups of scholars that probe the origin of academic resistance to members of disfavored social groups and question how these scholars handle the contradiction of using social bias to weed out members of certain groups and yet enunciating a value of pluralism.

This research has focused only on potential bias within academia. As noted in chapter 1, there are charges of bias in other important social institutions such as the media and the arts. Bolce and De Maio (2008) have shown that hostile attitudes toward fundamentalists are supported by the negative media coverage this group receives.

An exploration of whether the negative treatment of fundamentalists is a result of accurate reporting cannot be done without taking into account the possibility that this treatment is driven by a negative bias of the reporters. A systematic study of whether such a bias exists is necessary to fully understand the role the media plays in generating hostile attitudes toward fundamentalists. Likewise, it is quite plausible that bias against religious and political conservatives is also an important, but understudied, feature in other societal places such as certain types of businesses, religious settings, and social clubs.

Conclusion

I have substantiated the reality that religious and political conservatives face a level of rejection that other social groups do not experience in academia. The argument that the disproportionate representation of irreligious and politically progressive scholars in academia has no effect on the opportunities of religious and political conservatives is no longer sustainable without the generation of additional empirical work that shows otherwise. Previous work has shown that religious and political progressives possess power in academia due to their overrepresentation. This work indicates that at least some progressives use that power to filter out those with whom they disagree. If scientific knowledge is to grow in a more complete manner, then academia must become an institution where all ideas are explored, not merely ones that fulfill the desires of certain political or religious groups. Failure to create this openness threatens to turn scientific inquiry into a process of religious-like legitimization of progressive ideology.

This current research project is not perfect. It, like other empirical endeavors, has weaknesses that have to be accounted for. Those who do not want to confront the reality of scientific bias may use the fact that this research is not perfect to dismiss these results. Such an effort comes at a cost. Problems do not go away because we choose to ignore them. Often those problems merely become worse. Let us not be naïve to the fact that I am criticizing the institutions that serve scholars who may take issue with my work. Many of them will have legitimate concerns, but others may operate out of the same bias documented in this work to go out of their way to attack these findings. I welcome calls to produce better research that can update the results of the current studies. But I will reject negative assessments directed at this work that are born out of the desire to continue the status quo that ill serves our educational institutions. I have been around academia long enough to know, most of the time, the difference between these two types of criticisms.

To be a scientist means to be open to research and conclusions that potentially challenge our current level of knowledge. I am convinced that there are no major methodological or empirical shortcomings that challenge the basic finding in this work, which is that religiously and politically conservative academics face bias in their chosen profession. How pronounced this bias may be remains a point of debate, as I have acknowledged, but this study secures quite firmly the reality of such bias. Like any scientific conclusion, however, the results of this study are by no means unassailable. Should future systematic research adequately dealing with the problem of social desirability indicate that such a bias does not in fact exist, then I will accept the possibility that my conclusions here require revision. Absent such research, however, this study suggests that we acknowledge the bias against religious and political conservatives across most academic disciplines. Recognizing this reality is the scientific way to deal with this study. The unscientific way to handle this work is to ignore, or attempt to minimize without a scientific basis, its findings, allowing such biases in academia to continue unabated. Such efforts only reinforce the perception, and perhaps the unfortunate reality, that scientific institutions exist more to justify religiously and politically progressive ideas than to discover social and physical reality.

This study serves as an invitation, then, for religious and political progressives to practice the tolerance they profess. The essential measure of tolerance seems to lie not in dealing with groups or individuals with whom one shares deep affinities, but rather in offering opportunities to those with whom one shares little common ground. For religious and political progressives, true tolerance will come through developing alliances with conservatives in an effort to enact some, or all, of the measures listed in this chapter. For religious and political conservatives, verbal support for their inclusion in academia as well as recognition of the difficulties they may face would also be welcomed. The results of this research provide religious and political progressives the chance to show that they do not merely support marginalized groups with which they have ideological agreement but also those groups with which they disagree. Now is the time for professors, scholars, scientists, and the academy as a whole to take advantage of that chance and provide the rest of society with a model for what real tolerance can look like.

Appendix

Basic Methodology

The basic methodology used for studying sociologists was the methodology used for other disciplines. My basic strategy was to find a listing of the researchers in a given discipline. For sociologists, this was relatively easy since there is a directory of the members of the discipline's national organization. The name of the directory is the American Sociological Association (ASA) 2007 Directory of Members, and from it I developed a random list of faculty members. This listing does not include all sociologists, as some, like myself, are not current members of the ASA. But it is fair to argue that the vast majority of sociology professors are ASA members, and there is no reason to believe that using the directory created any sampling bias.

I only selected sociologists who were listed as regular or emeriti members of the American Sociological Association. I did not include student members because I wanted to minimize the chance of selecting graduate students for my research. Each eligible sociologist was numbered in the directory. Then a list of random numbers was generated for a subset of 1,500 sociologists. The sociologist assigned to the selected number was included in the sample. If there were duplicate numbers, if I accidentally assigned a number to someone who was not eligible for selection, or if I could not find an e-mail address for a respondent,[1] then I generated more random numbers until I had enough respondents. After sending out e-mails, I found that some went to accounts that were no longer operative. In that case, I first checked to see if the e-mail address was correctly recorded. I determined the college or university the person worked at and then went to the department Web site of that educational institution. At times I found that the e-mail address in the directory was different than the address on the Web site, and so I replaced it with the address on the Web site. Every reasonable attempt was made to ensure that I used the originally selected respondent. But if all of these efforts failed, then I used the random number generator to locate a replacement.

Only sociologists currently working in the United States were chosen, since I did not want to confound the findings with international cultural differences. Different social groups would have different meanings to scholars in other countries than they do for sociologists in the United States. For this reason, I eliminated all sociologists working at colleges and universities outside the United States.[2]

I sent the survey out twice. Each time I offered to share basic results with the respondents if they sent me an e-mail indicating interest. Since the respondents' e-mail addresses were kept confidential, some of the respondents who filled out the survey the first time received it a second time. In my second e-mail, I apologized in advance for this possibility and assured each respondent that they would not receive a third mailing. I also set the online instrument so that a respondent could only send in one survey from a single computer, although a respondent could come back to finish a survey that was previously started. This reduced the possibility that individuals who received the second request would send in multiple surveys.

Finally, it is worth noting that since I asked the respondents about where they worked, I was able to conduct research on only those that taught in an academic setting. Thus, the findings in chapter 3 only represent the responses of sociologists who work in some capacity at a college or university. Including the responses of sociologists who do not work in the academy did not produce significantly different results, but since I wanted to investigate the production of scientific knowledge, I chose to eliminate noncampus sociologists from my analysis. In a similar manner, when I analyzed the data on non-sociologists, I also eliminated those who did not indicate that they worked at an educational institution.

Information on Non-Sociology Disciplines

I wish I could state that I chose different disciplines for highly academic and scholarly reasons. The plain fact is that the availability of a listing of academics from a given discipline was the major factor that shaped my choices. I did take into consideration the need to obtain information from disciplines in the social sciences, humanities, and physical sciences. I decided to select three additional disciplines from the social sciences, three from the physical sciences, and two from the humanities. This gave me sufficient coverage of the academic disciplines, but it did produce less diverse information for the humanities than for other types of academic work. However, the choice of language academics allowed me to assess two different types of humanities (English and non-English), as the results in chapter 5 indicate.

The methodology for selecting possible scholars was basically the same as for selecting sociologists, regardless of the directory used. The only real difference was that, instead of surveying 1,500 scholars in each discipline, I only surveyed 500 respondents for each of the social and physical sciences and 750 for each discipline in the humanities. Ideally, each directory I obtained would have used the same criteria for inclusion. However, this was clearly not the case. As much as possible, I attempted to standardize my selection criteria by choosing individuals located in the United States and by attempting to avoid selecting graduate students who were teaching at their own university. Nevertheless it is important to look at each directory to understand some of the possible sampling biases inherent within them.

American Anthropological Association 2008–2009 Guide

This directory included an alphabetical listing of each college or university that has an anthropology department of some kind and listed the professors in that department. Many departments were linked to other disciplines, most notably sociology. Whenever possible, I eliminated names that I encountered where information indicated that the scholar was likely not an anthropologist. When I was unsure, I attempted to use the scholar's stated research areas to determine whether he or she was an anthropologist. But if that was not enough information to make a determination, I included the respondent. I did not include part-time faculty, who were listed separately from the full-time and emeritus faculty. My response rate for anthropologists was 17.1 percent.

American Chemical Society Directory of Graduate Research

This directory produced an alphabetical listing of each educational institution that provides a graduate degree in chemistry and contact information for the professors who work at them. Unfortunately, this eliminated chemists who work at institutions that do not provide graduate degrees. My response rate for chemists was 19.4 percent.

Directory of American Philosophers 2008–2009

This directory provided contact information for individuals in the philosophy departments in the United States. Each individual was grouped under his or her respective educational institution. Since colleges and universities not in the United States were excluded from this section of the directory and graduate students were set apart from the faculty, I was easily able to use this directory to create a list that met the criteria of the study. My response rate for philosophers was 27.9 percent.

Directory of History Departments, Historical Organizations, and Historians

This 2008–2009 directory provided an alphabetical listing of historians in a variety of occupational settings. Since it was often difficult to determine if the historians worked in an academic or nonacademic setting, I chose to be inclusive when it was unclear about the setting in which they worked. When there was insufficient contact information on a historian chosen at random, I eliminated that person from consideration. My response rate for historians was 27.8 percent.

Directory of Physics, Astronomy and Geophysics Staff

This directory provided information about scientists who work in a variety of departments connected to physics, astronomy, and geophysics. To concentrate on just physics, I eliminated any department that did not include physics within its name (e.g., Department of Geological Science) while I included those whose names contained the discipline of physics (e.g., Department of Geology and Physics). Furthermore, as I looked up contact information about each scientist, I eliminated a few of them when it was clear that physics was not their major research interest. This helped me to limit the number of scientists in the sample who do not study physics, but it did increase the possibility of missing some physics researchers. My response rate for physicists was 13 percent.

Directory of Political Science Faculty and Programs 2007–2008

This directory provided a list of colleges and universities with political science departments. It also provided a listing with the contact information of the instructors and professors in each department. Unfortunately, the directory did not provide information on two-year or community colleges, and prestigious professors at top-tier institutions were overrepresented in these findings. My response rate for political scientists was 15.4 percent.

Federation of American Societies for Experimental Biology Directory of Members 2008–2009

This directory included the members of sixteen different research groups.[3] There is a significant amount of variety among these associations, but they are connected by an interest in conducting experimental biological research. The members were listed alphabetically. I eliminated those from outside the United States and those that obviously did not work in academic settings.[4] I also eliminated any respondents that were clearly graduate students. My response rate for experimental biologists was 14.8 percent.

Publications of the Modern Language Association of America Directory

This directory provided a listing of scholars of the various languages. The sampling of 750 academics allowed me to capture enough English and non-English specialists to test for effects between the two groups. In this sense, I gained two different humanities groups out of this single directory. My response rate for language teachers was 18.8 percent.

These response rates are admittedly low. In fact, they are lower than the response rate for sociologists. Later in the appendix I will illustrate why these low response rates do not challenge the existence of social biases, but only the degree to which they influence members in a discipline.

Analysis of Non-Sociology Disciplines

Once the data were collected, I compared the attitudes that the scholars possessed toward the different social groups. As noted in chapter 5, there were clear differences in the attitudes of scholars from different disciplines. Thus, certain disciplines, such as anthropology and language, are more likely than other disciplines to demonstrate the biases documented in this book. However, it is plausible that demographic distinctions among the disciplines may account for these effects as well. Regression analysis is a valuable way to assess the power of discipline differences in determining attitudes toward different social groups as opposed to demographic variations among the disciplines.

I did analysis with the rating of each social group as the dependent variable of the model. The independent variables consisted of age, sex, and a dummy variable based on whether or not the respondent taught at a religious school. I also wanted to assess the prestige of the institution that each respondent taught at, so I included a five-category (doctorate, master, bachelor, associate, and other[5]) ordinal variable that assessed the level of degree offered in the respondent's field at his or her place of employment. I included the different scientific disciplines as dummy variables in each model. I used sociology as the reference group. Doing so helped me to compare how often membership in a certain discipline influenced the respondent's attitudes. The results of these models are in appendix table A.

An initial glance at the models indicates that sex and whether a respondent works at a religious institution are as influential as the discipline in which one works. In fact, as stated in the body of this book, sex and working in a religious institution are each significant in sixteen of the twenty-six regression models. In only fourteen of these models are any of the discipline variables significant. Considering that each model contained eight discipline variables,[6] the inability for discipline variables to predict attitudes toward certain social groups relative to sex and working at a religious school supports the argument that social characteristics of the members of the disciplines are at least as important as, if not more important than, institutional differences in the disciplines themselves in predicting social bias.

It may be useful to explore possible effects of the respondents' disciplines by looking at the social groups by categories of religion, politics, sexuality, and lifestyle. In the main body of the book, I argued that the most powerful biases were reserved for those who were seen as religiously conservative. We did observe some disciplinary influences on the degree of social stigma that the religiously conservative may face. Clearly anthropologists were eager to reject fundamentalists, evangelicals, and even mainliners, while they embraced atheists. Teachers of English and philosophy were also significantly more likely to reject fundamentalists than those in other disciplines. However, important nondisciplinary effects showed up as well. Working at a religious school helped to explain a respondent's acceptance of atheists, evangelicals, mainliners, Catholics, Jews, and Muslims. Men were more likely to accept evangelicals and Catholics, but less likely to accept Muslims, than women. Older scholars were more likely to accept atheists, but less likely to accept fundamentalists. It is fair to characterize the reaction of the respondents to the religious dimension as being influenced by both

Appendix Table A. Regression Estimates of the Assessment of the Attitudes of Academics toward Selected Social Groups

Variables	Democrat	Republican	Green Party	Libertarian	Communist Party	NRA	ACLU
Age	.02 (.01)	-.001 (.011)	.004 (.01)	-.01 (.009)	-.01 (.012)	-.068c (.013)	.041c (.011)
Male	-.201c (.05)	.172b (.052)	-.125b (.046)	.016 (.045)	-.241c (.058)	.329c (.063)	-.174b (.054)
School Prestige	-.014 (.026)	.022 (.026)	-.018 (.024)	.008 (.023)	-.036 (.03)	.04 (.032)	-.028 (.028)
Religious School?	-.013 (.066)	.137a (.069)	-.105 (.062)	.102 (.06)	-.3c (.078)	.116 (.084)	-.134 (.071)
Anthropology	.052 (.089)	-.021 (.093)	-.086 (.083)	.197a (.081)	-.054 (.104)	.038 (.113)	-.069 (.096)
History	-.115 (.096)	.129 (.99)	-.096 (.09)	.082 (.087)	-.229a (.112)	.104 (.123)	-.271b (.104)
Physics	-.286a (.119)	.397b (.123)	-.198 (.111)	.093 (.108)	-.306a (.14)	.202 (.151)	-.302a (.13)
Chemistry	-.136 (.095)	.172 (.098)	-.136 (.088)	.103 (.086)	.043 (.112)	.09 (.12)	-.079 (.103)
Exploratory Biology	-.162 (.111)	.26 (.115)	-.173 (.103)	.21a (.1)	-.072 (.129)	.167 (.141)	-.148 (.12)
Philosophy	-.109 (.077)	.091 (.08)	-.067 (.072)	-.031 (.07)	-.132 (.09)	.123 (.098)	-.178a (.083)
Language Non-English	-.347a (.144)	.274 (.15)	-.18 (.135)	.335a (.132)	-.05 (.171)	.053 (.192)	-.182 (.163)
Language English	.101 (.096)	.089 (.1)	-.051 (.09)	-.036 (.087)	-.1 (.113)	-.032 (.121)	-.099 (.103)
R^2	.04	.038	.019	.021	.05	.055	.039
N	1,006	1,006	1,004	1,002	1,000	1,005	1,003

[a] $p < .05$ level, [b] $p < .01$ level, [c] $p < .001$ level. Entries are betas, standard error in parentheses.

Appendix Table A. Regression Estimates of the Assessment of the Attitudes of Academics toward Selected Social Groups (*continued*)

Variables	Heterosexual	Homosexual	Bisexual	Transgendered	Atheist	Mormon
Age	.000 (.006)	-.001 (.007)	-.005 (.008)	-.006 (.01)	.018a (.009)	-.001 (.01)
Male	.028 (.027)	-.169c (.036)	-.141c (.038)	-.255c (.049)	-.078 (.042)	.008 (.047)
School Prestige	-.016 (.014)	.031 (.018)	.036 (.019)	.05a (.025)	.036 (.022)	.073b (.024)
Religious School?	.093a (.036)	-.268c (.047)	-.303c (.051)	-.351c (.065)	-.377c (.056)	-.088 (.063)
Anthropology	-.049 (.049)	.104 (.063)	.062 (.067)	.151 (.086)	.15a (.075)	-.144 (.084)
History	-.079 (.053)	-.042 (.068)	-.074 (.073)	.023 (.095)	.000 (.081)	.073 (.091)
Physics	.162a (.066)	-.145 (.086)	-.159 (.091)	-.064 (.117)	.019 (.102)	-.142 (.114)
Chemistry	-.018 (.052)	.011 (.068)	.008 (.072)	-.02 (.093)	.241b (.08)	.068 (.091)
Experimental Biology	-.048 (.061)	-.075 (.079)	-.069 (.084)	.027 (.109)	-.01 (.094)	.198 (.106)
Philosophy	-.035 (.043)	.005 (.055)	.001 (.059)	.134 (.076)	.091 (.065)	-.045 (.073)
Language Non-English	-.036 (.08)	-.085 (.103)	-.072 (.11)	.079 (.142)	.066 (.122)	.083 (.138)
Language English	.027 (.053)	.048 (.069)	.034 (.074)	.023 (.095)	.084 (.081)	-.128 (.091)
R^2	.022	.075	.069	.071	.07	.033
N	1,007	1,008	1,009	1,004	1,004	1,009

[a]$p < .05$ level, [b]$p < .01$ level, [c]$p < .001$ level. Entries are betas, standard error in parentheses.

Appendix Table A. Regression Estimates of the Assessment of the Attitudes of Academics toward Selected Social Groups (*continued*)

Variables	Jewish	Muslim	Catholic	Mainline	Evangelical	Fundamentalist
Age	.01 (.007)	-.005 (.007)	-.007 (.005)	.001 (.005)	-.022 (.014)	-.031[a] (.015)
Male	-.052 (.033)	-.091[b] (.034)	.052[a] (.026)	.047 (.026)	.286[c] (.068)	.118 (.071)
School Prestige	.006 (.017)	.014 (.018)	-.019 (.014)	-.02 (.013)	.002 (.035)	.036 (.036)
Religious School?	-.165[c] (.044)	-.219[c] (.046)	.075[a] (.035)	.129[c] (.034)	.414[c] (.091)	.163 (.095)
Anthropology	-.03 (.058)	.035 (.061)	-.074 (.047)	-.098[a] (.045)	-.47[c] (.121)	-.552[c] (.126)
History	.073 (.063)	.11 (.066)	.037 (.051)	-.026 (.049)	.016 (.132)	-.093 (.137)
Physics	.076 (.078)	-.127 (.082)	.135[a] (.063)	.122[a] (.061)	.098 (.163)	-.014 (.17)
Chemistry	.023 (.062)	.001 (.066)	-.022 (.05)	-.068 (.049)	.069 (.13)	.164 (.136)
Experimental Biology	-.018 (.073)	-.024 (.077)	-.031 (.059)	-.034 (.057)	.255 (.152)	.239 (.158)
Philosophy	-.008 (.051)	.000 (.053)	-.048 (.041)	-.077 (.04)	.016 (.105)	-.227[a] (.11)
Language Non-English	-.061 (.095)	.018 (.1)	-.021 (.076)	-.162[a] (.074)	.339 (.198)	.012 (.206)
Language English	.053 (.064)	.022 (.067)	-.012 (.051)	-.046 (.05)	-.194 (.131)	-.4[b] (.138)
R^2	.022	.04	.025	.04	.072	.053
N	1,009	1,007	1,006	1,005	1,008	1,007

[a] $p < .05$ level, [b] $p < .01$ level, [c] $p < .001$ level. Entries are betas, standard error in parentheses.

Appendix Table A. Regression Estimates of the Assessment of the Attitudes of Academics toward Selected Social Groups (*continued*)

Variables	Vegetarian	Hunter	Married	Divorced	Cohabitating	Single-Child	Under 30	Over 50
Age	.004 (.006)	-.032ᶜ (.009)	-.003 (.005)	.001 (.003)	.006 (.006)	.008 (.004)	.024ᶜ (.008)	.01 (.007)
Male	-.032 (.028)	.209ᶜ (.044)	.052ª (.024)	-.015 (.015)	-.094ᶜ (.027)	-.042 (.021)	-.113ᵇ (.037)	.024 (.035)
School Prestige	.003 (.014)	.003 (.023)	.009 (.012)	.022ᵇ (.008)	.034ª (.014)	.002 (.011)	.021 (.019)	.033 (.018)
Religious School?	-.086ª (.037)	.095 (.058)	.054 (.032)	-.058ᵇ (.02)	-.319ᶜ (.036)	.019 (.029)	-.049 (.049)	.178ᶜ (.046)
Anthropology	-.064 (.049)	.07 (.078)	.013 (.043)	.033 (.027)	.031 (.047)	.044 (.038)	.001 (.066)	-.054 (.061)
History	-.068 (.054)	.103 (.085)	.03 (.046)	.02 (.03)	-.009 (.051)	.007 (.041)	-.018 (.071)	-.007 (.067)
Physics	.014 (.066)	.157 (.105)	.305ª (.058)	.015 (.037)	-.041 (.064)	-.038 (.051)	-.129 (.088)	.082 (.082)
Chemistry	-.038 (.053)	.002 (.083)	-.054 (.046)	.013 (.029)	.038 (.051)	.01 (.041)	-.139ª (.071)	.018 (.066)
Experimental Biology	-.077 (.062)	.085 (.098)	.012 (.054)	-.016 (.034)	.000 (.06)	-.052 (.048)	-.009 (.082)	-.084 (.077)
Philosophy	.06 (.043)	.052 (.068)	.017 (.037)	.012 (.024)	-.049 (.041)	.018 (.033)	.054 (.057)	-.043 (.054)
Language Non-English	-.071 (.081)	.041 (.128)	-.013 (.07)	.036 (.044)	.022 (.078)	-.014 (.062)	.128 (.107)	.031 (.102)
Language English	.055 (.054)	-.028 (.085)	.061 (.047)	.081ᵇ (.03)	.045 (.052)	.012 (.042)	.045 (.072)	.092 (.067)
R^2	.018	.04	.041	.026	.113	.011	.031	.029
N	1,008	1,010	1,010	1,009	1,010	1,009	1,012	1,012

[a] $p < .05$ level, [b] $p < .01$ level, [c] $p < .001$ level. Entries are betas, standard error in parentheses.

disciplinary and nondisciplinary effects. However, most of the disciplinary effects were due to the strong aversion that anthropologists showed to religious conservatives. Without the effects generated by the anthropologists, there would have been relatively few disciplinary effects outside of the reaction to fundamentalists.

As concerns the political groups, it was the physicists that most influenced the disciplinary findings. They were significantly more supportive of Republicans and less supportive of Democrats, Communists, and the ACLU than other respondents. The non-English language teachers were also less supportive of Democrats, but tended to support libertarians. The experimental biologists supported libertarians more than other scholars. Thus most of the disciplinary effects came from groups that broke away from the progressive tendencies of sociologists. Nevertheless, there were also powerful nondisciplinary effects. In particular, men were less supportive of Democrats, Green Party members, Communists, and the ACLU, while they were more supportive of Republicans and the NRA than were women. Older scholars tended to have more support for the ACLU and less for the NRA. Academics at religious institutions were more likely to support Republicans but less likely to support Communists. Both disciplinary and nondisciplinary effects were evident in this work. The disciplinary effects were driven mostly by the inclusion of physicists, and the nondisciplinary effects were driven mostly by gender.

The disciplinary effects largely disappeared when I explored the reaction of scholars to social groups determined by sexuality. Only the physicists' support of heterosexuals was significant. However, there were several nondisciplinary effects that helped explain the reactions of scholars toward sexuality groups. Scholars at religious institutions predictably supported heterosexuals, but were less supportive of homosexuals, bisexuals, and transgendered individuals than other scholars. Men were also significantly less supportive of homosexuals, bisexuals, and transgendered individuals than were women. Finally, those at more prestigious schools were more supportive of transgendered individuals. The explanation of the support of the sexuality groups was clearly more dominated by nondisciplinary factors, most notably gender and working at a religious school, than by the uniqueness of the scientific disciplines.

An examination of the lifestyle groups suggests very few disciplinary effects. The physicists were significantly more likely to support those who were married, and English language professors were significantly more likely to support those who had been divorced than were other scholars. Otherwise, there were no significant effects due to differences in the disciplines. However, there were several nondisciplinary effects. Males were more supportive of hunters and the married, but were less supportive of cohabitating candidates than were women. Individuals teaching at religious schools were less supportive of vegetarians, the divorced, and cohabitators than were other scholars. Older scholars were less willing to hire hunters. Clearly nondisciplinary factors were more predictive of the scholars' responses to groups based on lifestyle than disciplinary factors.[7]

In the areas where this research indicates the most powerful evidence of bias—religious and political characteristics—membership in a certain discipline could be argued to have as powerful an effect on this bias as nondisciplinary factors. However, much of this effect was determined by the relative political conservatism of physicists and the anthropologists' distaste for religious conservatives. It is difficult to argue that these disciplinary effects are more powerful than factors such as sex, teaching at a religious school, and age. But concerning issues of sexuality and lifestyle, those nondisciplinary variables are much more important. Thus, one can tentatively claim that membership in a given discipline affects the type of biases that one has, but as it concerns an overall appreciation of the tendency of scholars to engage in social bias, sex and working at a religious institution are more important. This supports the conclusion in chapter 5 that we are more likely looking at general cultural attitudes within academia toward favored and disfavored groups rather than powerful effects from within certain disciplines. To the degree that there are differences among the disciplines, those differences are likely linked, at least partially, to the contrasting demographical and social elements within the disciplines.

Controlling for Positivity or Negativity Bias

There is a potential problem in using such rating scores to come to the conclusions I have drawn. It is possible that members from certain groups have a generalized positive or negative bias in assessing certain other groups. For example, it may be the case that social scientists are generally more critical of certain social groups than are physical scientists. This critical nature may make them more likely to downgrade members of social groups in general, and it is possible that this tendency has contributed to, or even determined, the higher tendency of those in the social sciences to downgrade religious and political conservatives relative to those in the physical sciences. I have already made the observation that the low scores of the disfavored social groups were further below the midpoint than the scores of the favored social groups were above it. This suggests that scholars may have a general tendency to make negative assessments of social groups. Such a propensity could potentially distort the quantitative findings of the earlier chapters.

The acceptable way of dealing with such a tendency is by making an adjustment of standardizing the bias measure. This is done by calculating the average of all the rating measures for each respondent and then subtracting the rating of a given group by that average to control for the tendency of each respondent to rate all groups high or low. With this new measure, any positive score indicates that the rating of a particular group is higher than the average rating of all groups. A negative score indicates that the rating of a particular group is lower than the average rating of all groups. The results of this adjustment can be seen in appendix table B.

The adjusted ratings in this table reinforce the general findings of chapter 5. For example, we see that the scores assessing Democrats are positive for all of the disciplines, while the scores assessing Republicans are negative for all of the disciplines. The same is respectively true when comparing all of the positive scores for ACLU members to the negative scores of NRA members. This supports the contention that academics have an overall favorable attitude toward progressive political groups and an overall

Appendix Table B. Comparison of Adjusted Means Indicating Whether Belonging to Selected Social Groups Damages or Enhances Acceptance of Job Applicants by Discipline

	Sociology (n = 372)	Political Science (n = 63)	Anthropology (n = 92)	History (n = 73)	Physics (n = 45)	Chemistry (n = 66)	Experimental Biology (n = 55)	Lang. English (n = 69)	Lang. Other (n = 25)	Philosophy (n = 160)
Democrat	.336	.121	.355	.2	.058	.167	.107	.443	.006	.209
Republican	-.5	-.339	-.438	-.306	-.008	-.257	-.202	-.267	-.234	-.295
Green Party	.207	.01	.105	.077	-.008	-.015	-.02	.124	.006	.094
Libertarian	-.312	-.133	-.112	-.169	-.164	-.196	-.093	-.31	-.074	-.223
Communist Party	-.175	-.498	-.188	-.402	-.453	-.242	-.311	-.252	-.154	-.338
NRA	-.68	-.466	-.634	-.443	-.342	-.545	-.438	-.731	-.794	-.41
ACLU	.352	.153	.301	.105	.103	.273	.162	.327	.286	.144
Heterosexual	-.019	.042	-.014	-.019	.169	-.045	-.057	.052	-.034	.000
Homosexual	-.046	.026	.04	-.115	-.253	-.09	-.147	-.006	-.114	-.115
Bisexual	-.067	-.006	-.004	-.169	-.297	-.121	-.166	-.064	-.154	-.151
Transgendered	-.218	-.275	-.08	-.293	-.408	-.333	-.257	-.267	-.154	-.287
Atheist	-.048	-.18	.116	-.128	-.053	.152	-.093	-.035	.006	-.036
Mormon	-.32	-.307	-.417	-.32	-.475	-.272	-.166	-.484	-.274	-.425
Fundamentalist	-.858	-.815	-1.33	-.854	-.875	-.651	-.584	-1.151	-.874	-.971
Evangelical	-.651	-.656	-1.047	-.512	-.475	-.515	-.384	-.745	-.394	-.474
Mainline	-.054	-.006	-.069	.009	.147	-.105	-.075	-.035	-.114	-.05
Catholic	-.073	.058	-.058	.009	.147	-.06	-.075	-.006	-.074	-.028
Muslim	-.067	-.069	.007	-.005	-.208	-.105	-.111	-.035	-.034	-.107
Jewish	-.027	.01	.018	.022	.08	-.015	-.093	.038	-.074	-.028
Vegetarian	-.003	-.037	-.036	-.074	.058	-.015	-.093	.052	-.074	.044
Hunter	-.339	-.148	-.21	-.156	-.142	-.302	-.202	-.339	-.314	-.143
Married	-.027	.026	.007	.009	.214	-.075	-.02	.023	-.074	.029
Divorced	-.078	-.133	-.036	-.074	-.097	-.09	-.111	-.035	-.074	-.064
Cohabitating	-.091	-.085	-.036	-.142	-.208	-.09	-.111	-.107	-.074	-.172
Single-Child	-.065	-.085	.007	-.046	-.164	-.075	-.129	-.064	-.074	-.036
Over 50	-.218	-.26	-.221	-.252	-.364	-.408	-.257	-.209	-.074	-.187
Under 30	-.014	.026	-.047	.009	.014	-.015	-.129	.052	-.034	-.05

unfavorable attitude toward conservative political groups. The differences between the adjusted means of Democrats and those of Republicans are significantly different for every discipline except for physics. The differences between the scores of NRA and ACLU members are significant for all the disciplines. There is little doubt that a real political dynamic is at work in the academics' evaluation of those with differing political beliefs. This finding is not due to any propensity academics have toward positive or negative assessments of groups in general.

Once again, transgendered individuals do not fare as well as the other sexual categories. All of the disciplines have negative scores for those who are transgendered, although in anthropology the score of –.08 indicates a relatively low tendency for a negative assessment of the transgendered in that discipline. However, assessment of transgendered individuals is exceptionally low among the physical sciences, with scores of –.408, –.333, and –.257, respectively, in physics, chemistry, and experimental biology.

We have seen throughout the course of this book that the assessment of conservative Christian groups has produced the highest level of rejection from academics. The adjusted scores for evangelicals are no exception, and range from a "high" of –.394 among non-English language teachers to a low of –1.047 among anthropologists. It gets worse for fundamentalists. Not only is this group's best score the –.584 rating of the experimental biologists, but two disciplines gave fundamentalists scores of less than –1 (anthropology and English language). Philosophers almost make it down to that level with their score of –.971. Five other disciplines have scores lower than –.8 for fundamentalists. Even after adjusting the ratings, the average academic discipline is nearly one entire rating point, on a seven-point scale, lower than the mean in their assessment of fundamentalists. The rejection of fundamentalists and, to a lesser degree, evangelicals is so much greater than the rejection of other social groups that it is easy to believe that a qualitatively greater level of hostility is experienced by religious conservative Christians in comparison to other social groups.

Appendix Table C. Comparison of Adjusted Means Indicating Whether Belonging to Selected Social Groups Damages or Enhances Acceptance of Job Applicants by Type of Discipline

	Social Sciences (n = 228)	Humanities (n = 234)	Physical Sciences (n = 166)
Democrat	.241	.255	.118[d]
Republican	−.369	−.279	−.171[b]
Green Party	.07	.093	−.015[d]
Libertarian	−.136	−.232	−.153
Communist Party	−.342	−.292	−.322
NRA	−.527	−.544	−.455
ACLU	.197	.212	.19
Heterosexual	.000	.011	.009
Homosexual	−.013	−.083	−.153[b]
Bisexual	−.057	−.125	−.183[a]
Transgendered	−.202	−.266	−.328
Atheist	−.044	−.031	.015
Mormon	−.399	−.355	−.292
Fundamentalist	−1.035	−1.01	−.689[bf]
Evangelical	−.768	−.544[a]	−.461[b]
Mainline	−.027	−.053	−.027
Catholic	−.005	−.027	−.009
Muslim	−.018	−.078	−.135[b]
Jewish	.017	−.014	−.015
Vegetarian	−.048	.033[a]	−.021
Hunter	−.176	−.219	−.226
Married	.013	.016	.021
Divorced	−.075	−.057	−.099
Cohabitating	−.084	−.143	−.129
Single-Child	−.035	−.049	−.117[ad]
Over 50	−.241	−.181	−.346[e]
Under 30	−.009	−.019	−.045

[a] Differs from Social Science at .05 level. [b] Differs from Social Science at .001 level. [c] Differs from Social Science at .01 level. [d] Differs from Humanities at .001 level. [e] Differs from Humanities at .05 level. [f] Differs from Humanities at .01 level.

Of course, these results need to be put into the context of the different types of disciplines that I have grouped together. In appendix table C, I once again group the disciplines by category into the social sciences, humanities, and physical sciences. We see a reinforcement of the general findings in chapter 5. For example, those in the physical sciences scored lower than the humanities in their assessment of Democrats and higher than the social sciences in their assessment of Republicans, replicating the finding in chapter 5 concerning the greater acceptance of political conservatism among the physical scientists. The physical scientists were also more supportive of traditional sexual norms than social scientists, having significantly lower levels of acceptance of homosexuals and bisexuals. They also were more accepting of Christian conservatives with their higher level of acceptance of fundamentalists and evangelicals than the social scientists and scholars of humanities. All of these findings follow the basic pattern found in the body of the book whereby those in the physical sciences have less bias against political and religious conservatives but more against sexual progressives than the social scientists and scholars of humanities.

I have dropped sociologists from this analysis so that the sheer number of sociology respondents would not dominate the findings concerning the social scientists. However, the results of the sociologists in appendix table B are similar to the results of the social scientists in appendix table C. Sociologists assessed Democrats more positively and Republicans more negatively than other social scientists. Including sociologists in the sample would likely have differentiated the social scientists even more from the physical scientists. Sociologists' scores assessing fundamentalists and evangelicals were a little higher than the scores of the other social scientists, but were still lower than the scores provided by the physical scientists and humanities scholars for evangelicals. Their scores for homosexuals and bisexuals were lower than those of other social scientists, but still not as low as the scores of the physical scientists. There is little reason to believe that including a representative number of sociologists would alter the results discussed in the preceding paragraph.

Thus the basic findings are upheld even after adjusting for the possibility that academics in certain disciplines may have the propensity to make a negative or positive general assessment of social groups. Even after we control for this propensity, politically and religiously conservative social groups face a generalized disapproval from scholars that their progressive counterparts do not have to deal with.

What about the Response Rate?

Finally, it is time to deal with the survey's low response rate. I bring it up specifically because it is the weakest empirical aspect of this study and I want to tackle it head-on. It is not surprising that there was a low response rate given the population I surveyed. Academics are busy people. I myself tend to turn down opportunities to take online surveys given that I have classes to prepare, papers and books to write, and committees to serve on. Since I had no monetary reward to offer the respondents, there was little I could do to induce them to take my survey unless they were curious about the preliminary results. The fact that sociologists had the highest response rate may attest to the fact that sociologists were more interested in social research and seeing the preliminary results than were those in other disciplines.

But there is another possible reason for this low response rate. I erred on the side of inclusion, and when there was any doubt about whether an academic was qualified, I sent a survey to a potential respondent. So I likely sent quite a few surveys to individuals working in nonacademic settings who perhaps did not fill out their surveys because they felt unqualified to do so. I know that this happened because some of them replied to inform me that this was why they were not returning the survey. I have no way of knowing how many other individuals were in the same situation and did not contact me. This may have accounted for some of the difference in response rates between the physical scientists and the other scholars. The chemists, physicists, and biologists were more likely than other academics to inform me that they worked in a research setting rather than at a college or university. It is likely that the higher propensity of the physical scientists to be in a setting where they were not teaching contributed to their low response rate. So it may be likely that I sent more surveys to unqualified individuals in those fields than in the social sciences and humanities. If this attempt at inclusion accounts for some of the reason why more scholars did not return their surveys, then my reported response rate is probably lower than the actual response rate of qualified respondents. It is unlikely that this actual response rate is high enough to ease the concerns many may have regarding the low response rate, but it is worth observing that the rate may not be as bad as at first it appears.

To understand how to deal with a low response rate, we must first consider why a low response rate is problematic. The results from quantitative surveys depend on the notion that the respondents accurately represent people in the general population. Using probability sampling techniques gives us some confidence that the original sample is representative. A low response rate raises the possibility that the sample is not representative. If 95 percent of the sample population fills out a survey, there cannot be much discrepancy from the original sample. Even if the entire 5 percent who do not fill out the survey are male, which means that the respondents underrepresent men in comparison to the original sample, we still will not have a large sex difference between the original sample and the final respondents. Generally scholars are comfortable with response rates above 50 to 60 percent and are ecstatic if they can get response rates of 75 percent. However, response rates of under 30 percent are looked at with suspicion since such low rates increase the possibility that the respondents are significantly different from the original sample and thus the general population.

I have clearly discussed why a low response rate is problematic so that the reader can make sense of my solution to this problem as well as perceive any weaknesses inherent in my solution. To comprehend this solution we have to go back to figures 3.5, 3.6, 3.7, 3.8, 3.9, and 3.10. In each of those figures, I broke the sample into different subgroups that allowed me to see if there were different types of biases linked to a specific subgroup. There were times I found that some subgroups (e.g., female sociologists, sociologists who study marginalized populations) had stronger biases than other subgroups. But in all subgroups, the basic biases I found among sociologists were documented. For example, in all of the subgroups, the same patterns of sociologists favoring Democrats over Republicans, ACLU members over NRA members, and everyone else over fundamentalists held true. Thus there is little reason to believe that a different, and possibly more accurate, demographic mix of sociologists would alter these basic findings.

Allow me to illustrate this in another way. The scores of male sociologists (m = 3.679) indicate that they were more accepting of Republicans than those under 65 (m = 3.582), whites (m = 3.663), sociologists at doctoral programs (m = 3.655), and sociologists not studying marginalized populations (m = 3.628). It is also clear that male sociologists scored lower than all of these subgroups in their acceptance of Democrats. Yet the scores for Democrats were significantly higher than the scores for Republicans (4.275 versus 3.679) among male sociologists at the .001 level. Male sociologists also scored lower than other subgroups in their support for ACLU members and higher than all other subgroups concerning their support of NRA members. Yet once again, the scores for ACLU members were higher than the scores for NRA members (4.309 versus 3.563) at the .001 level among male sociologists. Finally, male sociologists accepted evangelicals more, and atheists less, than these other subgroups. But they were more likely to accept atheists over evangelicals (3.963 versus 3.578) at the .001 level.[8] So even if I am badly underrepresenting male sociologists, I would still obtain the same basic findings if I did get an accurate sample of respondents. Even if only men answered the survey, the same basic findings would emerge from this work, and though those findings would be less pronounced, they would still be significant. In chapter 5, we saw that for non-sociology academics, the subgroups indicated the same basic pattern of bias in each respective discipline. So this effect is not limited to sociologists, and for all groups surveyed there is no evidence that these findings may be the result of sampling bias. While it is fair to question the strength of these findings, there is no empirical basis for questioning the findings themselves.

Please indulge me as I do a statistical experiment to drive this point home. Pretend that I am a card-carrying ACLU member atheist Democrat sociologist and I want to find some subgroup among sociologists where conservative groups do not face more negative bias than progressive groups. Does such a subgroup exist? Yes. Among sociologists who teach on conservative Protestant campuses, the rating of atheists is 2.8 compared to the 3.33 rating for fundamentalists and the astounding 5.333 rating for evangelicals. One could argue that perhaps this sample underrepresents such sociologists and that there is no real overall bias against fundamentalists and evangelicals relative to other religious groups.[9] My sample only found six sociologists on conservative Protestant campuses, so it is possible that they are underrepresented.

Appendix Table D. Comparison of Means of Atheists, Fundamentalists, and Evangelicals after Increased Weights for Sociologists on Conservative Protestant Campuses

Variables	Atheists	Fundamentalists	Evangelicals
Sociology	3.882 (400)	3.204[c] (416)	3.688[b] (413)
Political Science	3.833 (66)	3.292[b] (65)	3.391[a] (64)
Anthropology	4.139 (101)	2.64[c] (100)	2.91[c] (100)
History	3.913 (80)	3.15[c] (80)	3.532[b] (79)
Physics	4.0 (48)	3.18[c] (50)	3.56[a] (50)
Chemistry	4.219 (73)	3.361[c] (72)	3.507[c] (73)
Experimental Biology	3.981 (54)	3.481[c] (54)	3.685[b] (54)
Philosophy	3.993 (151)	2.987[c] (153)	3.516[c] (.153)
Language	4.037 (108)	2.889[c] (108)	3.321[c] (109)

[a] Differs from atheist at .05 level, [b] differs from atheist at .01 level, [c] differs from atheist at .001 level.

How badly might they be underrepresented? In my original data, sociologists at conservative Protestant campuses made up 1.3 percent of the sample. What if in reality they are twice that amount or three times that amount? Would it make a difference in the final results? Let us make sure they are fully represented. I will weight the responses of sociologists at conservative Protestant campuses so that their responses are multiplied twelve times more than in the normal sample. They now make up almost 16 percent of the sample. I do not actually believe that one out of every six sociologists works on a conservative Protestant campus, but these weights ensure that they will not be underrepersented. Given such weights, we can see in table D what the results would be for the sample as we look at the ratings of atheists, fundamentalists, and evangelicals. Do the weights affect the results? Barely. The difference between evangelicals and atheists decreases to the point that it is only significant at the .01 level, but otherwise the same basic results found in earlier chapters are substantiated. Even if I underrepresented what may be the most religiously conservative group of sociologists by a factor of 12, the same basic findings are undeterred. What about the other disciplines? As you can see in table D, the acceptance of atheists is significantly higher than the acceptance of fundamentalists and evangelicals for all other academic disciplines.[10] Even if my sample was so distorted that I underrepresented professors on conservative Protestant campuses by a factor of 12, after correcting for this distortion I still have the same basic findings. This is directly due to the power of those findings across all demographic and social groups.

No matter what the social or demographic makeup of the original sample, the same basic pattern of bias is likely to be found. As I stated before, this research represents the best current evidence concerning the absence or presence of bias within academia. Naturally one can conceive of future studies that will add to this evidence, and some of those studies may be able to incorporate response rates that provide us with more confidence in the strength of their findings. But until that happens, the critics of this current research must do more than point to its low response rates to dismiss these findings. They must also articulate why these low response rates invalidate the basic findings of this book, even though all subgroups of academics also exhibit those findings. An inability to do this indicates that criticism of low response rates is not a simple concern about inaccurate methodology but indicates a potentially powerful unwillingness to accept the implications of these findings. A truly insightful response to these results would be to construct a new research design able to overcome the weaknesses of this particular study that could either support the presence of these biases or refute the notion that the social biases of academics play a role in the formation of scientific inquiry.

Supplemental Material

Supplemental Table 5.1. Breakdown of Whether Belonging to Selected Social Groups Enhances or Damages Job Applicants by Discipline

	% Enhances Repub.	% Damages Repub.	% Enhances NRA	% Damages NRA	% Enhances ACLU	% Damages ACLU	% Enhances Fund.	% Damages Fund.
Political Science	0.0%	15.4%	1.5%	29.2%	18.5%	4.6%	1.5%	41.5%
Anthropology	1.0%	32.3%	3.0%	44.0%	24.0%	1.0%	1.0%	67.3%
History	6.2%	22.5%	3.8%	30.8%	16.5%	3.8%	1.3%	52.5%
Physics	8.0%	10.0%	4.0%	30.0%	20.4%	8.2%	4.0%	52.0%
Chemistry	1.4%	16.4%	0.0%	36.0%	22.2%	0.0%	0.0%	38.4%
Experimental Biology	0.0%	10.9%	0.0%	29.1%	20.0%	3.6%	0.0%	36.4%
Language – English	1.3%	26.9%	2.5%	43.0%	30.4%	3.8%	0.0%	71.4%
Language – Non-English	0.0%	16.1%	0.0%	39.3%	21.4%	0.0%	0.0%	41.9%
Philosophy	.7%	23.5%	2.0%	31.4%	21.1%	4.6%	0.0%	54.2%
Sociology	.9%	28.7%	1.9%	40.4%	29.6%	2.1%	.8%	49.2%

Supplemental Table 5.1. Breakdown of Whether Belonging to Selected Social Groups Enhances or Damages Job Applicants by Discipline (*continued*)

	% Enhances Evangel.	% Damages Evangel.	% Enhances Mormon	% Damages Mormon	% Enhances Atheist	% Damages Atheist	% Enhances Muslim	% Damages Muslim
Political Science	1.6%	39.1%	0.0%	21.5%	3.0%	10.6%	4.6%	7.7%
Anthropology	2.0%	58.8%	2.0%	34.3%	8.9%	0.0%	2.0%	1.0%
History	3.8%	29.1%	0.0%	20.0%	5.0%	8.8%	7.5%	2.5%
Physics	4.0%	38.0%	0.0%	28.6%	10.4%	8.3%	2.0%	14.0%
Chemistry	31.1%	0.0%	1.4%	20.5%	13.7%	0.0%	0.0%	2.7%
Experimental Biology	21.8%	0.0%	0.0%	9.1%	3.6%	3.6%	0.0%	3.6%
Language – English	1.3%	52.6%	0.0%	34.6%	6.5%	3.9%	9.1%	3.9%
Language – Non-English	3.2%	25.8%	0.0%	16.1%	3.2%	0.0%	3.2%	0.0%
Philosophy	3.3%	34.0%	1.9%	29.2%	9.9%	7.9%	7.8%	7.2%
Sociology	3.0%	38.8%	.6%	15.5%	6.4%	3.5%	6.2%	4.8%

Supplemental Table 5.2. Breakdown of Sex and Teaching at a Religious College or University by Discipline

	Male	Female	Secular	Religious
Political Science	60.0% (42)*	40.0% (28)	83.8% (57)	16.2% (11)
Anthropology	46.2% (49)	53.8% (57)	94.0% (94)	6.0% (6)
History	61.7% (50)	38.3% (31)	75.0% (57)	25.0% (19)
Physics	86.0% (43)	14.0% (7)	90.2% (46)	9.8% (5)
Chemistry	73.4% (58)	26.6% (21)	87.5% (70)	12.5% (10)
Experimental Biology	61.4% (35)	38.6% (22)	88.5% (46)	11.5% (6)
Language – English	65.1% (54)	34.9% (29)	81.3% (65)	18.8% (15)
Language – Non-English	18.2% (6)	81.8% (27)	91.2% (31)	8.8% (3)
Philosophy	68.8% (110)	31.3% (50)	77.6% (121)	22.4% (35)
Sociology	52.5% (203)	47.5% (184)	86.7% (327)	13.3% (50)

*Number of respondents in parentheses.

Supplemental Table 5.3. Comparison of Means Indicating Whether Belonging to Selected Social Groups Damages or Enhances Acceptance of Job Applicants by Discipline by Sex

	Political Science, Male (n = 42)	Political Science, Female (n = 28)	Anthropology, Male (n = 49)	Anthropology, Female (n = 57)	History, Male (n = 50)
Democrat	4.293	4.083	4.432	4.463	4.06
Republican	3.756	3.667	3.574	3.523	3.96
Green Party	4.098	4.0	4.114	4.226	4.041
Libertarian	3.927	3.917	3.932	3.963	3.98
Communist Party	3.275	3.917[b]	3.727	3.981	3.367
NRA	3.659	3.458	3.267	3.472	3.796
ACLU	4.22	4.167	4.378	4.352	4.1
Heterosexual	4.071	4.208	4.044	4.0	4.02
Homosexual	4.0	4.095	4.043	4.163	3.82
Bisexual	4.048	3.917	4.0	4.073	3.76
Transgendered	3.667	3.708	3.783	4.091[a]	3.617
Atheist	3.810	3.875	4.217	4.074	3.8
Mormon	3.707	3.667	3.543	3.545	3.7
Fundamentalist	3.244	3.375	2.636	2.655	3.24
Evangelical	3.35	3.458	3.111	2.759	3.7
Mainline	4.024	4.083	3.935	3.945	4.1
Catholic	4.146	4.083	3.957	3.964	4.14
Muslim	3.951	3.917	3.978	4.074*	4.02
Jewish	4.024	4.0	3.978	4.055	4.08
Vegetarian	4.048	4.0	4.0	4.0	3.918
Hunter	3.857	3.833	3.822	3.782	4.08
Married	4.048	4.125	4.044	4.036	4.122
Divorced	3.881	3.958	4.0	4.0	3.959
Cohabiting	3.905	3.958	4.0	4.0	3.82
Single-Child	3.976	3.958	4.022	4.055	3.98
Over 50	3.762	3.833	3.674	3.982[a]	3.86
Under 30	4.024	4.12	3.957	3.964	4.08

* Differs from male at .1 level, [a] differs from male at .05 level, [b] differs from male at .01 level, [c] differs from male at .001 level.

Supplemental Table 5.3. Comparison of Means Indicating Whether Belonging to Selected Social Groups Damages or Enhances Acceptance of Job Applicants by Discipline by Sex (*continued*)

History, Female (n = 31)	Physics, Male (n = 43)	Physics, Female (n = 7)	Chemistry, Male (n = 58)	Chemistry, Female (n = 21)	Experimental Biology, Male (n = 35)
4.633[b]	4.025	4.286	4.264	4.053	4.19
3.333[b]	4.05	3.857	3.755	3.895	3.848
4.31*	4.0	4.143	4.094	4.053	3.97
3.586[a]	3.875	3.714	3.811	4.056*	3.938
4.0[b]	3.538	3.286	3.827	3.899	3.788
3.069[b]	3.675	3.286	3.545	3.421	3.606
4.172	4.103	4.143	4.327	4.211	4.188
4.0	4.275	4.0	4.074	4.0	4.03
4.033	3.769	4.0	3.981	4.0	3.879
3.967	3.75	3.857	3.962	3.947	3.848
3.867	3.625	3.714	3.679	3.842	3.697
4.1[a]	4.026	3.857	4.264	4.105	4.03
3.767	3.59	3.429	3.755	3.737	3.909
3.0	3.25	2.857	3.292	2.64	3.455
3.241*	3.65	3.143	3.481	3.556	3.697
3.933	4.2	4.0	3.981	3.947	4.0
4.0	4.2	4.0	4.019	4.0	4.0
4.1	3.825	3.857	3.962	4.0	3.939
4.067	4.125	4.0	4.075	4.0	3.97
4.067	4.1	4.0	4.019	4.0	3.969
3.567[b]	3.925	3.571	3.796	3.789	3.824
4.0*	4.375	4.143	4.0	4.0	4.091
4.0	4.0	3.857	3.981	4.0	3.939
4.0*	3.9	3.857	3.981	4.0	3.939
4.033	3.95	4.0	4.0	4.0	3.909
3.7	3.732	3.714	3.623	3.842	3.667
3.967	4.122	4.143	4.075	4.056	3.97

* Differs from male at .1 level, [a] differs from male at .05 level, [b] differs from male at .01 level, [c] differs from male at .001 level.

Supplemental Table 5.3. Comparison of Means Indicating Whether Belonging to Selected Social Groups Damages or Enhances Acceptance of Job Applicants by Discipline by Sex (*continued*)

	Experimental Biology, Female (*n* = 22)	Language, Male (*n* = 35)	Language, Female (*n* = 82)	Philosophy, Male (*n* = 110)	Philosophy, Female (*n* = 50)
Democrat	4.182	4.452	4.377	4.179	4.404[a]
Republican	3.905	3.677	3.688	3.774	3.532[a]
Green Party	4.19*	4.129	4.211	4.123	4.255
Libertarian	4.048	3.613	3.947[a]	3.802	3.638
Communist Party	3.714	3.742	3.89	3.613	3.872*
NRA	3.65	3.452	3.213	3.623	3.447
ACLU	4.368	4.258	4.373	4.143	4.319
Heterosexual	4.0	4.194	4.039	4.057	4.064
Homosexual	4.0	3.903	4.079*	3.821	4.174[b]
Bisexual	4.0	3.903	4.013	3.792	4.128
Transgendered	4.0*	3.645	3.934*	3.686	4.089[b]
Atheist	3.905	4.129	4.0	3.924	4.152
Mormon	3.905	3.419	3.649	3.63	3.589
Fundamentalist	3.524	2.714	2.937	3.057	2.83
Evangelical	3.667	3.355	3.299	3.651	3.213[a]
Mainline	4.0	3.968	3.96	4.0	3.978
Catholic	4.0	4.032	4.013	4.038	3.957
Muslim	4.0	3.839	4.092[b]	3.887	4.064
Jewish	4.0	4.0	4.092	3.953	4.106
Vegetarian	4.0	4.096	4.066	4.076	4.149
Hunter	3.952	3.806	3.649	3.876	3.809
Married	4.0	4.129	4.039	4.093	4.0*
Divorced	4.0	4.0	4.039	3.944	4.0*
Cohabitating	4.0	3.839	4.039	3.776	3.979*
Single-Child	4.0	4.0	4.013	3.991	4.043
Over 50	4.048[a]	3.806	3.961	3.879	3.787
Under 30	3.905	4.226	4.04	3.991	4.0

* Differs from male at .1 level, [a] differs from male at .05 level, [b] differs from male at .01 level, [c] differs from male at .001 level.

Supplemental Table 5.4. Comparison of Means Indicating Whether Belonging to Selected Social Groups Damages or Enhances Acceptance of Job Applicants by Discipline by Whether at Religious School

	Political Science, Secular ($n = 57$)	Political Science, Religious ($n = 11$)	Anthropology, Secular ($n = 94$)	Anthropology, Religious ($n = 6$)	History, Secular ($n = 50$)
Democrat	4.189	4.182	4.432	4.8	4.286
Republican	3.736	3.727	3.523	3.8	3.696
Green Party	4.075	3.818*	4.17	4.4	4.196
Libertarian	3.943	3.818	3.955	4.0	3.873
Communist Party	3.577	3.182	3.841	4.2	3.571
NRA	3.585	3.727	3.348	3.4	3.473
ACLU	4.245	4.091	4.364	4.667	4.182
Heterosexual	4.056	4.455[a]	4.022	4.0	4.0
Homosexual	4.093	3.636[a]	4.122	4.0	3.982
Bisexual	4.056	3.455[b]	4.044	4.0	3.893
Transgendered	3.741	3.091[a]	3.944	4.0	3.815
Atheist	3.963	3.182[c]	4.135	4.333	4.036
Mormon	3.792	3.273[a]	3.511	3.667	3.839
Fundamentalist	3.208	3.909*	2.584	3.0	3.125
Evangelical	3.34	3.8	2.889	3.0	3.418
Mainline	4.038	4.091	3.933	4.0	3.982*
Catholic	4.075	4.364*	3.956	4.0	4.018
Muslim	4.0	3.636[a]	4.011	4.333[b]	4.036
Jewish	4.057	3.818	4.0	4.033	4.054
Vegetarian	4.019	4.091	4.0	4.0	3.964
Hunter	3.87	3.909	3.8	3.833	3.875
Married	4.074	4.091	4.045	4.0	4.036
Divorced	3.926	3.818	4.0	4.0	4.0
Cohabitating	4.0	3.545[c]	4.0	4.0	3.982
Single-Child	3.963	4.0	4.044	4.0	3.947
Over 50	3.759	3.909	3.811	4.167	3.893
Under 30	4.055	4.0	3.922	4.5[b]	3.982

* Differs from secular at .1 level, [a] differs from secular at .05 level, [b] differs from secular at .01 level, [c] differs from secular at .001 level.

Supplemental Table 5.4. Comparison of Means Indicating Whether Belonging to Selected Social Groups Damages or Enhances Acceptance of Job Applicants by Discipline by Whether at Religious School (*continued*)

	History, Religious (*n* = 20)	Physics, Secular (*n* = 47)	Physics, Religious (*n* = 5)	Chemists, Secular (*n* = 71)	Chemists, Religious (*n* = 10)
Democrat	4.158	4.093	4.0	4.281	4.0
Republican	3.842	3.977	4.0	3.797	4.0
Green Party	3.944	4.023	4.0	4.094	4.0
Libertarian	3.833	3.814	4.0	3.873	3.889
Communist Party	3.682	3.548	3.0	3.857	3.778
NRA	3.722	3.558	4.0	3.477	3.889
ACLU	3.895	4.143	3.8	4.375	4.0
Heterosexual	4.053	4.233	4.0	4.062	4.0
Homosexual	3.632[a]	3.762	3.8	4.015	3.75[a]
Bisexual	3.632	3.721	3.8	3.985	3.75
Transgendered	3.421	3.628	3.4	3.769	3.375
Atheist	3.526[b]	4.024	3.75	4.215	4.25
Mormon	3.421[b]	3.476	4.0	3.797	3.75
Fundamentalist	3.158	3.07	4.0	3.375	3.625
Evangelical	3.842	3.512	4.0	3.523	3.75
Mainline	4.211	4.163	4.0	3.985	3.875
Catholic	4.316[a]	4.163	4.0	4.015	4.0
Muslim	4.105	3.814	3.8	4.0	3.75
Jewish	4.158	4.093	4.2	4.062	4.0
Vegetarian	4.0	4.07	4.0	4.046	4.0
Hunter	3.947	3.907	4.2	3.889	3.754
Married	4.211[a]	4.279	4.6	4.0	4.0
Divorced	3.895*	3.977	4.0	3.985	4.0
Cohabitating	3.597[c]	3.884	3.8	3.985	4.0
Single-Child	4.018	3.93	3.8	3.984	4.125
Over 50	3.474[b]	3.659	3.8	3.656	3.889
Under 30	4.211*	4.136	4.2	4.063	4.111

* Differs from secular at .1 level, [a] differs from secular at .05 level, [b] differs from secular at .01 level, [c] differs from secular at .001 level.

Supplemental Table 5.4. Comparison of Means Indicating Whether Belonging to Selected Social Groups Damages or Enhances Acceptance of Job Applicants by Discipline by Whether at Religious School (*continued*)

Experimental Biologists, Secular ($n = 48$)	Experimental Biologists, Religious ($n = 7$)	Language, Secular ($n = 98$)	Language, Religious ($n = 18$)	Philosophy, Secular ($n = 124$)	Philosophy, Religious ($n = 35$)
4.4	4.178	4.404	4.389	4.259	4.212
3.844	4.0	3.652	3.833	3.664	3.818
4.022	4.4*	4.182	4.222	4.19	4.061
3.978	4.0	3.864	3.778	3.733	3.788
3.8	3.4	3.845	3.833	3.836	3.152[c]
3.622	3.4	3.345	3.167	3.526	3.697
4.267	4.0	4.356	4.167	4.278	3.939[a]
4.022	4.0	4.034	4.333[a]	4.043	4.121
3.978	3.4[b]	4.057	3.833*	4.043	3.529[c]
3.978	3.2[c]	4.011	3.778*	4.034	3.394[c]
3.889	3.0[b]	3.909	3.5[a]	3.938	3.333[c]
4.0	3.8	4.091	3.778[a]	4.167	3.394[c]
3.911	4.0	3.596	3.611	3.655	3.412
3.4	4.0	2.83	3.167	3.017	2.909
3.667	4.0	3.233	3.824[a]	3.379	4.061[b]
4.0	4.0	3.943	4.059	3.957	4.125[a]
4.0	4.0	4.011	4.059	3.983	4.125
3.978	3.8*	4.068	3.722[b]	4.043	3.576[b]
4.022	4.0	4.012	3.833[a]	4.06	3.788
3.978	4.0	4.096	4.066	4.148	3.939[a]
3.844	4.0	3.719	3.667	3.826	3.939
4.022	4.4[b]	4.045	4.167	4.034	4.176[a]
3.978	3.8*	4.034	4.0	3.991	3.853[c]
3.978	3.8*	4.034	3.722	3.991	3.294[c]
3.933	4.0	4.011	4.0	4.017	3.971
3.822	3.8	3.955	3.722*	3.853	3.824
3.978	3.8	4.057	4.278	3.957	4.118[a]

* Differs from secular at .1 level, [a] differs from secular at .05 level, [b] differs from secular at .01 level, [c] differs from secular at .001 level.

Supplemental Table 5.5. Percent of Each Group That States That Knowing That an Applicant Is a Fundamentalist Is Extremely Damaging to Their Ability to Support That Person's Job Candidacy

Discipline	Percent that states it is extremely damaging if candidate is a fundamentalist	Approximate probability that any given member of the discipline possesses such animosity toward fundamentalists
Sociology	7.8	1 in 12
Political Science	10.8	1 in 9
Anthropology	22.8	1 in 4.5
History	8.8	1 in 11
Physics	14.0	1 in 7
Chemistry	5.5	1 in 18
Experimental Biology	1.8	1 in 55
English Language	9.1	1 in 11
Non-English Language	12.9	1 in 8
Philosophy	13.1	1 in 8

Collegiality Survey

1. The following is a list of traits that most people find enjoyable. Please rank how desirable is each trait to you for a colleague in your department.

    1—Not Desirable at All

    2—Fairly Desirable

    3—Somewhat Desirable

    4—Very Desirable

    5—Extremely Desirable

Kindness_____

Patience_____

Caring_____

Sense of Humor_____

Friendly_____

Tolerant_____

Generous_____

Communicative_____

Easygoing_____

Forgiving_____

Teachable_____

Humble_____

Compliant_____

Selfless_____

Gentle_____

Gives Compliments_____

Honest_____

Dependable_____

Trustworthy_____

Hard-Working_____

2. The following is a list of traits that most people find distasteful. Please rank how distasteful is each trait to you for a colleague in your department.

    1—Not Distasteful at All

    2—Fairly Distasteful

    3—Somewhat Distasteful

    4—Very Distasteful

    5—Extremely Distasteful

Hot Temper_____

Arrogant_____

Sarcastic_____

Humorless_____

Shyness_____

Discourteous_____

Greedy_____

Irritable_____

Talkative_____

Lazy_____

Perfectionist_____

Narrow-Minded_____

Uncooperative_____

Bossy_____

Gossip_____

Argumentative_____

Loud_____

Dishonest_____

Rude_____

Undependable_____

3. Please evaluate each statement as it concerns you as it concerns the collegiality of the faculty you work with. If you are not part of a faculty on an academic campus, then evaluate the social atmosphere in your workplace. On a scale of 1 to 7, where 1 indicates that the statement is absolutely not true, 4 indicates that the statement is equally true and untrue, and 7 indicates that the statement is absolutely true.

Absolutely Untrue   **Equally True and Untrue**   **Absolutely True**

The people I work with tend to like each other

1   2   3   4   5   6   7

There is little or no interpersonal conflict at work

1   2   3   4   5   6   7

The people at work tend to socialize with each other outside of work

1   2   3   4   5   6   7

People at work are very tolerant of coworkers who differ from them

1   2   3   4   5   6   7

People at work are willing to help each other out

1   2   3   4   5   6   7

Everyone at work feels comfortable with each other

1   2   3   4   5   6   7

4. Assume that your facility is hiring a new professor. Below is a list of possible characteristics of this new hire. Many of them are characteristics that you can not directly inquire of prospective candidates. However, if you were able to learn of these characteristics about a candidate, would that make you more or less likely to support their hire? Please rate your attitude on a scale in which 1 indicates that the characteristic greatly damages your support to hire a candidate, 4 is that the characteristic does not make a difference, and 7 indicates that the characteristic greatly enhances your support to hire the candidate. If you do not understand the characteristic, then please indicate such with "n/a."

1—Extremely damages support of candidate

2—Moderately damages support of candidate

3—Slightly damages support of candidate

4—Does not make a difference

5—Slightly enhances support of candidate

6—Moderately enhances support of candidate

7—Extremely enhances support of candidate

8—N/A

The candidate is a Democrat_____

The candidate is a Republican_____

The candidate is a Green Party member_____

The candidate is a Libertarian_____

The candidate is a Communist party member_____

The candidate is a member of the NRA_____

The candidate is a member of the ACLU_____

The candidate is heterosexual_____

The candidate is homosexual_____

The candidate is bisexual_____

The candidate is transgendered_____

The candidate is an atheist_____

The candidate is a Mormon_____

The candidate is a Fundamentalist_____

The candidate is an Evangelical Protestant_____

The candidate is a Mainline Protestant_____

The candidate is a Catholic_____

The candidate is Muslim_____

The candidate is Jewish_____

The candidate is a vegetarian_____

The candidate likes to hunt_____

The candidate is married_____

The candidate is divorced_____

The candidate is in a cohabitating relationship_____

The candidate is single with children_____

The candidate is over 50 years old_____

The candidate is under 30 years old_____

5. *The following is a list of possible ways that a department can improve the collegiality among the faculty. Please place a check by the suggestion that you think is most helpful.*

_____Have more social functions between faculty members.

_____More interpersonal training for faculty members to help them improve their relationships with each other.

_____More collaborative projects between faculty members.

_____Reduce the use of titles that denote rank (Assistant Professor, Full Professor, etc.).

_____A more democratic organization of the department.

_____A chair who is supportive of creating a more collegial atmosphere.

_____Place the offices of the faculty closer together to facilitate interaction.

6. *The same list in the first question [the same list from question 5] is included in this question. Please place a check by the suggestion that you feel is the second most important way a department can become more collegial.*

_____Have more social functions between faculty members.

_____More interpersonal training for faculty members to help them improve their relationships with each other.

_____More collaborative projects between faculty members.

_____Reduce the use of titles that denote rank (Assistant Professor, Full Professor, etc.).

_____A more democratic organization of the department.

_____A chair who is supportive of creating a more collegial atmosphere.

_____Place the offices of the faculty closer together to facilitate interaction.

7. *The same list in the first question [the same list from questions 5 and 6] is included in this question. Please place a check by the suggestion that you feel is the third most important way a department can become more collegial.*

_____Have more social functions between faculty members.

_____More interpersonal training for faculty members to help them improve their relationships with each other.

_____More collaborative projects between faculty members.

_____Reduce the use of titles that denote rank (Assistant Professor, Full Professor, etc.).

_____A more democratic organization of the department.

_____A chair who is supportive of creating a more collegial atmosphere.

_____Place the offices of the faculty closer together to facilitate interaction.

8. *Are there any suggestions that you have for improving the collegiality of a department that were not included in these questions?*

9. *What is your age? (Circle one)*

Below 25	36–40	51–55	66–70
26–30	41–45	56–60	Over 70
31–35	46–50	61–65	

10. *What is your sex? (Circle one)*

Female   Male

11. *What is your race? (Circle one)*

White	Black	Latino
Asian	Native American	Middle Eastern
Multiracial	Other	

12. *Highest Level of Education? (Circle one)*

Bachelor's Degree   Master's Degree   Doctorate

13. *What sort of place do you work at? (Circle one)*

Self-Employed	College/University with M.A. but no Ph.D. Program	Your own private business
Federal or State Government		In a private business where you are not the owner
Private Industry	4-year College/University w/o grad program	
Private Foundation, Institute, or Charitable Org.	Community college	Other
College/University with Ph.D. Program	Other academic setting	

14. *If you teach at a college or university, then what is the religious orientation of that college or university? (Circle one)*

Public nonreligious school	Mainline Protestant	Jewish
	Conservative Protestant	Other
Private nonreligious school	Catholic	

15. Please list your top sociological research and/or teaching area. (Circle one)

Aging and the Life Course

Alcohol, Drugs, and Tobacco

Animals and Society

Asia and Asian America

Children and Youth

Collective Behavior and Social Movements

Communication and Information Technologies

Community and Urban Sociology

Comparative and Historical Sociology

Crime, Law, and Deviance

Culture

Economic Sociology

Education

Emotions

Environment and Technology

Ethnomethodology and Conversation Analysis

Evolution and Sociology

Family

History of Sociology

International Migration

Labor and Labor Movements

Latino/a Sociology

Law

Marxist Sociology

Mathematical Sociology

Medical Sociology

Mental Health

Methodology

Organizations, Occupations, and Work

Peace, War, and Social Conflict

Political Economy of the World-System

Political Sociology

Population

Race, Gender, and Class

Racial and Ethnic Minorities

Rationality and Society

Religion

Science, Knowledge, and Technology

Sex and Gender

Sexualities

Social Psychology

Sociological Practice

Teaching and Learning

Theory

16. Please list your second most important sociological research and/or teaching area. (Circle one)

Aging and the Life Course

Alcohol, Drugs, and Tobacco

Animals and Society

Asia and Asian America

Children and Youth

Collective Behavior and Social Movements

Communication and Information Technologies

Community and Urban Sociology

Comparative and Historical Sociology

Crime, Law, and Deviance

Culture

Economic Sociology

Education

Emotions

Environment and Technology

Ethnomethodology and Conversation Analysis

Evolution and Sociology

Family

History of Sociology

International Migration

Labor and Labor Movements

Latino/a Sociology

Law

Marxist Sociology

Mathematical Sociology

Medical Sociology

Mental Health

Methodology

Organizations, Occupations, and Work

Peace, War, and Social Conflict

Political Economy of the World-System

Political Sociology

Population

Race, Gender, and Class

Racial and Ethnic Minorities

Rationality and Society

Religion

Science, Knowledge, and Technology

Sex and Gender

Sexualities

Social Psychology

Sociological Practice

Teaching and Learning

Theory

17. Please list your third most important sociological research and/or teaching area. (Circle one)

Aging and the Life Course

Alcohol, Drugs, and Tobacco

Animals and Society

Asia and Asian America

Children and Youth

Collective Behavior and Social Movements

Communication and Information Technologies

Community and Urban Sociology

Comparative and Historical Sociology

Crime, Law, and Deviance

Culture

Economic Sociology

Education

Emotions

Environment and Technology

Ethnomethodology and Conversation Analysis

Evolution and Sociology

Family

History of Sociology

International Migration

Labor and Labor Movements

Latino/a Sociology

Law

Marxist Sociology

Mathematical Sociology

Medical Sociology

Mental Health

Methodology

Organizations, Occupations, and Work

Peace, War, and Social
Conflict

Political Economy of the
World-System

Political Sociology

Population

Race, Gender, and Class

Racial and Ethnic
Minorities

Rationality and Society

Religion

Science, Knowledge, and
Technology

Sex and Gender

Sexualities

Social Psychology

Sociological Practice

Teaching and Learning

Theory

Notes

Chapter 1

1   Of course, one can be both a drug addict and a professor. But I suggest that a person's actions as a professor likely add more positive social good than one's actions as a drug addict.

2   Obviously, individuals with little or no religious faith are going to be less likely to value the importance of maintaining a religious culture. However, they may have other social or political cultural aspects they desire to be maintained in their family. One can easily conceptualize a politically progressive atheist who becomes just as upset at his or her child marrying a devotee of Rush Limbaugh as the person of faith becomes with a child marrying a nonbeliever.

3   For example, work based on the authoritarian personality (Adorno, Frenkel-Brunswik, Levinson, & Sanford, 1950) indicated that political conservatives and the highly religious are less tolerant. However, this work has generally used members of progressive social groups as potential targets of such prejudice. Thus measures of right-wing authoritarianism (Altermeyer, 1968) indicate potential hostility against atheists, feminists, and homosexuals, but not against fundamentalists, Republicans, and hunters. In such research potential progressive bias against conservative social groups may not be captured.

4   Some academics freely admit that their conclusions are shaped by their own personal biases. This can be seen in postmodern academic literature (Lyotard, 1984; Rorty, 1994; Seidman & Wagner, 1992)

that acknowledges the social and political biases of researchers and removes the "burden" of attempting to be objective.

5   It should also be noted that this anthropologist has a natural incentive not to find evidence of such bias. Evidence of bias would cast doubt on the research of anthropology in general, which could result in a loss of prestige for the anthropologist. Likewise scientists who construct measurements for detecting bias within their field, or even in science in general, possess motivation to find no bias in the field. It is unlikely that such scientists would overtly distort findings, but it is not unreasonable to assert that such individuals may be less able to construct adequate measures for assessing bias due to their own belief in the value of science.

6   A future study ideally would conduct in-depth quantitative and qualitative analysis of several disciplines as a logical extension of this work. However, the strength of the quantitative findings of the disciplines examined in this work indicates that there is little chance that including more respondents or qualitative assessments of scholars other than sociologists will produce results distinct from these current findings. Nevertheless, such an analysis may be useful in illustrating the process by which social biases develop among academics and the degree of those biases in different types of academic disciplines.

7   The term *fundamentalist* throughout will refer to a particular type of Protestant Christian that originated in the early twentieth century.

8   I discovered in my dissertation (1994) that individuals from the South and from lower socioeconomic status are underrepresented among sociologists.

Chapter 2

1   In fact, sociology has been called a multiparadigmal discipline because of the competing paradigms that reside within it.

2   That is, if objective reality is something that truly exists. Theories of postmodernism contend that objective reality is a myth in and of itself. I tend to resist such reasoning because I find no need for scientific work if there is not a reality out there that needs to be discovered.

3   It has been argued that the Catholic hierarchy was less upset about the claims Galileo made and more concerned with his unwillingness to admit to the weaknesses of his claims (Woods, 2005). Such an argument may put the Catholic church in a little better light, but it does not detract from my general contention that the Catholic church was restrictive to certain forms of scientific inquiry. This historical event

still serves as an illustration of early conflict between science and Christianity.

4   This is not to state that groups that do have small numbers of highly educated individuals should be excluded. The Hmong tend to have lower levels of educational attainment, but no one seriously believes that they should be excluded from participation in science. Members of this ethnic group that do obtain the necessary levels of education should be allowed to engage in scientific inquiry. It is only if a group is inherently defined by having lower levels of educational attainment, such as high school dropouts, that such limitations apply.

Chapter 3

1   The demographic transition is the process by which societies move from having high birth and death rates to having low birth and death rates. It generally happens with a fall in the death rate, which creates high population growth, to be followed by a lowering of the birth rate as societies adjust to new technologies and mores.

2   Some may argue that this design uses an unwarranted level of deception. It is unlikely that I would obtain an honest assessment by directly asking scholars about their social biases. Nevertheless, I challenge the assertion that this method involves deception. The social biases that academics bring into their work clearly affect the collegiality of that environment. This is especially the case for members of disfavored social groups. Obviously I put a lot more emphasis on one part of the survey and look at a limited aspect of collegiality, but this emphasis on only a few survey questions does not mean that I am totally ignoring issues that affect collegiality in academia.

3   Whenever possible I will illustrate the results with graphs rather than detail tables.

4   This likely underestimates the true response rate, as several individuals e-mailed me and stated that they did not feel qualified to fill out the survey since they were not a faculty member at a college or university. It is impossible to determine how many others also decided that they were not qualified to fill out the survey and thus chose to ignore it.

5   It is reasonable to ask whether the score of 4 could also indicate no knowledge about the group; however, my uncertainty of this assertion led to my decision to exclude these individuals from analysis. To be on the safe side, however, I also ran the analysis with those indicating no knowledge scored as a 4. At no point did the inclusion of these individuals alter the basic results of this research.

6   It may be argued that I am only assessing an initial reaction to a survey and not real bias for or against a given social group. Most respondents may have only given themselves a few moments of thought before answering the question rather than deliberately considering their own social bias. Yet given the propensity of the highly educated to exhibit a social desirability effect, it is unlikely that many of them would indicate a bias if allowed a considerable amount of time to think through such a question. Thus the quick reactions to these questions are likely a better indicator of an academic's basic biases than a more deliberate reaction. Such basic biases can easily influence the reaction a scholar has toward members of a disfavored group whether the scholar realizes he or she has the bias or not.

7   This is operationalized by summing the percentages of sociologists who state that membership in a given social group either extremely, moderately, or slightly damages their support of the candidate. So it is not the case that nearly half of all sociologists completely reject fundamentalists, but about half of all respondents do punish, to some degree, a prospective fundamentalist candidate for his or her faith.

8   Once again, these figures are from summing up the slightly, moderately, and extremely agree categories.

9   It might have been possible to construct a question with less of a social desirability effect by asking the respondent if he or she thought that most members of the department would have a problem with that candidate. In such a question, the respondent would be able to attribute any bias that he or she might have to others. However, such a question does not directly get at the potential bias of the respondent, which is the focus of this work. A person who is unbiased may truly believe that others in his or her department are biased, and thus the question would not always determine whether an individual is intolerant of certain social groups. There would be no way to determine what percentage of the respondents indicated the perceived bias of the department versus the percentage that indicated their own personal bias. Thus I believe the original question is the best approach. Because of the possibility of a social desirability effect, the original question likely underestimates the degree of bias that exists in academia, but this only strengthens the general findings of this research.

10   Individuals who studied marginalized populations were less likely to state that none of the characteristics mattered to them. I cannot determine why this is the case with this quantitative work since I did not ask individuals why they decided to accept or reject certain groups. But future research may be able to determine why the study of marginalized groups may lead to a higher tendency to engage in social bias.

11 It is notable that a fair number of respondents (n = 23) stated that Islamic beliefs enhanced their support of a potential candidate. In contrast, there were only two sociologists perceiving Mormon beliefs, only eleven sociologists perceiving evangelical beliefs, and only three sociologists perceiving fundamentalist beliefs as enhancing a candidate's position. This research found substantially more support for Muslims than for other conservative religious groups.

12 However, it should be pointed out that this is only true if I am capturing a cohort effect. If what I am recording is the fact that younger cohorts are less likely to be intolerant or to act on their biases, then over time we will see less of a bias effect. It is possible, however, that I am recording a time effect in that sociologists in general may tend to become more biased as they grow older. Thus these younger sociologists may become less tolerant as they grow older and more set in their ways. Finally, it is also possible that younger sociologists may have a higher propensity to hide their biases from social surveys than older sociologists. They may possess, and act on, their biases just as much as older sociologists, but they have grown up in an era when admitting to have biases is not commonly accepted. If this is true, then fundamentalist, NRA, evangelical, and Republican job candidates may be no more likely to be fairly evaluated by younger sociologists than by older ones.

13 More than four-fifths, or 86.0 percent, of the sociologists responding to the survey who work on college campuses are white. The next highest percentage is Hispanic sociologists at 4.7 percent, followed by blacks, who make up 4.4 percent of the population. No other racial group is more than 3 percent of the sample.

14 Ironically, it may not be whether one defines oneself as a fundamentalist or evangelical that helps determine one's level of social progressiveness. Smith (2000) finds on some social and political measures that evangelicals are more conservative than fundamentalists. What is likely just as, or more, important in determining a person's level of social and political conservatism is the degree of religiosity a conservative Protestant possesses. However, such distinctions are likely lost on most academics who answered this survey, as many of them are unaware of the literature that explores the social and political contours of conservative Protestants.

15 Evidence for such an assertion can be seen in the fact that sociologists who studied religion (n = 31) were not significantly more likely to reject fundamentalists than other sociologists (3.355 versus 3.202: p = .414). However, sociologists who studied religion were significantly less likely to reject evangelicals than other sociologists (3.774 versus

3.391: $p = .05$). Sociologists who study religion may be in a position to understand the less radical nature of evangelicalism relative to fundamentalism and thus may determine that evangelicals are more acceptable than fundamentalists.

16 Some may argue that early in the twentieth century, the ideas of functionalism were conservative in orientation and that the Chicago school contained sociologists who were sympathetic to individuals of faith. Yet Smith (2003) argues that many of these sociologists kept their antipathy toward conventional religion hidden in an effort to lessen resistance to societal reform. Furthermore, it is indisputable that sociologists have generally pushed progressive political and religious ideas as much as or more than traditional ones even in times when the field was relatively conservative in comparison to other periods of the discipline. Thus traditional religious interests have never had a stronghold among sociology professors.

Chapter 4

1 The date I started to examine the blogs was September 29, 2008. I went back twenty blog posts from that date.

2 I found a few blog entries of interest in 2009 that I analyzed as well.

3 SocProf, "Book Review—Heart of Diamonds," The Global Sociology Blog, September 23, 2008, http://globalsociology.com/2008/09/23/book-review-heart-of-diamonds.

4 Jesse Fagan, "Karl Rove and Obama Got SNA," Orbital Teapot, July 23, 2008, http://orbitalteapot.blogspot.com/2008/07/karl-rove-and-obama-got-sna.html.

5 Timothy Shortell, "Worst Ever," What Would Durkheim Do? September 24, 2008, http://www.shortell.org/node/285.

6 johneglass, "actions or results?" not your typical sociologist, July 11, 2008, http://socinsight.blogspot.com/2008/07/actions-or-results-occurred-to-me-this.html (emphasis in original).

7 Jose Marichal, "Personality, Geography, and the Presidential Campaign," thickculture, September 11, 2008, http://contexts.org/thickculture/2008/09/11/personality-geography-and-the-presidential-campaign/ (emphasis added).

8 Drek, "Just in case you were curious," Total Drek, September 29, 2008, http://totaldrek.blogspot.com/2008/09/just-in-case-you-were-curious.html.

9   johneglass, "well, okay, i actually had more to say," not your typical sociologist, April 28, 2008, http://socinsight.blogspot.com/2008/04/well-okay-i-actually-had-more-to-say.html.

10 J. Miller, "The Cancer of Conservatism," Uncommon Thought Journal, December 21, 2008, http://www.uncommonthought.com/mtblog/archives/2008/12/21/the-cancer-of-c.php. Originally published on the author's blog.

11 Ron Anderson, "Pistol-packing Sarah Palin shoots herself in her community service foot—denigrating volunteers," sociological eye, September 25, 2008, http://contexts.org/eye/2008/09/25/pistol-packing-sarah-palin-shoots-herself-in-her-community-service-foot-denigrating-volunteers/.

12 An admittedly secondhand story I heard reinforces this point. When I presented some of these preliminary findings, a Christian student told me that her major professor once remarked at a party that he would try to remove any student that he found out to be a Christian. His reasoning was that anyone who was foolish enough to believe in a Christian God was not smart enough to be in academia. Naturally she has not revealed her religious beliefs to him. While I cannot confirm the accuracy of this story, given the results of my analysis of the blogs it does not seem unreasonable that such a professor would make such a statement in an environment where he did not anticipate offending any Christians.

13 Corey, "Too much snark," My Confused Muse, November 1, 2007, http://cc_muse.blogspot.com/2007/11/too-much-snark.html.

14 Randy Lynn, "My Boss's Spouse's Friend Made Me Do It," Potato Chipping, May 27, 2008, http://www.potatochipping.com/2008/05/my-bosss-spouses-friend.

15 Jason Miller, "Winning the Battle for their Souls," Thomas Paine's Corner, July 8, 2006, http://civillibertarian.blogspot.com/2006/07/rendition-of-christ.html.

16 Drek, "*Total Drek* is experiencing technical difficulties," Total Drek, September 24, 2008, http://totaldrek.blogspot.com/2008/09/total-drek-is-experiencing-technical.html.

17 Ron Anderson, "President Bush, Comic Envoy to the World," sociological eye, May 22, 2008, http://contexts.org/eye/2008/05/22/president-bush-comic-envoy-to-the-world/.

18 Jesse Fagan, "Evolution = Natural Selection," Orbital Teapot, July 30, 2008, http://orbitalteapot.blogspot.com/2008/07/evolution-natural-selection.html.

19 Erin, "Shaky Political Coalitions: Christians and Conservatives," Prairie Sociology, April 8, 2005, http://prairiesociology.blogspot .com/2005/04/shaky-political-coalitions-christians.html.

20 Rowan Wolf, "Who is running for President," Uncommon Thought Journal, February 22, 2004, http://www.uncommonthought.com/ mtblog/archives/2004/02/22/who-is-running.php.

21 Shamus Khan, "my final disappointment," scatterplot, December 18, 2008, http://scatter.wordpress.com/2008/12/18/my-final-disappointment.

22 Rowan Wolf, "What Message is Obama Sending with Rick Warren," Uncommon Thought Journal, December 18, 2008, http:// uncommonthought.com/mtblog/archives/2008/12/18/what -message-is.php.

23 Ecklund (2010) finds a general tendency among some scientists to con- ceptually link religious activity to right-wing fundamentalist activ- ism. Given this reality, it is not surprising that sociologists also engage in such stereotyping.

24 Jay Livingston, "Palin and Torture, Party and Gender," Montclair Socioblog, September 9, 2008, http://montclairsoci.blogspot.com/2008/09/palin -and-torture-party-and-gender.html.

25 Jessie, "Sarah Palin and White Women's Racism," the color line, September 10, 2008, http://contexts.org/colorline/2008/09/10/sarah -palin-and-white-women%e2%80%99s-racism/ (emphasis in original).

26 Jay Livingston, "Ressentiment, Baby, Ressentiment," Montclair Socioblog, October 11, 2008, http:/montclairsoci.blogspot.com/2008/10/baby-for- ressentiment.html.

27 Jason Miller, "Of Moral Regression, Heartland Extremism, and Solidarity against the Wicked Witch," Thomas Paine's Corner, August 4, 2006, http://civillibertarian.blogspot.com/2006/08/evolution-that- would-blow-darwins-mind.html.

28 Rowan Wolf, "Fires Are Harder to Put Out Than They Are to Start," Uncommon Thought Journal, October 12, 2008, http://www .uncommonthought.com/mtblog/archives/2008/10/12/fires_are _harde_1.php.

29 I did get some entries from searches that were embedded in the blogs. This allowed me to find relevant blog entries from years in the past. I had a choice of ignoring those entries so that all of the blogs were examined in a similar time frame. But I chose not to do so under the idea that the more information I obtain, the better analysis I can conduct.

30 Jeff Larson, "Enlightenment as Mass Destruction," Dried Sage, November 12, 2006, http://driedsage.blogspot.com/2006/11/war -industry-enlightenment-as-mass.html.

31 Rachel, "Xenophobia and Racism Affect Black School Children in Ireland," RachelsTavern.com, September 3, 2007, http://www .rachelstavern.com/uncategorized/xenophobia-and-racism-in -ireland-affect-black-school-children.html.

32 Jeremy Freese, "hey jeremy, where do *you* draw the line?" Jeremy Freese's Weblog, November 2, 2004, http://jeremyfreese.blogspot .com/2004/11/hey-jeremy-where-do-you-draw-line.html.

33 Andrew Perrin, "the new l-word," scatterplot, September 25, 2008, http://scatter.wordpress.com/2008/09/25/the-new-l-word/.

34 Changeseeker, "What Would Malcolm Say?" Why Am I Not Surprised? November 28, 2008, http://whyaminotsurprised.blogspot .com/2008/11/what-would-malcolm-say.html (emphasis in original).

35 Monte Bute, "Yesterday Jennifer met Amy Goodman and the riot police," a backstage sociologist, September 3, 2008, http://contexts .org/monte/2008/09/03/yesterday-jennifer-met-amy-goodman-and -the-riot-police/.

36 Bute, "Yesterday Jennifer."

37 Sue Greer-Pitt, "understanding the nomos," Sociological Stew, July 2, 2008, http://suesstew.blogspot.com/2008/07/understanding-nomos .html.

38 Jessie Daniels, "Racism (and other issues) among Gay Marriage Supporters," Racism Review, November 12, 2008, http://www .racismreview.com/blog/2008/11/12/racism-and-other-issues-among -gay-marriage-supporters/.

39 Seth Wagerman, "Questions/Answers/More Questions re: Prop 8," thickculture, November 21, 2008, http://contexts.org/ thickculture/2008/11/21/questionsanswersmore-questions-re- prop-8/.

40 Grad School Mommy, "voting NO on Prop 8," October 22, 2008, http:// gradmommy.wordpress.com/2008/10/.

41 Wolf, "Fires Are Harder to Put Out" (emphasis in original).

42 Shamus Khan, "not an arab/muslim," scatterplot, October 13, 2008, http://scatter.wordpress.com/2008/10/13/not-an-arabmuslim.

43 Jessie Daniels, "As Economic Crisis Worsens, is Racism a 'Luxury' Whites Can No Longer Afford?" RacismReview, October 8, 2008, http://www.racismreview.com/blog/2008/10/08/racism-a-luxury.

44 Eszter, "Which one?" Eszter's Blog, October 8, 2008, http://www
.esztersblog.com/2008/10/08/which-one.

45 Jay Livingston, "Shake . . . Or Not," Montclair Socioblog, October 8,
2008, http://montclairsoci.blogspot.com/2008/10/shake-or-not.html.

Chapter 5

1 The major exception to this would be arguments surrounding evolution versus creationism. However, this conflict is not as pervasive as
the conflict between the social sciences/humanities and traditional
groups. In the case of the social sciences/humanities, almost every
issue studied lends itself to conflict from traditional social groups as
opposed to the single major issue of evolution.

2 A list of these directories, and information about them, can be found
in the appendix on pages 188–90.

3 As it concerns the atmosphere in academia, the lack of inclusion of
nonscientific fields is not trivial. There is work indicating that professors in these fields are more likely to be politically conservative
than other professors (Ladd & Lipset, 1975; Zipp & Fenwick, 2006).
Extending this work to look at some of these fields would allow us to
make a more informed assessment about the atmosphere in academia
in general as well as to comprehend the nature of scientific bias.

4 Only 5.6 percent of the sociologists returning the survey did so after
the November 4 elections.

5 It is difficult to test for the Mormon effect since data for most of the
disciplines were collected entirely after the November 4 elections.
However, data collection for sociologists and chemists did begin before
the elections, and thus I can get some idea about whether the election results may have influenced the reaction of these scholars toward
Mormons. Looking at these two disciplines, I did find that sociologists
and chemists who rated Mormons after the election provided a lower
rating than those who did so before the election (3.65 versus 3.758),
but this difference was not significant. So there is a possibility that the
elections did influence the scholars' attitude toward Mormons, but the
evidence for this is by no means conclusive.

6 The scores of Mormons and evangelicals were only significantly different among political scientists, historians, and English language
faculty, though they were also significantly different at the .1 level
for chemists and experimental biologists. Thus it is reasonable to
think of the level of acceptance for evangelicals and Mormons as
roughly similar.

7   Race was not included because in some of the disciplines there were so few nonwhites that there was not any variation of the dependent variable.

8   One reviewer of the book suggested an alternative thesis. The reviewer suggested that any slight biases that scholars have may be overcome by the scholarship of those from disfavored groups. I quote the example the reviewer gave to illustrate this point. "I know of a case where the majority of a department voted against a candidate who had a commendable record but a disapproved affiliation. But the department chair overruled the majority, took the decision to the tenured professors who voted to extend an offer, and the university administration backed the department head. An offer was made and the candidate accepted the position." However, the reviewer misses the entire point. I never claim that it is impossible for those from disfavored groups to be hired. My argument is that they face barriers with which those from favored groups do not have to deal. In this example, we see that the candidate had to have the chair of the department intervene to get hired. If the candidate had not had this particular affiliation, then he or she would have been offered the position without the intervention. There is no guarantee that all department chairs would have intervened or even would have had the power to intervene. It is not unrealistic to imagine that this situation could have been very different if the candidate had not had the support of the chair, tenured faculty, or administration. Are we to believe that every situation like this one is handled in such a manner? Finally, I assume that the candidate had a clearly superior academic record to all other candidates. Would the chair have gone to bat for the candidate if his or her academic record had been very similar to the other candidates'? Why would the chair have utilized political capital if it was not to gain a superior scholar? So this candidate likely had to have a better record than candidates without the questionable affiliation. Thus the reviewer's example illustrates my very point, which is that scholars from disfavored groups face higher barriers than other scholars. Sometimes they can overcome those barriers; at other times they cannot. So those affiliations influence, but do not determine, their abilities to obtain the academic positions they seek.

Chapter 6

1   This is not unlike the work that has been done on symbolic racism (McConahay & Hough, 1976; Weigel & Howes, 1985). That work suggests that some whites may have subtle animosity toward people of color but do not show this hostility on issues that directly impact race.

But if they can find nonracial reasons to oppose people of color, they will tend to do so and express their disfavor of racial minorities in this manner. Such a process is plausible for scholars given the tension between the value of tolerance that many of them espouse and the reality that they also have mistrust for religious and political conservatives.

2   Furthermore, contemporary Christian biologists appear to have fewer problems with the concept of evolution than their predecessors. A good example of this can be found in the work of Francis Collins, who affirms an evangelical Christian faith but also supports the idea of evolution over the notion of intelligent design (McCarthy, 2006).

3   I am not the only one to make such an assertion. Gould (1997) argues that there are areas best situated for scientific inquiry and areas best left to those with religious expertise. He contends that while there may be some overlap, those in the sciences should be careful about portraying themselves as having religious expertise and vice versa. I tend to agree with his basic arguments, although I recognize that the overlap is likely greater with the social sciences than with the physical sciences, in which Gould was an expert.

4   It should also be noted that membership in the NRA can be seen as a proxy for adherence to extreme conservative political ideology, in much the same way that fundamentalism is such a proxy.

5   Let us look at this in another way. Assume that every sociologist has a one-in-twelve chance of feeling that a candidate's fundamentalist beliefs extremely damage the support that sociologists will provide a candidate. Assume that we have a six-person search committee who examines the candidates. There is a 91.6 percent chance that a particular sociologist will not have such strong views. But if we take into account the fact that we have six sociologists, then we must multiply .916 by six. This leaves only a 40.66 percent chance that the committee will be free of anyone with a high level of animosity toward fundamentalists. While each person has only one vote, clearly the powerful feelings of one member of the committee can influence the one or two more individuals needed to derail a potential candidate's opportunity. We must be careful not to allow what may be a small number of individuals with high hostility toward religious conservatives to tempt us to minimize the serious nature of this problem.

6   There are ways to "force" individuals to make a choice about whether a social group is acceptable or not. For example, if I had used a six-point scale, then the respondent would have had to choose whether group membership helped or hurt a person's candidacy for a position. Then there would have been no midpoint by which a person could

have stated that membership in a social group did not help or hurt. Such a scale undoubtedly would have increased the percentages of respondents that either supported an approved group or rejected a disapproved group. But I wanted the midpoint in the scale to allow the respondent to state that group membership was unimportant.

7   Thus this effect may be ameliorated if scholars have religiously and politically conservative friends outside of their occupation. Future research should investigate such a question and whether such interpersonal contact may reduce the degree of social bias academics express.

8   Furthermore, even if there are some cultural conservatives in their departments, such individuals may not feel free to express their beliefs. Ecklund (2010) documents that there is a social atmosphere among scientists which discourages the discussion of religious issues and thus may work to silence religious conservatives.

9   However, one exception to this might be seen in a recent article by Lilla (2009), an ex-conservative, contending that conservative political ideas should be taken seriously. Perhaps the fact that Lilla was once a conservative helped him to appreciate the perspectives of conservatives more earnestly.

10   The Summers episode also indicates why it is important to account for the humanities as well as the traditional scientific disciplines. Many of the pressures that operated to remove Summers came from disciplines that are more properly located in the humanities than in the traditional sciences. Thus scholars from the humanities often are able to influence the type of scientific work that is conducted, even if those scholars do not conduct the scientific work themselves.

11   For example, Oliver and Shapiro (1995) document how the historical accumulation of wealth has created an often unseen advantage for whites. They illustrate how wealth allows whites to sustain financial hardships and gain additional resources. Furthermore, they document that even at similar income levels, whites have more wealth than blacks since their families have historically been able to accumulate this wealth. This is one way in which whites can have an advantage in society even if there is little or no racial animosity directed at blacks.

Chapter 7

1   There actually has been an attempt to create a similar document that addresses the privileges that Christians have (Schlosser, 2003). The argument is made that Christians enjoy a level of acceptance and respect not given to those of other faiths or who have no faith at all. While such an argument may make sense if we are discussing

Christians in the larger society, this research has indicated that conservative Christians enjoy no such advantages in academia.

2   This assumes that such individuals have been able to obtain such academic positions. The additional barriers they have encountered can
easily have stopped many of them from reaching a position where they
are protected by tenure.

3   Indeed, even the term "fundamentalist" is used in a derogatory manner at times when it is used to describe all conservative Protestants. It
implies that belief in a conservative version of Protestantism is akin to
having an extremist religious perspective. Fundamentalism is a term
that accurately describes the beliefs of members of certain segments
of Protestantism, and ideally it would be used for nothing more than
to describe those segments. But because it is a term that has actual
useful applications, unlike the term "bible thumper," I chose not to
use this word as an example of derogatory terminology, although
I have no doubt that at times it is used to dehumanize conservative
Protestants.

4   It is possible that such groups receive a good deal of discrimination outside of academia but that the very biases documented in this research
have hindered the ability of social scientists to perceive the reality
of such discrimination. For example, it is possible that members of
these disfavored groups may face similar barriers in areas where they
are relatively low in number, such as in the media or the entertainment industry. Future research may be able to document the degree
to which this is the case or whether the majority group status of these
groups is only challenged in academia.

5   This is not to say that religious and political conservatives, whites,
and males truly relate to racism or sexism, as there are economic, historical, and structural components to such inequalities that are not
captured by conservatives' experiences in academia. But to the degree
that they face intergroup stigmatization and rejection, religious and
political conservatives experience, as out-group members in academia, rejection that is likely similar to what a black perceives in an
all-white country club or what a woman perceives in a "good old boy"
business office. In both cases, the members of the stigmatized group
are allowed to participate but likely pick up signals that they are still
part of the out-group.

Appendix

1   To find the e-mail addresses, I went to the home page of the respondent's discipline at his or her school of employment. If that did not

provide me with the needed information, then I searched the university's Web site for the given name. If that did not provide the e-mail address, then I looked no further. Usually it was emeritus professors for whom I was unable to find the proper information, perhaps because they are less likely to possess an e-mail account than other professors.

2   Those who were socialized in the United States but worked at a college or university outside the United States were excluded by this method. However, I suspect that this excluded relatively few academics. I did include those scholars socialized in other countries but currently working in the United States. I suspect that this is not an insignificant number of sociologists. However, these individuals have likely been in the United States long enough to have picked up on social cues as to which social groups are acceptable, and thus their answers should reflect the values of the larger discipline.

3   Those groups included the American Physiological Society, the American Society for Biochemistry and Molecular Biology, the American Society for Pharmacology and Experimental Therapeutics, the American Society for Investigative Pathology, the American Society for Nutrition, the American Association of Immunologists, the American Association of Anatomists, the Protein Society, the Society for Developmental Biology, the American Peptide Society, the American Society for Bone and Mineral Research, the Society for the Study of Reproduction, the Endocrine Society, and the American Society of Human Genetics.

4   If there was any doubt, I erred on the side of including the respondent in the sample.

5   It is most likely that "other" refers to some type of certificate or minor in that field since any other training more powerful than an associate-level degree would likely fit into an easily describable category. This justifies putting "other" as the lowest category. Fortunately only 31, or 2.8 percent of respondents, listed "other" instead of one of the more recognizable categories, so it is unlikely that inclusion of this category altered the major results of this work.

6   Multicollinearity is not an explanation for this finding, as the highest correlation with the discipline variables is between philosophy and anthropology at −.133. This level of correlation is not high enough to raise concerns of multicollinearity.

7   I chose not to discuss responses toward job candidates under 30 or over 50 in any of these groupings, as they did not easily fit into religious, political, sexuality, or lifestyle dimensions. However, a look at the last two models clearly indicates that nondisciplinary variables

were more predictive of the attitudes of scholars toward the young or old than disciplinary factors.

8   I used evangelicals instead of fundamentalists for this exercise since fundamentalists were even less acceptable than evangelicals. If evangelicals do not experience the same level of acceptance as atheists, then certainly fundamentalists will not be accepted. The use of evangelicals instead of fundamentalists should have made it more difficult to document a statistical difference between a religious group and atheists. This fact should strengthen the findings of this study.

9   The ratings among such sociologists are 4.333 for Democrats and 3.833 for Republicans. While we can argue that perhaps the bias against religious conservatives is overhyped, even among sociologists on conservative Protestant campuses there is no chance that an underrepresentation distorts my findings concerning political bias.

10   I combined the English and non-English languages because there were no non-English language professors on conservative campuses.

Bibliography

Abramowitz, Alan, and Kyle L. Saunders. 2005. "Why Can't We All Just Get Along? The Reality of a Polarized America." *The Forum: A Journal of Applied Research in Contemporary Politics* 3 (2): Article 1. http://www .bepress.com/forum/vol3/iss2/art1.

Aby, Stephen H. 2007. "Academic Freedom in Perilous Times." In *The Academic Bill of Rights Debate*, ed. Stephen H. Aby, 1–16. Greenwood Press.

Adorno, Theodor W., Else Frenkel-Brunswik, Daniel Levinson, and Nevitt Sanford. 1950. *The Authoritarian Personality*. Harper & Row.

Alba, Richard. 2006. "Diversity's Blind Spot." *Ethnicities* 6 (4): 518–54.

Alterman, Eric. 2004. *What Liberal Media? The Truth about Bias and the News*. Basic Books.

Altermeyer, Bob. 1968. *Right-Wing Authoritarianism*. University of Manitoba Press.

Altermeyer, Bob, and Bruce Hunsberger. 1992. "Authoritarianism, Religious Fundamentalism, Quest, and Prejudice." *International Journal for the Psychology of Religion* 2 (2): 113–33.

American Council of Trustees and Alumni. 2006. "How Many Ward Churchills?" Washington, D.C.

Ames, Barry, David C. Barker, Chris W. Bonneau, and Christopher J. Carman. 2005. "Hide the Republicans, the Christians, and the Women:

A Response to 'Politics and Professional Advancement among College Faculty.'" *Forum* 3 (2): 1–7.

Arnold, Dean E. 2006. "Why Are There So Few Christian Anthropologists? Reflections on the Tensions between Christianity and Anthropology." *Perspectives on Science and Christian Faith* 58 (4): 266–82.

Asante, Molefi K. 1998. *The Afrocentric Idea*. Temple University Press.

Ashmore, Karen. 2008. "Is Your World Too White? A Primer for Whites Trying to Deal with a Racist Society." In *The Matrix of Race, Class, Gender, and Sexuality: Examining the Dynamics of Oppression and Privilege*, ed. Abby L. Ferber, Christina M. Jimenez, Andrea O'Reilly Herrera, and Dena R. Samuels, 638–43. McGraw-Hill.

Astin, H. S., A. L. Antonio, C. M. Cress, and A. W. Astin. 1997. *Race and Ethnicity in the American Professoriate, 1995–96*. Higher Education Research Institute, Graduate School of Education & Information Studies.

Aveling, Nado. 2002. "Student Teachers' Resistance to Exploring Racism: Reflections on 'Doing' Border Pedagogy." *Asia-Pacific Journal of Higher Education* 30:119–30.

Balch, Stephen H. 2006. "Words to Live by: How Diversity Trumps Freedom on Academic Websites." A report by the National Association of Scholars, June 29, 2006.

Batson, C. Daniel, Patricia Schoenrade, and W. Larry Ventis. 1993. *Religion and the Individual: A Social-Psychological Perspective*. Oxford University Press.

Bednar, Nancy L., and Allen D. Hertzke. 1995. "Oklahoma: The Christian Right and Republican Realignment." In *God at the Grass Roots: The Christian Right in the 1994 Elections*, ed. Mark J. Rozell and Clyde Wilcox, 91–108. Rowman & Littlefield.

Bell, Michael M. 2008. *An Invitation to Environmental Sociology*. Pine Forge.

Benokraitis, Nijole. 1997. *Subtle Sexism: Current Practice and Prospects for Change*. Sage Publications.

Benokraitis, Nijole, and Joe R. Feagin. 1995. *Modern Sexism: Blatant, Subtle and Covert Discrimination*, 2nd ed. Prentice-Hall.

Berger, Helen A. 1999. *A Community of Witches: Contemporary Neo-Paganism and Witchcraft in the United States*. University of South Carolina Press.

Berger, Peter. 1986. *The Capitalist Revolution*. Basic Books.

Bergman, Gerald. 2001. "Religion and Medicine: The Christian Science Holocaust." *New England Journal of Skepticism* 4 (4): 10–14.

Beutel, Ann M., and Donna J. Nelson. 2006. "The Gender and Race-Ethnicity of Faculty in Top Social Science Research Departments." *Social Science Journal* 43 (1): 111–25.

Bishop, Ronald. 2007. *Taking on the Pledge of Allegiance: The Media and Michael Newdow's Constitutional Challenge*. State University of New York Press.

Bobo, Lawrence, James R. Kluegel, and Ryan A. Smith. 1997. "Laissez-Faire Racism: The Crystallization of a Kinder, Gentler, Antiblack Ideology." In *Racial Attitudes in the 1990s: Continuity and Change*, ed. Steven A. Tuch and Jack K. Martin, 15–42. Praeger.

Bobo, Lawrence, and Frederick C. Licari. 1989. "Education and Political Tolerance: Testing the Effects of Cognitive Sophistication and Target Group Affect." *Public Opinion Quarterly* 53:285–308.

Bogardus, Emory. 1968. "Comparing Racial Distance in Ethiopia, South Africa, and the United States." *Sociology and Social Research* 52:149–56.

Bohm, R. M. 1998. "American Death Penalty Opinion: Past, Present, and Future." In *America's Experiment with Capital Punishment*, ed. J. R. Acker, R. M. Bohm, and C. S. Lanier, 25–46. Carolina Academic.

Bolce, Louis, and Gerald De Maio. 1999. "The Anti-Christian Fundamentalist Factor in Contemporary Politics." *Public Opinion Quarterly* 63 (4): 508–42.

———. 2008. "A Prejudice for the Thinking Classes." *American Politics Research* 36 (2): 155–85.

Bonilla-Silva, Eduardo. 2001. *White Supremacy and Racism in the Post–Civil Rights Era*. Lynne Rienner.

———. 2003. *Racism without Racists: Color-Blind Racism and the Persistence of Racial Inequality in the United States*. Rowman & Littlefield.

Bonvillian, Nancy. 2006. *Women and Men: Cultural Constructs of Gender*. Prentice-Hall.

Bourdieu, Pierre. 1988. *Distinction: A Social Critique of the Judgment of Taste*. Harvard University Press.

Bozell, L. Brent. 2008. "A Media Veep Double Standard." *New York Post*, September 4.

Brock, David. 2004. *The Republican Noise Machine: Right-Wing Media and How It Corrupts Democracy*. Crown.

Buell, Emmett H., and Lee Sigelman. 1985. "An Army that Meets Every Sunday? Popular Support for the Moral Majority in 1980." *Social Science Quarterly* 66:427–34.

Burtchaell, James T. 1998. *The Dying of the Light: The Disengagement of Colleges and Universities from Their Christian Churches*. Eerdmans.

Calvert, Clay. 2006. "Hate Speech and Its Harms: A Communication Theory Perspective." *Journal of Communication* 47 (1): 4–19.

Capeheart, Loretta, and Dragon Milovanovic. 2007. *Social Justice: Theories, Issues, and Movements*. Rutgers University Press.

Carr, Leslie G. 1997. *Color-Blind Racism*. Sage Publications.

Catton, William J. 1961. "The Functions and Dysfunctions of Ethnocentrism: A Theory." *Social Problems* 8 (3): 201–11.

Caudron, Shari, and Cassandra Hayes. 1997. "Are Diversity Programs Benefiting African Americans?" *Black Enterprise* 27 (7): 121–32.

Cetina, Karin K. 1999. *Epistemic Cultures: How the Sciences Make Knowledge*. Harvard University Press.

Chandler, Charles R. 2001. "Social Factors Influencing Immigration Attitudes: An Analysis of Data from the General Social Survey." *Social Science Journal* 38 (2): 177–88.

Chaney, Carole K. 1998. "Explaining the Gender Gap in U.S. Presidential Elections, 1980–1992." *Political Research Quarterly* 51 (2): 311–39.

Chodorow, Nancy. 1999. *The Reproduction of Mothering*. University of California Press.

Christerson, Brad, Korie L. Edwards, and Michael O. Emerson. 2005. *Against All Odds: The Struggle for Racial Integration in Religious Organizations*. New York University Press.

Clayton-Pedersen, Alma R., Sharon Parker, Daryl G. Smith, Jose F. Morena, and Daniel Hiroyuki Teraguchi. 2007. *Making a Real Difference with Diversity: A Guide to Institutional Change*. Association of American Colleges and Universities.

Coenders, Marcel, and Peer Scheepers. 2003. "The Effect of Education on Nationalism and Ethnic Exclusionism: An International Comparison." *Political Psychology* 24 (2): 313–43.

Cohen-Cole, Ethan B., and Steven N. Durlauf. 2005. "Evaluating Claims of Bias in Academia: A Comment on Klein and Western's 'How Many Democrats per Republican at UC-Berkeley and Stanford?'"

Colson, Charles. 2007. "Stem-Cell Breakthrough: A Battle of Worldviews." *Florida Baptist Witness*, December 12.

Comte, Auguste. 1896. *Positive Philosophy*. Bell.

Cooperman, Alan. 2007. "Is There Disdain for Evangelicals in the Classroom?" *Washington Post*, May 5.

Corsun, David L., and Wanda M. Costen. 2001. "Is the Glass Ceiling Unbreakable?" *Journal of Management Inquiry* 10 (1): 16–25.

Cotter, David A., Joan M. Hermsen, Seth Ovadia, and Reeve Vanneman. 2001. "The Glass Ceiling Effect." *Social Forces* 80 (2): 655–82.

Coulter, Ann. 2004. *How to Talk to a Liberal (If You Must): The World according to Ann Coulter.* Crown.

D'Souza, Dinesh. 1991. *Illiberal Education: The Politics of Race and Sex on Campus.* Free Press.

Dalton, Russell J., Paul A. Beck, and Robert Huckfeldt. 1998. "Partisan Cues and the Media: Information Flows in the 1992 Presidential Election." *American Political Science Review* 92:111–26.

Davis, Richard. 2005. "Feminist Logic Leads Only to Disaster." MichNews. Com. http://michnews.com, April 27.

Dawkins, Richard. 1986. *The Blind Watchmaker.* W. W. Norton.

———. 2006. *The God Delusion.* Houghton Mifflin.

de Wijze, Stephen. 2000. "The Family and Political Justice: The Case of Political Liberalisms." *Journal of Ethics* 4 (3): 257–82.

Deegan, Mary Jo. 1988. *Jane Addams and the Men of the Chicago School, 1892–1918.* Transaction Publishers.

Demerath III, N. J. 2005. "The Battle over a U.S. Culture War: A Note on Inflated Rhetoric versus Inflamed Politics." *The Forum: A Journal of Applied Research in Contemporary Politics* 3 (2): Article 6.

Desmond, Adrian, and James Moore. 1992. *Darwin: The Life of a Tormented Evolutionist.* Warner.

Doerflinger, Richard M. 1999. "The Ethics of Funding Embryonic Stem Cell Research: A Catholic Viewpoint." *Kennedy Institute of Ethics Journal* 9 (2): 137–50.

Domke, David, Mark D. Watts, Dhavan V. Shah, and David Fan. 1999. "The Politics of Conservative Elites and the 'Liberal Media' Argument." *Journal of Communication* 49:35–59.

Durkheim, Emile. 1965. *The Elementary Forms of the Religious Life.* Free Press.

Eckhardt, William. 1991. "Authoritarianism." *Political Psychology* 12 (1): 97–124.

Ecklund, Elaine H. 2010. *Science vs. Religion: What Do Scientists Really Think?* Oxford University Press.

Ecklund, Elaine H., Jerry Z. Park, and Phil T. Veliz. 2008. "Secularization and Religious Change among Elite Scientists." *Social Forces* 86 (4): 1805–40.

Ecklund, Elaine H., and Christopher P. Scheitle. 2007. "Religion among Academic Scientists: Distinctions, Disciplines, and Demographics." *Social Problems* 54 (2): 289–307.

Edlund, Lena, and Rohini Pande. 2002. "Why Have Women Become Left-Wing? The Political Gender Gap and the Decline in Marriage." *Quarterly Journal of Economics* 117 (3): 917–61.

Edwards, Richard C., Michael Reich, and Thomas E. Weisskopf. 1978. "Sexism." In *The Capitalist System*, ed. Richard C. Edwards, Michael Reich, and Thomas E. Weisskopf, 331–41. Prentice-Hall.

Ehrenreich, Barbara, and John Ehrenreich. 1977. "The Professional Managerial Class." *Radical America* 11:7–31.

Elder, Larry. 2003. *Showdown: Confronting Bias, Lies and the Special Interests That Divide America*. St. Martin Griffin.

Ellison, Christopher G., Samuel Echevarria, and Brad Smith. 2005. "Religion and Abortion Attitudes among U.S. Hispanics: Findings from the 1990 Latino National Political Survey." *Social Science Quarterly* 86 (1): 192–208.

England, Paula. 2001. "Gender and Access to Money: What Do Trends in Earnings and Household Poverty Tell Us?" In *Reconfigurations of Class and Gender*, ed. Janine Baxter and Mark Western, 131–53. Stanford University Press.

Farley, John E. 2010. *Majority-Minority Relations*. Prentice-Hall.

Feagin, Joe. 2000. *Racist America: Roots, Current Realities, and Future Reparations*. Routledge.

———. 2006. *Systemic Racism: A Theory of Oppression*. Routledge.

Feagin, Joe, and Clairece Feagin. 1986. *Discrimination American Style: Institutional Racism and Sexism*. Krieger Publishing Company.

Feagin, Joe, and Hernan Vera. 2002. "Confronting One's Own Racism." In *White Privilege: Essential Readings on the Other Side of Racism*, ed. Paula S. Rothenberg, 121–25. Worth Publishers.

Fetto, John. 2000. "Interracial Friendships Slip?" *American Demographics* 22 (1): 23.

Fico, Frederick, and Stan Soffin. 1995. "Fairness and Balance of Selected Newspaper Coverage of Controversial National, State and Local Issues." *Journalism and Mass Communication Quarterly* 72 (3): 21–33.

Finke, Laurie A. 2005. "Performing Collegiality, Troubling Gender." *Symploke* 13 (1–2): 121–33.

Fiorina, Morris. 2005. *Culture War? The Myth of a Polarized America*. Pearson Longman.

Folbre, Nancy. 1985. "The Pauperization of Motherhood." *Review of Radical Political Economics* 16 (4): 80–82.

Forrest, Barbara, and Glenn Branch. 2005. "Wedging Creationism into the Academy." *Academe Online.* http://www.aaup.org/AAUP/pubsres/academe/2005/JF/Feat/forr.htm.

Fulton, A. S., Richard L. Gorsuch, and E. A. Maynard. 1999. "Religious Orientation, Antihomosexual Sentiment, and Fundamentalism among Christians." *Journal for the Scientific Study of Religion* 38 (1): 14–22.

Furrow, James L., Pamela E. King, and Krystal White. 2004. "Religion and Positive Youth Development: Identity, Meaning, and Prosocial Concerns." *Applied Developmental Science* 8 (1): 17–26.

Gallagher, Charles. 2004. "Racial Redistricting: Expanding the Boundaries of Whiteness." In *The Politics of Multiracialism: Challenging Racial Thinking,* ed. Heather M. Dalmage, 59–76. State University of New York Press.

Garrison, Jessica, and Joanna Lin. 2008. "Prop. 8 Protesters Target Mormon Temple in Westwood." *Los Angeles Times,* November 7.

Gartner, John D. 1986. "Antireligious Prejudice in Admission to Doctoral Programs in Clinical Psychology." *Professional Psychology: Research and Practice* 17 (5): 473–75.

Gartner, John D., Morton Harmatz, Ann Hohmann, David Larson, and Alison Fishman Gartner. 1990. "The Effect of Patient and Clinician Ideology on Clinical Judgment: A Study of Ideological Countertransference." *Psychotherapy* 27 (1): 98–106.

Geertz, Clifford. 1966. "Ethos, Worldview and the Analysis of Sacred Symbols." *Antioch Review* (Winter): 421–37.

Gey, Steven G. 2006. "Atheism and the Freedom of Religion." In *The Cambridge Companion to Atheism,* ed. Michael Martin, 250–66. Cambridge University Press.

Gieryn, Thomas. 1999. *Cultural Boundaries of Science: Credibility on the Line.* University of Chicago Press.

Gilligan, Carol. 1993. *In a Different Voice: Psychological Theory and Women's Development.* Harvard University Press.

Giroux, Henry. 2006. "Academic Freedom under Fire: The Case for Critical Pedagogy." *College Literature* 33 (4): 1–42.

Goldberg, Bernard. 2001. *Bias: A CBS Insider Exposes How the Media Distort the News.* Regnery.

Goldberg, Jonah. 2008. *Liberal Fascism: The Secret History of the American Left, from Mussolini to the Politics of Meaning.* Doubleday.

Goodman, Diane J. 2000. *Promoting Diversity and Social Justice: Educating People from Privileged Groups.* Sage Publications.

Gordon, Scott. 1995. *The History and Philosophy of Social Science.* Routledge.

Gorski, Eric. 2008. "Anger over Gay Marriage Vote Directed at Mormons." *USA Today,* November 13.

Gould, Kenneth A., and Tammy L. Lewis. 2008. *Twenty Lessons in Environmental Sociology.* Oxford University Press.

Gould, Stephen J. 1997. "Nonoverlapping Magisteria." *Natural History* 106 (2): 16–22.

Gouldner, Alvin W. 1978. "The New Class Project." *Theory and Society* 6:153–204.

Greeley, Andrew M. 1972. *The Denominational Society.* Scott, Foresman.

———. 1973. "'The Religious Factor' and Academic Careers: Another Communication." *American Journal of Sociology* 78 (5): 1247–55.

Grey, Thomas C. 1991. "Civil Rights vs. Civil Liberties: The Case of Discriminatory Verbal Harassment." *Journal of Higher Education* 63 (5): 485–516.

Griffin, Glenn A., Richard L. Gorsuch, and Andrea L. Davis. 1987. "A Cross-Cultural Investigation of Religious Orientation, Social Norms, and Prejudice." *Journal for the Scientific Study of Religion* 26 (3): 358–65.

Grosz, Elizabeth A., and Marie de Lepervanche. 1988. "Feminism and Science." In *Crossing Boundaries: Feminisms and the Critique of Knowledges,* ed. E. A. Grosz and M. de Lepervanche, 5–27. Allen & Unwin.

Grumbach, Kevin, Janet Coffman, Emily Rosenoff, and Claudia Munoz. 2001. "Trends in Underrepresented Minority Participation in Health Professions Schools." In *The Right Thing to Do, the Smart Thing to Do,* ed. Herbert W. Nickens and Brian D. Smedley, 185–207. National Academies Press.

Gunther, Al C. 1992. "Biased Press or Biased Public? Attitudes toward Media Coverage of Social Groups." *Public Opinion Quarterly* 56 (2): 147–67.

Hall, Marie Boas. 1958. *History of Science.* Macmillan.

Hamilton, Richard F., and Lowell I. Hargens. 1993. "The Politics of the Professors: Self-Identifications, 1969–1984." *Social Forces* 71 (3): 603–27.

Harding, Sandra. 1986. *The Science Question in Feminism.* Cornell University Press.

———. 1987. "Introduction: Is There a Feminist Method?" In *Feminism and Methodology,* ed. Sandra Harding, 1–14. Indiana University Press.

Harper, Marcel. 2007. "The Stereotyping of Nonreligious People by Religious Students: Contents and Subtypes." *Journal for the Scientific Study of Religion* 46 (4): 539–52.

Hayes, Bernadette C. 1995. "The Impact of Religious Identification on Political Attitudes: An International Comparison." *Sociology of Religion* 56 (2): 177–94.

Heinemann, Thomas, and Ludger Honnefelder. 2002. "Principles of Ethical Decision Making Regarding Embrionic Stem Cell Research in Germany." *Bioethics* 16 (6): 530–43.

Hemphill, Helen, and Ray Haines. 1997. *Discrimination, Harassment, and the Failure of Diversity Training: What to Do Now?* Quorum.

Hertzke, Allen D. 2008. "The Faith-Based Human Rights Quest: Missing the Story." In *Blind Spot: When Journalists Don't Get Religion*, ed. Paul Marshall, Lela Gilbert, and Roberta Green-Ahmanson, 65–86. Oxford University Press.

Hochschild, Arlie, and Anne Machung. 2003. *The Second Shift*. Penguin.

Hodge, David R. 2002. "Does Social Work Oppress Evangelical Christians? A 'New Class' Analysis of Society and Social Work." *Social Work* 47 (4): 401–14.

Hodge, David R., Lisa M. Baughman, and Julie A. Cummings. 2006. "Moving towards Spiritual Competency: Deconstructing Religious Stereotypes and Spiritual Prejudices in Social Work Literature." *Journal of Social Service Research* 32 (4): 211–31.

Horowitz, David. 2006. *The Professors: The 101 Most Dangerous Academics in America*. Regnery.

Horowitz, David, and Eli Lehrer. 2003. "Political Bias in the Administrations and Faculties of 32 Elite Colleges and Universities." Center for the Study of Popular Culture.

Howard, Don. 2003. "Two Left Turns Make a Right: On the Curious Political Career of North American Philosophy of Science at Midcentury." In *Logical Empiricism in North America*, ed. Gary L. Hardcastle and Alan W. Richardson, 25–93. University of Minnesota Press.

Howard, Lawrence C. 1958. "The Academic and the Ballot." *School and Society* 86:415–19.

Howse, Brannon, and Michael Reagan. 2005. *One Nation under Man? The Worldview War between Christians and the Secular Left*. B & H Publishing Group.

Hubbard, Ruth. 1983. "Have Only Men Evolved?" In *Discovering Reality: Feminist Perspectives on Epistemology, Metaphysics, Methodology and*

Philosophy of Science, ed. Sandra Harding and M. Hintikka, 45–69. D. Reidel Publishing Company.

Hunsberger, Bruce. 1995. "Religion and Prejudice: The Role of Religious Fundamentalism, Quest, and Right-Wing Authoritarianism." *Journal of Social Issues* 51 (2): 113–29.

Hunter, James Davison. 1991. *Culture War: The Struggle to Define America*. Basic Books.

———. 1994. *Before the Shooting Begins: Searching for Democracy in America's Culture War*. Simon & Schuster.

Hurtado, Sylvia, Jeffrey F. Milem, Alma R. Clayton-Pedersen, and Walter R. Allen. 1998. "Enhancing Campus Climates for Racial/Ethnic Diversity: Educational Policy and Practice." *Review of Higher Education* 21 (3): 279–302.

Iacobbo, Karen, and Michael Iacobbo. 2004. *Vegetarian America: A History*. Praeger.

Ince, John. 2005. *The Politics of Lust*. Prometheus.

Johnson, Allan. 1997. *The Gender Knot: Unraveling Our Patriarchal Legacy*. Temple University Press.

Joyner, Kara, and Grace Kao. 2000. "School Racial Composition and Adolescent Racial Homophily." *Social Science Quarterly* 81 (3): 810–25.

Kahn, Richard, and Douglas Kellner. 2004. "New Media and Internet Activism: From the 'Battle of Seattle' to Blogging." *New Media and Society* 6 (1): 87–95.

Kane, Emily W. 1995. "Education and Beliefs about Gender Inequality." *Social Problems* 42:74–90.

Kann, Mark E. 1998. *A Republic of Men*. New York University Press.

Karenga, Maulana. 2001. "Introduction to Black Studies." In *Racism*, ed. Ellis Cashmore and James Jennings, 209–16. Sage Publications.

Kassing, Leslee R., Denise Beesley, and Lisa L. Frey. 2005. "Gender Role Conflict, Homophobia, Age, and Education as Predictors of Male Rape Myth Acceptance." *Journal of Mental Health Counseling* 27 (4): 311–28.

Katz, Judith. 2003. *White Awareness: A Handbook for Anti-Racism Training*, 2nd ed. University of Oklahoma Press.

Kaufmann, Karen M., and John R. Petrocik. 1999. "The Changing Politics of American Men: Understanding the Sources of the Gender Gap." *American Journal of Political Science* 43 (3): 864–87.

Keller, James R. 2002. *Queer (Un)Friendly Film and Television*. McFarland.

Kelley, Dean M. 1972. *Why Conservative Churches Are Growing*. Harper & Row.

Kimball, Roger. 1990. *Tenured Radicals: How Politics Has Corrupted Our Higher Education*. Harper & Row.

Kimmel, Michael, and Thomas Mosmiller. 1992. *Against the Tide: Pro-Feminist Men in the United States, 1776–1990: A Documentary History*. Beacon.

Kimura-Walsh, Erin. 2008. "Encroaching on Autonomy: The Influence of the Academic Bill of Rights on U.S. Higher Education." *InterActions: UCLA Journal of Education and Information Studies* 4 (1): 1–27.

Kinder, Donald R., and Nicholas Winter. 2001. "Exploring the Racial Divide: Blacks, Whites, and Opinion on National Policy." *American Journal of Political Science* 45 (2): 439–56.

Klein, Daniel B., and Charlotta Stern. 2004–2005. "Political Diversity in Six Disciplines." *Academic Questions* 18 (2): 40–52.

Klein, Daniel B., and Andrew Western. 2004–2005. "Voter Registration of Berkeley and Stanford Faculty." *Academic Questions* 18 (1): 53–65.

Knuckey, Jonathan. 1999. "Religious Conservatives, the Republican Party and Evolving Party Coalitions in the United States." *Party Politics* 5 (4): 485–96.

———. 2005. "A New Front in the Culture War? Moral Traditionalism and Voting Behavior in U.S. House Elections." *American Politics Research* 33 (5): 645–71.

Koenig, Harold G. 1997. *Is Religion Good for Your Health*? Haworth.

Kohn, Bob. 2003. *Journalistic Fraud: How the* New York Times *Distorts the News and Why It Can No Longer Be Trusted*. WND Books.

Korgen, Kathleen Odell. 2002. *Crossing the Racial Divide: Close Friendships between Black and White Americans*. Praeger.

Kristol, Irving. 1979. "The Adversary Culture of Intellectuals." In *The Third Century*, ed. Seymour Martin Lipset, 327–43. Hoover Institution Press.

Krugman, Paul. 2005. "An Academic Question." *New York Times*, April 5.

Kuhn, Thomas. 1962. *The Structure of Scientific Revolutions*. University of Chicago Press.

Kuruvila, Matthai. 2008. "Mormons Face Flak for Backing Prop. 8." *San Francisco Chronicle*, October 27.

Ladd, Everett C., and Seymour M. Lipset. 1975. *The Divided Academy: Professors and Politics*. McGraw-Hill.

Larson, Edward J., and Larry Witham. 1998. "Leading Scientists Still Reject God." *Nature* 394:313.

Lawrence, Charles R., III. 1993. "If He Hollers Let Him Go: Regulating Racist Speech on Campus." In Matsuda and Lawrence, 53–58.

Laythe, Brian, Deborah Finkel, and Lee A. Kirkpatrick. 2001. "Predicting Prejudice from Religious Fundamentalism and Right-Wing Authoritarianism." *Journal for the Scientific Study of Religion* 40 (1): 1–10.

Lazarsfeld, Paul F., and Wagner Thielens. 1958. *The Academic Mind: Social Scientists in a Time of Crisis.* Free Press.

Lazere, Donald. 2004. "The Contradictions of Cultural Conservatism in the Assault on American Colleges." *Chronicle of Higher Education* 50 (43): B–15.

Lechuga, Vicente M. 2005. "Protecting Academic Freedom in a Time of Crisis." *Navigator* 5 (1): 1–3.

Lee, John. 2006. "The Faculty Bias Studies: Science or Propaganda." Report by American Federation of Teachers, AFL-CIO.

Lee, Tien-Tsung. 2005. "The Liberal Media Myth Revisited: An Examination of Factors Influencing Perceptions of Media Bias." *Journal of Broadcasting & Electronic Media* 49 (1): 43–64.

Lehman, Edward C. 1972. "The Scholarly Perspective and Religious Commitment." *Sociological Analysis* 33 (4): 199–213.

Leland, John. 2000. "Shades of Gay." *Newsweek*, March 20.

Leuba, James H. 1921. *The Belief in God and Immortality.* Open Court.

———. 1934. "Religious Beliefs of American Scientists." *Harper's Magazine*, August.

Levin, Jeffrey S. 1996. "How Religion Influences Morbidity and Health: Reflections on Natural History, Salutogenesis and Host Resistance." *Social Science and Medicine* 43 (5): 849–64.

Levin, Jeffery S., and L. M. Chatters. 1998. "Research on Religion and Mental Health: An Overview of Empirical Findings and Theoretical Issues." In *Religion and Prevention in Mental Health: Research, Vision and Action*, ed. H. G. Koenig, 33–50. Haworth.

Lilla, Mark. 2009. "Taking the Right Seriously: Conservatism Is a Tradition, Not a Pathology." *Chronicle of Higher Education* 56 (4/5): B6–B8.

Limbaugh, David. 2004. *Persecution: How Liberals Are Waging War against Christianity.* Harper Paperbacks.

Lincoln, C. Eric, and Lawrence H. Mamiya. 1990. *The Black Church in the African American Experience.* Duke University Press.

Lincoln, Yvonna S., and Gaile S. Cannella. 2004. "Qualitative Research, Power and the Radical Right," *Qualitative Inquiry* 10 (2): 175–201.

Loftus, Jeni. 2001. "America's Liberalization in Attitudes towards Homosexuality, 1973 to 1998." *American Sociological Review* 66:762–82.

Long, Gary T., and Faye E. Sulton. 1987. "Contributions from Social Psychology." In *Male and Female Homosexuality: Psychological Approaches*, ed. Louis Diamant, 221–37. Hemisphere.

Longenecker, Justin G., Joseph A. McKinney, and Carlos W. Moore. 2004. "Religious Intensity, Evangelical Christianity, and Business Ethics: An Empirical Study." *Journal of Business Ethics* 55 (4): 371–84.

Lynch, James. 1987. *Prejudice Reduction and the Schools*. Cassell.

Lyotard, Jean-Francois. 1984. *The Postmodern Condition*. University of Minnesota Press.

Maira, Sunaina. 2004. "Youth Culture, Citizenship and Globalization: South Asian Muslim Youth in the United States after September 11th." *Comparative Studies of South Asia, Africa and the Middle East* 24 (1): 221–35.

Mannheim, Karl. 1954. *Ideology and Utopia: An Introduction to the Sociology of Knowledge*. Harcourt Brace.

Marsden, George M. 1996. *The Soul of the American University: From Protestant Establishment to Established Nonbelief*. Oxford University Press.

Marsiglio, William. 1993. "Attitudes towards Homosexual Activity and Gays as Friends: A National Survey of Heterosexual 15- to 19-Year-Old Males." *Journal of Sex Research* 30 (1): 12–17.

Martin, John Levi. 2001. "The Authoritarian Personality, 50 Years Later: What Lessons Are There for Political Psychology?" *Political Psychology* 22 (1): 1–26.

Martin, Patricia Yancey, Marie Withers Osmond, Susan Hesselbart, and Meredith Wood. 1980. "The Significance of Gender as a Social and Demographic Correlate of Sex Role Attitudes." *Sociological Focus* 13 (4): 338–96.

Massey, Douglas S., and Nancy Denton. 1996. *American Apartheid: Segregation and the Making of the Underclass*. Harvard University Press.

Matsuda, Mari J., and Charles R. Lawrence III. 1993. *Words That Wound: Critical Race Theory, Assaultive Speech and the First Amendment*. Westview.

Mayhew, Matthew J., Heidi E. Grunwald, and Eric L. Dey. 2005. "Curriculum Matters: Creating a Positive Climate for Diversity from the Student Perspective." *Research in Higher Education* 46 (4): 389–412.

McCarthy, Deborah, and Leslie King. 2005. *Environmental Sociology: From Analysis to Action*. Rowman & Littlefield.

McCarthy, John F. 2006. "Francis S. Collins and *The Language of God*." *Living Tradition* 125.

McChesney, Robert. 2004. *The Problem of the Media: U.S. Communication Politics in the Twenty-first Century*. Monthly Review Press.

McColgan, Aileen. 2005. *Discrimination Law: Text, Cases and Materials*. Hart.

McConahay, John B., and Joseph C. Hough. 1976. "Symbolic Racism." *Journal of Social Issues* 32 (2): 23–46.

McElroy, Wendy. 2006. "Campuses Pay High Price for PC Policies." FoxNews .com. http://www.foxnews.com/story/0,2933,186528,00.html.

McIntosh, Peggy. 2002. "White Privilege: Unpacking the Invisible Knapsack." In *White Privilege: Essential Readings on the Other Side of Racism*, ed. Paula S. Rothenberg, 97–102. Worth Publishers.

McKay, Hollie. 2009. "Tom Hanks Says Mormon Supporters of Proposition 8 'Un-American.'" FoxNews.com. http://www.foxnews.com/ entertainment/2009/01/16/tom-hanks-says-mormon-supporters -proposition-american.

McPherson, Miller, Lynn Smith-Lovin, and James M. Cook. 2001. "Birds of a Feather: Homophily in Social Networks." *Annual Review of Sociology* 27:415–44.

Medved, Michael. 1993. *Hollywood vs. America*. Harper Paperbacks.

Mervis, Jeffrey. 2001. "New Data in Chemistry Show 'Zero' Diversity." *Science* 292:1291–92.

Mildorf, Jarmila. 2005. "Words That Strike and Words That Comfort: Discursive Dynamics of Verbal Abuse in Roddy Doyle's 'The Woman Who Walked into Doors.'" *Journal of Gender Studies* 14 (2): 107–22.

Mills, Sara. 2008. *Language and Sexism*. Cambridge University Press.

Moon, J. Donald. 2004. "Political Liberalism: Agency Rights and Tragic Conflicts." In *Political Liberalism*, ed. Shaun P. Young, 79–102. State University of New York Press.

Mowles, Jessica M. 2008. "Framing Issues, Fomenting Change, 'Feminist-ing': A Contemporary Feminist Blog in the Landscape of Online Political Activism." *International Reports on Socio-Informatics* 5 (1): 29–49.

Musick, M. A. 1996. "Religion and Subjective Health among Black and White Elders." *Journal of Health and Social Behavior* 37 (3): 221–37.

Neumann, Joseph K., William Thompson, and Thomas W. Woolley. 1992. "Evangelical vs. Liberal Christianity: The Influence of Values on the Nonclinical Professional Decisions of Social Workers." *Journal of Psychology and Christianity* 11 (1): 57–67.

Newman, Katherine S. 2003. *A Different Shade of Gray: Midlife and Beyond in the Inner City*. New Press.

Niebuhr, Reinhold. 1949. *Moral Man and Immoral Society: A Study in Ethics and Politics*. Scribner's Sons.

Niebuhr, H. Richard. 1957. *The Social Sources of Denominationalism*. Meridian.

Nieli, Russell K. 2005. "Enhancing Intellectual Diversity on Campus—The James Madison Program at Princeton." *Academic Questions* 18 (2): 20–48.

Nielsen, Laura B. 2002. "Subtle, Pervasive, Harmful: Racist and Sexist Remarks in Public as Hate Speech." *Journal of Social Issues* 58 (2): 265–80.

Nisbet, Robert. 1971. *The Degradation of the Academic Dogma*. Basic Books.

Niven, David. 2002. *Tilt? The Search for Media Bias*. Greenwood Press.

Noffke, Jacqueline L., and Susan H. McFadden. 2002. "Denominational and Age Comparisons of God Concepts." *Journal for the Scientific Study of Religion* 40 (4): 747–56.

Novak, Robert. 2006. "Stem Cell Politics." *Lincoln Tribune*, July 7.

Olasky, Marvin. 1988. *Prodigal Press: The Anti-Christian Bias of the American News Media*. Crossway.

Oldfield, Duane M. 1996. *The Right and the Righteous: The Christian Right Confronts the Republican Party*. Rowman & Littlefield.

Oliver, Melvin L., and Thomas M. Shapiro. 1995. *Black Wealth/White Wealth: A New Perspective on Racial Inequality*. Routledge.

Olson, Laura R., Wendy Cadge, and James T. Harrison. 2006. "Religion and Public Opinion about Same-Sex Marriage." *Social Science Quarterly* 87 (2): 340–60.

Padilla, Yolanda. 2004. *Gay and Lesbian Rights Organizing: Community-Based Strategies*. Routledge.

Paglia, Camille. 2006. "Academic, Heal Thyself." *New York Times*, March 6.

Patton, Tracey O. 2004. "Reflections of a Black Woman Professor: Racism and Sexism in Academia." *Howard Journal of Communication* 15:185–200.

Peek, Charles W., George D. Lowe, and L. Susan Williams. 1991. "Gender and God's Word: Another Look at Religious Fundamentalism and Sexism." *Social Forces* 69 (4): 1201–21.

Pengree, Gregory C. 2006. "Rhetorical Holy War." *American University Journal of Gender, Social Policy & the Law* 14:313.

Phelan, Jo, Bruce G. Link, Ann Stuene, and Robert E. Moore. 1995. "Education, Social Liberalism, and Economic Conservatism: Attitudes toward Homeless People." *American Sociological Review* 60:126–40.

Plummer, Kenneth. 1995. *Telling Sexual Stories: Power, Change and Social Worlds*. Routledge.

Polanyi, Michael. 1958. *Personal Knowledge: Towards a Post-Critical Philosophy*. University of Chicago Press.

Pope, Liston. 1942. *Millhands and Preachers*. Yale University Press.

Priest, Robert J. 2001. "Missionary Positions: Christian, Modernist, Postmodernist." *Current Anthropology* 42 (1): 29–68.

"Psychoanalysis Q and A: Steven Pinker." 2005. *Harvard Crimson*, January 19. http://www.thecrimson.com/article/2005/1/19/psychoanalysis-q-and-a-steven-pinker-in-an.

Quebedeaux, Richard. 1978. *The Worldly Evangelicals*. Harper & Row.

Railey, John. 2009. "Stem-Cell Research: Does President Obama's Position on This Controversial Topic Change the Game? Can Embryonic Stem-Cell Research Now Live Up to Its Promise? *Winston-Salem Journal*, March 29.

Ressler, Lawrence E., and David R. Hodge. 2003. "Silenced Voices: Social Work and the Oppression of Conservative Narratives." *Social Thought* 22 (1): 125–42.

Riccardi, Nicholas. 2008. "Mormon Church Feels the Heat over Proposition 8." *Los Angeles Times*, November 17.

Ringenberg, William C. 1984. *The Christian College: A History of Protestant Higher Education in America*. Eerdmans.

Roof, Wade Clark, and William McKinney. 1987. *American Mainline Religion: Its Changing Shape and Future*. Rutgers University Press.

Rorty, Richard. 1994. "Method, Social Science, and Social Hope." In *The Postmodern Turn: New Perspectives on Social Theory*, ed. Steven Seidman, 46–64. Cambridge University Press.

Rose, Stephen J., and Heidi I. Harmann. 2004. *Still a Man's Labor Market: The Long-Term Earnings Gap*. Institute of Women's Policy Research.

Rosser, Sue V. 2004. *The Science Glass Ceiling: Academic Women Scientists and the Struggle to Succeed*. Routledge.

Rothman, Stanley, S. Robert Lichter, and Neil Nevitte. 2005. "Politics and Professional Advancement among College Faculty." *The Forum: A Journal of Applied Research in Contemporary Politics* 3 (1): Article 2.

Ruether, Rosemary R. 1975. *New Women, New Earth*. Seabury.

Ruiz-Canela, M. 2002. "Embryonic Stem Cell Research: The Relevance of Ethics in the Progress of Science." *Medical Science Monitor* 8 (5): 21–26.

Saroglou, Vassilis, Isabelle Pichon, Laurence Trompette, Marijke Verschueren, and Rebecca Dernelle. 2005. "Prosocial Behavior and Religion: New Evidence Based on Projective Measures and Peer Ratings." *Journal for the Scientific Study of Religion* 44 (3): 323–48.

Schaefer, Richard T. 1996. "Presidential Address: Education and Prejudice; Unraveling the Relationship." *Sociological Quarterly* 37 (1): 1–16.

Schlosser, Lewis. 2003. "Christian Privilege: Breaking a Sacred Taboo." *Journal of Multicultural Counseling and Development* 31:44–51.

Schmalzbauer, John. 2003. *People of Faith: Religious Conviction in American Journalism and Higher Education.* Cornell University Press.

Scott, D. Travers. 2007. "Pundits in Muckrakers' Clothing: Political Blogs and the 2004 U.S. Presidential Election." In *Blogging, Citizenship, and the Future of Media*, ed. Mark Tremayne, 39–57. CRC Press.

Seidman, Steven, and David G. Wagner. 1992. *Postmodernism and Social Theory.* Blackwell.

Seltzer, Richard, Jody Newman, and Melissa Leighton. 1997. *Sex as a Political Variable: Women as Candidates and Voters in U.S. Elections.* Lynne Rienner.

Semmes, Clovis E. 1981. "Foundations of an Afrocentric Social Science: Implications for Curriculum-Building, Theory and Research in Black Studies." *Journal of Black Studies* 12 (1): 3–17.

Shariff, Azim F., and Ara Norenzayan. 2007. "God Is Watching You: Priming God Concepts Increases Prosocial Behavior in an Anonymous Economic Game." *Psychological Science* 18 (9): 803–9.

Sharfstein, Steven S. 2006. "Presidential Address: Advocacy as Leadership." *American Journal of Psychiatry* 163 (10): 1712–15.

Sidanius, Jim, Felicia Pratto, and Lawrence Bobo. 1996. "Racism, Conservatism, Affirmative Action, and Intellectual Sophistication: A Matter of Principled Conservatism or Group Dominance?" *Journal of Personality and Social Psychology* 70 (3): 476–90.

Sidanius, Jim, Pam Singh, John J. Hetts, and Chris Federico. 2000. "It's Not Affirmative Action, It's the Blacks." In *Racialized Politics: The Debate about Racism in America*, ed. David O. Sears, Jim Sidanius, and Lawrence Bobo, 191–235. University of Chicago Press.

Sinha, Jill W., Ram A. Cnaan, and Richard J. Gelles. 2007. "Adolescent Risk Behaviors and Religion: Findings from a National Study." *Journal of Adolescence* 30 (2): 231–49.

Smith, Christian. 2000. *Christian America? What Evangelicals Really Want.* University of California Press.

———. 2003. "Secularizing American Higher Education: The Case of Early American Sociology." In *The Secular Revolution: Power, Interests, and Conflict in the Secularization of American Public Life*, ed. Christian Smith, 97–159. University of California Press.

Smith, Christian, Michael Emerson, Sally Gallagher, Paul Kennedy, and David Sikkink. 1998. *American Evangelicalism: Embattled and Thriving*. University of Chicago Press.

Smith, William, Philip G. Altbach, and Kofi Lomotey. 2002. *The Racial Crisis in American Higher Education*. State University of New York Press.

Song, Tae-Hyon. 1991. "Social Contact and Ethnic Distance between Koreans and the U.S. Whites in the United States." Western Illinois University Press.

Stark, Rodney. 1963. "On the Incompatibility of Religion and Science." *Journal for the Scientific Study of Religion* 3 (1): 3–20.

Stark, Rodney, and Roger Finke. 2000. *Acts of Faith: Explaining the Human Side of Religion*. University of California Press.

Statham, Anne, Laurel Richardson, and Judith A. Cook. 1991. *Gender and University Teaching*. State University of New York Press.

Steinman, Kenneth J., and Marc A. Zimmerman. 2004. "Religious Activity and Risk Behavior among African American Adolescents: Concurrent and Developmental Effects." *American Journal of Community Psychology* 33 (3–4): 151–61.

Studlar, Donley T., Ian McAllister, and Bernadette C. Hayes. 1998. "Explaining the Gender Gap in Voting: A Cross-National Analysis." *Social Science Quarterly* 79 (4): 779–98.

Sumner, William G. 1906. *Folkways*. Ginn.

Swim, Janet K., Robyn Mallett, and Charles Stangor. 2004. "Understanding Subtle Sexism: Detection and Use of Sexist Language." *Sex Roles* 51 (3–4): 117–28.

Sykes, Charles J. 1990. *The Hollow Men: Politics and Corruption in Higher Education*. Regnery Gateway.

Taifel, Henri. 1981. *Human Groups and Social Categories*. Cambridge University Press.

Thernstrom, Stephan. 2005. "Harvard's Crucible: A Question of Academic Freedom, and Meritocracy, and Sense." *National Review* 57 (6): 34–36.

Tichner, J. A. 2002. "Gendering World Politics: Issues and Approaches in the Post–Cold War Era." *Political Science Quarterly* 117 (2): 336–37.

Turner, C. S., and S. L. Myers. 2000. *Faculty of Color in Academe: Bittersweet Success*. Allyn & Bacon.

Vogt, W. P. 1997. *Tolerance and Education: Learning to Live with Diversity and Difference*. Sage Publications.

Washington, Joseph R. 1964. *Black Religion*. Beacon.

Weaver, David, and G. Cleveland Wilhoit. 1993. "The American Journalist in the 1990s: Traits, Education, Work, and Professional Attitudes." Presented at the 76th annual conference of the Association for Education in Journalism and Mass Communication, Kansas City, August 11–14.

Weber, Max. 1958. *The Protestant Ethic and the Spirit of Capitalism*. Scribner's Sons.

Weigel, Russell H., and Paul W. Howes. 1985. "Conceptions of Racial Prejudice: Symbolic Racism Reconsidered." *Journal of Social Issues* 41 (3): 117–38.

Wharton, Amy. 2004. "Gender Inequality." In *Handbook of Social Problems: A Comparative International Perspective*, ed. George Ritzer. Sage Publications.

White, Andrew D. 2004. *A History of the Warfare of Science with Theology in Christendom*. Kessinger.

Wilmore, Gayrand S. 1972. *Black Religion and Black Radicalism*. Doubleday.

Woods, Thomas E. 2005. *How the Catholic Church Built Western Civilization*. Regnery.

Wuthnow, Robert. 1985. "Science and the Sacred." In *The Sacred in a Secular Age*, ed. Phillip E. Hammond, 187–203. University of California Press.

Xu, Yonghong J. 2008. "Gender Disparity in STEM Disciplines: A Study of Faculty Attrition and Turnover Intentions." *Research in Higher Education* 49 (7): 607–24.

Yancey, George. 1994. "The Utilization of Weber's Elective Affinity to Reconcile the Macro and Micro Schools within Sociology of Science." Ph.D. dissertation, University of Texas.

———. 1998. "Differential Attitudes of American Sociologists in Assessment of NOW: A Test of the Gender Gap in a Progressive Subculture." *Sociological Imagination* 35 (2–3): 119–36.

———. 2003. *Who Is White? Latinos, Asians, and the New Black/Nonblack Divide*. Lynne Rienner.

Zipp, John F., and Rudy Fenwick. 2006. "Is the Academy a Liberal Hegemony? The Political Orientations and Educational Values of Professors." *Public Opinion Quarterly* 70 (3): 304–26.

Index